WILD
guide

Andalucía
Hidden Places, Great Adventures
and the Good Life

Edwina Pitcher

WILD
guide

Contents

Regional Overview

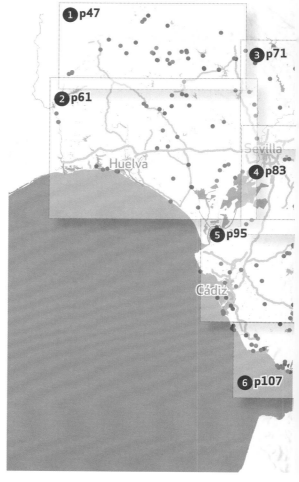

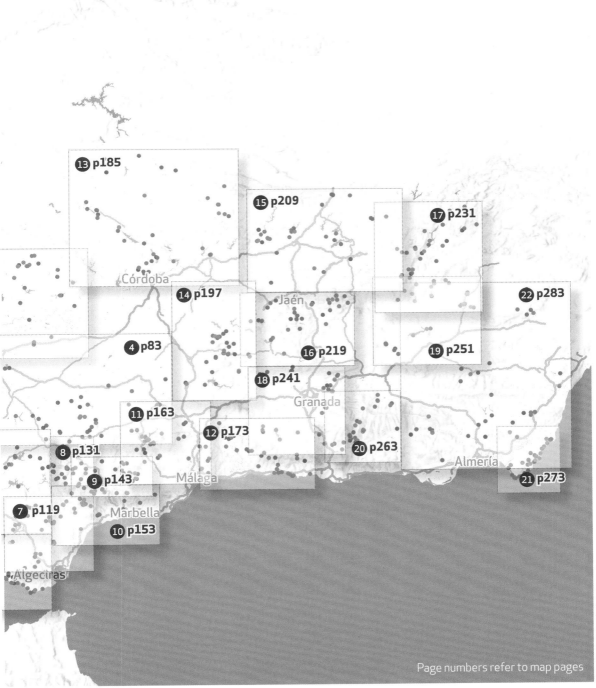

13 p185
15 p209
17 p231
22 p283
14 p197
Córdoba
Jaén
4 p83
16 p219
19 p251
18 p241
Granada
11 p163
12 p173
20 p263
Almería
8 p131
9 p143
Málaga
21 p273
7 p119
Marbella
10 p153
Algeciras

Introduction

I first came to Andalucía having crossed the border from Portugal, in the spring of 2017, looking for its prehistoric sites which lay hidden under cork and oak trees. As the low woodland spread across this ancient frontier nothing seems to mark the territory but the river. As we reached the first villages it quickly came apparent this was Andalucía. Holy Week celebrations had begun, and balconies heaved with families leaning over to catch glimpses of the *paso*. Inching past us along the narrow street and threatening to fall with each sway was the Virgin, long gold cloak spread out, surrounded by tall candles, and decked in flowers. These processions became a recurrent theme of my journeys, caught in the crowds, armfuls of petals thrown from rooftops, incense, trumpets and drumming.

Nowhere embodies the idea of Spain as much as Andalucía. Flamenco, Holy Week, bullfighting, sherry, cigars, it is easy to reduce the area to cliché, but while it is *all* these things, it is also a whole lot more. You only need to scratch the surface to reveal a history rich with characters who knew its wild places. A visit to caves in Jaén province, once filled with thousands of bronze goddess idols, the early Christian chapels carved into soft rock in dusty olive groves, or the remains of an Islamic fortress by a lakeside, the haunt of the 9th-century rebel leader Umar ibn Hafsun, will all conjure an Andalucía that escapes these stereotypes.

Before the first Brits came to the Costa del Sol seeking sun and sea, Andalucía was already, in 1845, 'the most popular destination for travellers to Spain', and yet it is incredible how little-known Andalucía remains today. The vast wilderness of the Sierra Morena, home to a slowly recovering population of Iberian lynx, the ever-shifting wetlands of Doñana or the snow-capped mountain Mulhacen in the Sierra Nevada are some of Europe's richest and most important natural areas and remain relatively unknown. For those willing to go on foot, horseback or cycle these wild places offer beautiful natural treasures.

Ancient history and wildlife

Andalucía has been subjected to endless romanticised versions. In the 19th century notions of the bandits living in wild hills and gypsies in picturesque caverns took root. But the Romantic travellers were just one of many successive waves of invasions and migrations that have each brought with them their own myths and fictions. The golden hoard of El Carambolo pulled from river mud outside Seville has shed more light on the semi-mythical harbour city of Tartessos, said to have been built beyond the Pillars of Hercules, or Straits of Gibraltar, around the 8th century BC. Serious historians even today make speculative links between this site and the Atlantis myth. And the region would come to be reconquered and reimagined once again when Tariq, a general from Tangier, sailed across the Straits on a quiet morning in 711, ushering in eight centuries of Islamic rule and the kingdom of Al-Andalus.

As more artefacts and hidden treasures emerge from these cultures, it is difficult to separate muddied facts from fiction. What we do know is that Andalucía, the gateway between Africa and Europe, has always been in flux. Just like the skies above. We only need to look up to see the heavens filled with bird migrations between the two continents. At just 13km at its narrowest point, the Straits are a crucial crossing point for birdlife. Visit in early autumn to see blue skies flecked with thousands of griffon vultures spiralling up on thermals. It is a thrilling experience to see these incredibly earthy creatures of feather, flesh, and claws, soaring overhead to Africa.

Stunning places to watch for wildlife continue across the region's eight provinces. Head to the sheer ravines and deep forests of Sierra de Cazorla in autumn to listen for *la Berrea*, the bellows of stags during mating season, or watch for hundreds of pink flamingos in the salt marshes of Fuente de Piedra in Málaga. Fearless ibex, a wild mountain goat, crown the most vertical of plunges in the Sierra Nevada and in late summer you can look for whales, orcas and dolphins gliding between the Mediterranean Sea and Atlantic ocean.

Food and places to stay

Andalucía is as rich in adventures over mountains, lakes, cliffs, deserts, caves, rivers and sea, as it is rich in the food and wine to fuel these adventures. In the mountains, feast on grilled local meats or *embutidos*, chorizos, sausages, and cured hams. If you visit the Sierra de Grazalema, whose hills receive the most annual rainfall in Spain, be sure to try *queso de payoyo*, a cheese produced by the goats grazing on its green grass. By the rivers try freshwater fish. At the coast, feast on grilled prawns, heaped plates of fried fish or bubbling seafood rice dishes to share. Kept in caves and cellars are the region's hallowed wines: sip on dry white *manzanillas* by the mouth of Andalucía's great river Guadalquivir, and sherries ranging from opaque gold *palo cortados* to darker ambers of *amontillados*, *olorosos* and sweet *pedro ximénez* in the bodegas of Jerez de la Frontera. Head to La Axarquía mountains in Málaga for intense *moscatels* and the deserts of Almería or villages of the Sierra Nevada for deep dark reds.

You will discover the best places to eat, dishes made to recipes handed down through generations, but also rural havens perfect for romantic escapes. Spend a week in a characterful mountain village with sparkling stone fountains or a wild retreat to a working farm. There are safari tents hidden in pine woodland with birdsong in trees overhead or wilder campsites from which to stargaze.

Andalucía is a place woven over with paths and stories left by Iberian tribes, Andalusí kings, Christian crusaders and sea-faring traders. It is crossed by Roman roads and pilgrims' pathways connecting sacred mountain chapels. Enduring all of this are much older footprints stamped on stone – dinosaur footprints some 230 million years old, calluses pushed into mud-prints as though they were here yesterday (see North Jaén). A visit to these wild sites, woodland, hills, rivers and caves, will be thronged with a thousand stories from different times. Often just a hike away, they'll transport you to an ancient, wilder time.

The result of these journeys and nights sleeping under stars is this compendium of wild, hidden and exceptionally beautiful places across Andalucía. It is packed with memories of cool rivers, thundering waterfalls, hidden springs, flashes of wildlife and sunsets seen from sacred sites. I hope that inspires love for these precious places and many more adventures.

Edwina Pitcher

Finding your way

Each wild place can be located using the overview map provided at the end of each chapter, along with the detailed directions, but to be sure of finding your way you'll need to use the latitude and longitude provided. This is given in decimal degrees (WGS84) and can be entered straight into any web-based mapping program, such as Google or Bing. Print out the map before you go, or save a 'screen grab' and email it to yourself. You can also enter the co-ordinates into your GPS, car satnav (enable 'decimal degrees') or your smartphone, if it has GPS. All maps apps will take decimal degrees, and the ViewRanger app will even give you turn-by-turn instructions to guide you to your point. Approximate walk-in times are given, for one way only (we allow about 15 mins per km), and abbreviations in the directions refer to left and right (L, R) and north, east, south and west (N, E, S, W).

Wild & responsible

1. High risk of forest fires in the summertime. Don't leave any glass out in the sunshine. Even the smallest shard can spark a flame in the sun. If you see discarded bottles, please collect them.

2. During this time campfires are prohibited in all rural areas as well as in the picnic parks or *áreas recreativas*.

3. If you wash in streams or rivers, only use biodegradable soap or none at all.

4. Park considerately.

5. Take map, compass, whistle and a water bottle when venturing into remote areas and always tell someone where you are going – do not rely on your mobile phone.

Useful phrases

Hello!	¡Hola!
Good morning	buenos días
Good afternoon	buenas tardes
Please	por favor
Thank you	muchas gracias
Where is?	¿Dónde está…?
the beach	la playa
the river	el río
the lake	el lago/ el embalse
the castle	el castillo
the forest	el bosque
the footpath	el sendero
a bothy	el refugio
right	derecha
left	izquierda
roadside inn	una venta
a glass of wine	una copa de vino
a bottle of wine	una botella de vino
a beer	una cerveza
some tapas	unas tapas
a larger dish for sharing	un ración
bread	pan
cheese	queso
cured ham	jamón ibérico
fried fish	pescaito frito
olives	aceitunas

Best for
Beaches & coast

Andalucía is well known for its long golden sandy beaches. This epic coastline, reaching from Huelva, and its border with Portugal, in the west to the ancient volcanic coast at Almería in the east, is riddled with secret coves, windswept dunes, colossal cliffs and hidden sea caves.

The coastline differs dramatically from place to place. The Costa de la Luz, running from Huelva into Cádiz provinces, offers golden sands, wild dunes and fabulous hiking routes following fishermen's paths with detours to secret coves. At Playa de Bolonia the bleached white pillars of a Roman amphitheatre look out to golden shores, secret natural pools, and great snorkelling. Nearby at Duna de Valdevaqueros you can roll down immense sand dunes and look out to the not-so-distant African coastline. From here to Tarifa, wild winds make the coast a haven for kite surfers.

Go wild! Follow smugglers' routes to cliffside cascades and rock pools teeming with life along the Cádiz coast or discover hidden beaches perfect for a skinny dip along Flecha de Nueva Umbría. Head to Cabo de Gata where volcanic rock scoops underwater, alive with coral reefs, bright seagrass and hundreds of shimmering fishes. Kayak to sea caves in Nerja or skinny dip at Playa de Calaiza where mountains meet the sea.

Best for
Skinny dipping

Stripping bare and diving into a sparkling lake, forest river or a thrillingly deep clear mountain pool is one of the most immediate ways to immerse yourself in nature. It's beneficial too as we emerge feeling reinvigorated, energised, and empowered.

Open your eyes under clear mountain streams in Sierra de Grazalema to see shimmering shoals of barbel fish at Charco la Bomba. Lie back and float like a star in the soft green lake under the watchtower at Embalse de la Torre de Águila or dry-off on sun-warmed rocks at Río Guadiato while bright pink and yellow dragonflies dip and dart over the river. Feel your pulse race as you dive into icy mountain pools in the Serranía de Ronda or feel your body melt in wild thermal pools at Granada. Swim across the Portuguese border from smugglers' footpaths in Huelva or bravely under thundering waterfalls that pummel your shoulders in Sierra de Huétor. Water gives our bodies freedom of movement and a good number of Andalucía's waterfalls, lakes and rivers – and many beaches where nudism is the norm – are in secluded spots, perfect for a skinny dip which only adds to this unhindered freedom.

Be safe

1 Never swim alone, and do keep a constant watch on weak swimmers.

2 Know your limits and stay close to the shoreline. Cold water will decrease your swimming range and can lead to cold cramps. People with a heart condition should avoid rapid entry into cold water.

3 Never jump into water you have not thoroughly checked for depth and obstructions.

4 Avoid strong currents, such as those found under large waterfalls, rapids or weirs: they can drag you under.

5 Always make sure you know how you will get out before you get in.

6 Wear footwear if you can.

7 Watch out for boats on any navigable river. Wear a coloured swim hat so you can be seen.

8 Avoid direct contact with blue-green algae and be wary of water quality in lowland areas during droughts and heavy rain. Cover cuts with plasters if worried, and if you develop flu-like symptoms tell your doctor you have been wild swimming.

Best for
Ancient & sacred

On the cusp of Europe, looking to Africa, guarding the gateway between the Atlantic Ocean and Mediterranean Sea, Andalucía has always been a meeting place of cultures. With rock carvings and standing stones, ancient roman roads and early cave chapels, hilltop castles and hidden watchtowers, the landscape is a tapestry of hallowed places and territorial markings. Start to unpick a little of its history and it will begin to unravel in all directions, towards Africa, the Middle East and even America.

Long before the first Phoenician longboats touched Cádiz's golden sands in the 12th century BC, ancient Iberian tribes had built settlements, erecting rock tombs and cave paintings. Gaze up at vulture colonies living in the limestone crags from the mysterious tombs at Betis, they say once used for sky burials. Hike up behind the roman ruins at Bolonia to pre-roman steps carved in rock, a hidden stairway to heaven. Look out for ritual offerings, flowers or grain, left on these holy stones.

The search for Andalucía's prehistoric and ancient sites will lead you to exceptionally beautiful and wild places. The elemental moonscape of desert gullies surrounding the burial sites at Los Millares saw some of the first humans to cross from Africa. See the landscape through ancient eyes at Dolmen de Menga, one of Europe's largest passage graves, whose shadowy recesses look out to summer sunrise over the sleeping profile of Peña de los Enamorados.

Best for
Sunset hill forts & highpoints

From the lush green Sierra de Grazalema to the soaring peaks of the Sierra Nevada, the mountains and hilltops of Andalucía are scattered with lost ruins and standing stones, perfect for a sunset. Climb up to Castillo de Luna in the golden hour and see the land fall away spread like an antique map below. As the light diffuses to a deep marmalade orange over the hills from Silla del Papa, you can listen for the tinkling of bells as goat herds return home.

At Cueva de los Letreros, its ochre cave paintings are perfectly aligned for the sunset over the pink-hued desert gullies below. Sit at its rocky outcrop as griffon vultures wheel overhead. Andalucía has many hilltop castles and watchtowers, once part on the 12th century *Banda Morisca*, the old frontier between Muslim and Christian kingdoms. Now deserted, you can watch the sunset from time-worn steps and ghostly grey archways looking out over olive groves.

Fill your lungs with sea air as you watch the sun set into the Mediterranean from the coastal watchtower Torre Vigía de Cerro Gordo, still watching for marauding pirates. Feel the wind in your hair from Pico del Terril, the highest peak in Seville. Breathe in the mountain air from Castillo de Miramontes, built during Muslim rule and left to the wild, where eagles soar and sheep graze by its scattered rock.

Best for
Caves & Grottoes

From the subterranean cathedral formed at Cueva del Hundidero to the shadowy recesses of Cueva de Belda, the bedrock of Andalucía is riddled with underground rivers, passageways to chambers, catacombs and cavities. Often a small scramble down into these caves can lead to caverns hollowed out by water over a dizzying expanse of time.

Mysterious ochre paintings of stags and wild animals can be spied at Cueva de Bacinete while 20,000-year-old paintings are partially hidden behind several millennia worth of flowstone at Cueva de la Pileta. Rivers have eaten into the porous limestone in the Sierra de Huétor, carving echoing caves and sparkling grottoes behind curtains of waterfalls. For caving enthusiasts, Cueva de Sorbas offers thrilling belly crawls through narrow tunnels.

Not all these underground hollows are natural. At Osuna you can find pre-roman burial chambers in catacombs along the dusty roadside while at Tholos de El Romeral, a Bronze Age passage grave in Málaga, you can play with its ancient acoustics. Visit the Phoenician quarries dug deep under the springtime flowers in the Sierra de San Cristobal to find cool chambers with impenetrable shadows. Many of these caves provide shelter for native bat colonies whose enduring presence in these netherworlds eclipses all human activity.

Best for
Wildlife

From eagles soaring over hilltop castles to ancient bat colonies living in dark caves, Andalucía's wild places are home to a wealth of wildlife. Colonies of griffon vultures nest in dramatic limestone gorges in the Sierra de Cádiz and hundreds of pink flamingos can be seen in shimmering marshlands at Doñana. Come in autumn to see blue skies filled with thousands of vultures migrating over the narrow strip of sea to the rocky coast of Morocco.

Encountering this wildlife is exhilarating; whether you catch a glimpse of deer at Cazorla, spy the elusive Iberian lynx in Huelva, or hear eagles' wingbeats in high places, these moments are sure to stay with you. While the Sierra Morena north of Jaén has not heard the howl of a wolf for several decades, rewilding plans are in place and endangered Iberian lynx are tentatively returning home in Doñana and the Sierra de Andújar.

Set out to climb Mulhacén in the dawn half-light and you'll be sure to share your way with sure-footed wild ibex. Or wait at twilight by cool springs at Cerrada de la Malena for solitary mouflon, an ancient species of wild sheep, who come down from the hills to drink. Look out for pygmy marbled newts in the Sierra de las Nieves, or dolphins and orcas in the Straits; you'll need patience and sharp eyes but the thrill of seeing these creatures only deepens the joy of these wild places.

Best for
Picnics & foraging

Fresh and seasonal local produce can be the highlight of any picnic, it also reveals fascinating insights into the area's cultural and natural history. With its sun-drenched fields and rich earth, Andalucía is often called the garden of Spain. Visit the Seville region in late spring for roadside asparagus and fields popping with wildflowers. In early spring, after the bitter oranges have fallen, the lanes and streets of villages across Andalucía are filled with the scent of *azahar*, orange blossom.

Spy out wild mushrooms and sculptural fungi in the Picos de Aroche after the first rains, pick wild figs by the wayside in Málaga or feast on chestnuts in the Genal valley. Wind up mountain paths in spring and breathe in the heady scent of rockrose and wild herbs. Feast on cherries, strawberries or sweet *chirimoya*, custard apples, from pop-up roadside stalls or local shops and farmers' markets. If picking mushrooms remember to take little and leave the roots.

Andalucía also has a joyful culture of picnicking, with many mossy stone tables often made from ancient millstones, sheltered under wizened oak trees. These *áreas recreativas* are usually signed from the road and next to a cool river, or hidden waterfall. Chill a bottle of *vino de jerez* wedged between river stones and pack a picnic to feast by the riverbank.

Best for
Mountain villages

Scattered across Andalucía are timeless villages whose rhythm and pace of life works in harmony with their natural surroundings. The *pueblos blancos*, or white villages, with a cluster of dazzling houses on green hills, crowned by castles, make up some of the most iconic scenes in Cádiz and Málaga provinces. Their winding and narrow streets, filled with flowering pot plants, resemble villages in northern Morocco. With roots in the medieval Islamic kingdom of Al-Andalus, their history still resounds in their placenames, Grazalema, Benamahoma, Benaocaz or Zahara de la Sierra.

The olive groves, forests and hills surrounding these villages hide lost ruins, hillforts and Roman roads. Ramble along the footpaths which link the villages, making use of droving paths, roman roads and riverways, to find these wild sites. Follow river Majaceite as it flows from Benamahoma under dappled woodland into El Bosque. Or wander along worn Roman flagstones connecting Ubrique to Benaocaz.

Head east to the Alpujarran villages to find medieval rammed-earth walls, uneven thatched eaves, narrow passageways with chestnut beams and windows looking out to the Sierra Nevada. Nearly forgotten trade routes known as *escarihuelas* connect them with the sea and make enchanting footpaths to follow. Arriving on untarmacked paths, without a car or road in sight, lends an extra sense of stillness and peace to their streets.

Best for
Fiestas & pilgrimage

A land of sharp contrasts, Andalucía is famous for its colourful flamenco *ferias* and candlelit Holy Week processions. These festivals are famous in its cities, *Semana Santa* in Seville and even the irreverently joyful *Carnaval de Cádiz*, where raucous costumed groups parade through town performing subversive songs and visual puns. But head into the rural areas for a wild and heady, irreverent mix of sacred and profane.

Romerías, pilgrimages to a shrine, happen across the countryside and the *Romería de El Rocío* to the sanctuary in the Doñana wetlands draws pilgrims nationwide. Catch glimpses of their garlanded bow top wagons, horses plunging into rivers and flamenco dresses dragging on cracked mud, as they make their way to the shrine. Or pay a visit to the hilltop sanctuary of the Virgen de la Cabeza, the Queen of the Sierra Morena mountain range. Her *romería* in late April is the oldest in Spain. At Epiphany, come to Huelva to see the *Cabalgata de Higuera de la Sierra*, where the three kings arrive in regal costume throwing armfuls of sweets into crowds.

A more contemporary festival of art rejuvenates the whitewashed streets of Genalguacil in the Genal valley during the summer months. While old superstitions are given new life in Soportújar at the *Fería del Embrujo* or witchcraft festival.

Best for
Slow food & wine

Food in Andalucía is celebration. With olive oil like liquid gold, finely cut *jamón*, sherry from dark oak barrels and fried fish like crisp sea-spray – you can hold the landscape in your glass and explore the flavours of the mountains and sea without leaving the table.

Tapas, or small bites, can be enjoyed across the region but around the Granada province they are served along with your drinks. In Cádiz feast on *choco frito*, fried cuttlefish, as the sea washes in under your beach bar. At local markets you can try fresh sea urchins. Head to Barbate to gorge on tuna caught in ancient fish traps during the annual migrations.

Hike up to Trevélez in the Sierra Nevada where the salty scent of curing *jamón* comes in waves on the mountain air. The Arabic influence can be tasted in Málaga's *ajo blanco*, delicious cold almond and garlic soup, Córdoban *salmorejo*, a denser gazpacho perfect for summer, as well as in the almond and honey pastries and biscuits such as *alfajors* and *polvorones*.

This abundance of flavours and dishes is matched by the region's wines. At Sanlucar de Barrameda try a glass of dry *manzanilla* with a plate of grilled prawns. At Jerez sip on a dry *fino* or *palo cortado*, swill a glass of richer *oloroso*, *amontillado* or sweet *Pedro Ximénez*. Discover dark reds in Granada and lighter reds in Almería, fortified wines in Montilla, sweet moscatels in Málaga or anis liquors in Cazalla de la Sierra.

Best for
Places to stay

Sleeping out under the stars in Andalucía is a magical experience, and several campsites have made this experience all the more romantic. Stargaze from a safari lodge hidden away in pine woodland outside Jerez. Wake up to birdsong at secret yurts near Tarifa and its wild coast. Or open your shutters to dawn over the Sierra Norte de Sevilla and start your day with a wild horse trek at Cortijo El Berrocal. If you are travelling in midsummer, look up for the beautiful annual meteor showers – the Perseids – when stars shoot across dark skies.

Wild does not have to mean roughing it – enjoy the sensual side of nature on luxurious daybeds in coastal gardens at La Joya de Cabo de Gata or watch the moonrise from the pool at Cortijo La Molina. Retreat to Alpujarran villages in spring and follow cobbled streets into the mountains passing ancient threshing grounds and sparkling fountains. Bed down in the evening with a book under old eaves and log fires.

The deserts of Granada and Almería hide hundreds of cave houses. Stay at Cuevas Al Jatib with chimneys emerging from desert rock, cosy hearths hollowed deep into the soft stone. Or escape to elegant farmhouses, *cortijos* and *fincas*, surrounded by vineyards, olive groves and fruit trees and wake to breakfast on local breads, honey, olive oil, fresh fruit and cakes.

ARACENA Y PICOS DE AROCHE

Our perfect weekend

→ **Forage** for autumn mushrooms in Picos de Aroche, a great place to spot *gurumelos* or *amanita ponderosa*

→ **Listen** for the clatter of hooves on stone at Christmas and catch a glimpse of the Magi lit up under a streetlamp

→ **Hike** through a tangle of cork oak woodland to the forest plunge pool of Charco Malo

→ **Run** along a rope bridge and follow the old smugglers' route between Spain and Portugal

→ **Marvel** at a murmuration of starlings from the battlements of Santa Olalla del Cala

→ **Climb** up Mirador Piedra de Utrera and look out across the mountains to Portugal

→ **Cycle** down to Puente de la Peramora and look up for the black vultures who live in the rocks at nearby Sierra Pelada

→ **Sip** on a glass of *onubense* wine at Bodega los Curros in the pretty village of Higuera de la Sierra

→ **Bed** down under old chestnut beams at Casa Rural El Alamillo and wake up to birdsong from the rafters

Mossy walls wind along the lanes and valleys of the northern Huelva province, black pigs and cattle resting under the shade of twisted cork oaks and mighty holm oaks. Bordered by Portugal's Alentejo region to the west and by Spain's Extremadura region to the north, this region sits between some of the oldest borders in Europe, with nothing to mark them but wild rivers and ruins. It is famous for its black pigs from which Spain's highest-quality *jamón* is produced. This locally cured meat can be enjoyed at many an *onubense* bar, surrounded by flowering plazas, proud balconies and often exuberant festivities.

These sleepy villages rest on wild and turbulent histories. Defensive border castles at Aracena, Santa Olalla del Cala and Cortegana crown the hills and once defended the land against Portuguese attack and a centuries-long Christian conquest from the north. After its last Muslim rulers were expelled in the 13th century, the land was re-christened the *Banda Gallega*, the Galician Belt, as it was repopulated by people from northern Spain. But the names of the beautiful white villages of Alájar, Zufre and Almonaster keep the echo of their Arabic past.

Many of these villages are hidden in the Picos de Aroche, and you can hike or bike through its oaken woodland, its peaks home to black vulture colonies. At Almonaster a 10th-century mosque sits proudly above a tangle of jasmine-perfumed streets with rows of white houses and orange trees. Weeping willows hang over a cobbled Roman road by its river. Follow a footpath to Santa Ana la Real, a haven for hikers with its signed stargazing footpaths, geological trails or forest footpaths to book swaps hidden in trees.

Smuggling was a way of life for centuries for the towns on each side of the border, and you can follow these old contraband routes along the Chanza river. Something wild lives on in the spirit of the people here and if you're lucky enough to be in Rosal de la Frontera in mid-May, head down to the riverbanks to see hundreds of horses and colourful wagons celebrating the feast of San Isidro el Labrador. And if you want a really wild festival, head to Zufre to see horseback races up the ancient, cobbled streets, cheered on from crowded balconies.

The long-distance Ruta de la Plata trail passes through many of these towns. It was once the commercial silver trade route but is now one of the quieter pilgrim ways to Santiago de Compostela in Galicia. Ancient ways of life continue in Castañuelo, a tiny hamlet where locals still cook on fires in large metal plates on their porches. Hike out of the village to see the much older remains of a Celtic hillfort with incredible views of the Sierra Morena.

If you visit during Epiphany, be sure to stop at Higuera de la Sierra for the oldest and most extravagant Cabalgata in Andalucía. The three kings – Balthasar, Melchior and Gaspar – arrive after dark on horseback in full Al-Andalus-inspired Magi costume. The main event is the parade, where townsfolk dress as nativity characters. The stage sets are built throughout the year and include real donkeys, lambs and olive trees. Once ready, the entire scene is constructed on the backs of trucks, dramatically lit and paraded slowly through the town. Armfuls of sweets are thrown into the crowd.

You can't pass these villages without trying a plate of finely cut *jamón*, especially at Jábugo. *Jamón ibérico* is the original slow food, produced from the black pigs that live free range in the *dehesa*, eating acorns under the oaks. Savour the cured meat with a glass of the local *tinto*; it's the best way to bring out the flavour.

SMUGGLERS' SWIMS

1 MOLINO DE LA LAGUNA

Years ago, life in these hills revolved around the River Chanza. Whether smuggling contraband along its wild paths or waiting your turn to grind flour at these old mills, both the Portuguese and the Spanish would have trodden these paths to the mills.

→ From Paymogo follow the HU-7400 towards Portugal. After 7km, and just before you cross the Chanza river, there is a slip road on the L. Park here, the mill is 400m downstream. The beginning of the 8km Ruta del Contrabando is signed 'Inicio Senda' to more mills and hanging bridges.

5 mins, 37.7591, -7.4142 🏊🚻🎣🚶‍♂️

2 PUENTE COLGANTE DE RÍO CHANZA

This rope bridge over a tributary in the Chanza river is a good place for a dip.

→ See directions to Molino de la Laguna and follow the path upstream for 1.5km.

20 mins, 37.7663, -7.3936 🏊⛰🚶‍♂️🎣🚻➰

3 MOLINO DE PABLO

Locals say this ruined mill is haunted by the ghosts of two ill-fated lovers, Teresinha and Leohel. Follow the river path upstream for

another 2km to find the ruins of another mill, Molino de la Cirujana.

→ See directions to Molino de la Laguna and follow the path upstream for 2km.

30 mins, 37.7704, -7.3914 🏊⛰🚶‍♂️🎣🚻➰⬦

4 RÍO MÚRTIGAS

A beautiful bridge spans the wide River Múrtigas, which continues its journey, meandering over the Portuguese border. This last stretch of river, the Valle de Múrtigas, is bordered by verdant fields and woodland. It lies along the Ruta de los Contrabandistas trail, which begins in Encinasola and ends in the Portuguese village of Barranco.

→ Follow Carretera del Contrabandista out of Encinasola and then follow footpath signs to the River Múrtigas, about 4km. For the track and more info see Turismosierradearacena.com

1 hr, 38.1111, -6.8968 🏊🎣🚻🚶‍♂️

5 ARROYO DE PEDRO GIL

This small lake is perfect for a swim along the Ruta de los Contrabandistas footpath. Continue towards Portugal from this lake for 1.5km to reach a pretty bridge over the Valquemado river.

→ See directions to Río Múrtigas. The lake lies about 8km along the 17km Ruta de

los Contrabandistas trail, which starts in Encinasola.

2 hrs, 38.0971, -6.9111 🏊🚶‍♂️⛰

HIDDEN WATERFALLS

6 LOS CHORROS DE JOYARANCÓN

A beautiful and gentle walk through cork oak woodland filled with birdsong. The waterfall falls about 15m into several little pools and runs over the path. It is deep enough for a refreshing splash and paddle. It's best to visit after rain.

→ From Santa Ana la Real take the HU-8105 for 2km towards Alájar. After the tiny bridge turn L and park. Follow the path on the L along the river, keeping L at crossroads, for 1km to reach the waterfall. Or see directions to Risco de Levante and follow a signed 1.5km detour.

15 mins, 37.8758, -6.7125 🚶‍♂️🐕🥾

7 CHARCO MALO

The setting of this small, dark pool, formed under the mossy rocks in the Arroyo de Guijarra, is like something from a fairy tale. Surrounded by ash, alders, chestnut and oak, the footpath leaves from the pretty village of Cortelazor and follows the old lane along drystone walling. A good plunge pool.

11

7

8

→ The circular 5km footpath is signed from the end of Calle Olivos in Cortelazor. Follow the path for 1.7km to the waterfall.
30 mins, 37.9292, -6.6146

RIVERS AND ROMERÍAS

8 RECINTO ROMERO ROSAL DE LA FRONTERA

For most of the year this is a peaceful spot by the old bridge, chapel and wide green River Alcalaboza. However, the chapel of San Isidro Labrador is also the site of the annual festivities celebrated on the weekend closest to 15 May. It is known locally as the 'second Rocío' as the space fills with horses, wagons and tents, following the cross-border pilgrimage of the brotherhood of the Alentejo-Gothic chapel of Nuestra Señora de la Paz de Ficalho.

→ From Rosal de la Frontera, follow the A-495 S for 7km and cross the river. Continue for 100m and park where you can on the R. You will see the chapel and the river.
5 mins, 37.9153, -7.1994

9 EMBALSE DE ARACENA

A muddy beach leads to this cool, clear reservoir, perfect for some longer swims and surrounded by pastureland that slopes gently to the water. There are a couple of good restaurants at this spot too.

→ From Aracena take the N-433 to Valdezufre. Turn L onto the HU-8130 and continue for 7km. Turn L at signs for 'pantano' then immediately L at the fork. Continue for 200m until you see the restaurants and lake. Park where you can and head down to the water.
5 mins, 37.9121, -6.4604

HIKING & BIKING

10 PUENTE DE LA PERAMORA

This pretty stone bridge over the Alcalaboza stream is a lovely place for a picnic and rest along the 29km cycle trail from Aroche to El Mustio, the abandoned forest village. You will pass holm oaks, farmland, granite boulders and great views of the Peñas de Aroche mountains, as well as the Sierra Pelada, home to one of Spain's most important black vulture colonies. The cycle path is called Aroche-El Mustio Eco de la Naturaleza; you can download the track from Rfec.com.

→ From Puente Felipe II in Aroche follow green signs for the Calle Corredera. After about 300m turn R after the restaurant and you will

find yourself on the track. After 2km keep L at the fork. The bridge is on your R after 6km.
2 hrs, 37.9021, -7.0112 🏕🎣🚶🌲🏊

11 RISCO DE LEVANTE
This wonderful rocky outcrop with its Tibetan bridge is popular with climbers and lies along the signed 8km, circular footpath from Santa Ana la Real. One of the most beautiful walks in the province, it passes through cork oak woodland and by mossy stone bridges, streams, forest book exchange chests, starlight observation decks and has great views of the Sierra Morena. A detour takes you to the Chorros de Joyarancón.

→ Sendero Risco de Levante is signed from Fuente de los Tres Caños in Santa Ana la Real. It is about 4km to the crag.
1 hr, 37.8541, -6.6945 🚶🎣🚲🏞🌲🏔🚶

ANCIENT & SACRED

12 CROMLECH PASADA DEL ABAD
Just before the border with Portugal, this small but ancient cromlech lies along the old livestock road connecting Sierra Morena with Alentejo. It dates from the Bronze Age and locals today refer to it as the Devil's Stones, but they are thought to have once been used for charting seasonal cycles, equinoxes and solstices as well as marking the old *vereda* (droving path). Part of the symbolic and cultural landscape, the stones sit close to the Ribera de Chanza, which becomes the Chança river in Portugal, defining a stretch of the frontier.

→ From Aroche take the N-433 towards Rosal de la Frontera and at km145,5 turn L and the cromlech is on the roadside.
1 min, 37.9773, -7.1434 🚲🏞⛪🏕🌲

13 CUIDAD ROMANA DE TURÓBRIGA
In the meadows, surrounded by the wooded hills of the Sierra de Huelva and a short stroll from the banks of the Chanza river, stand the ruins of this 1st-century Roman city. Turóbriga was built to protect an area called Baeturia Céltica, important for its mining and mineral wealth. It was abandoned in the 3rd century and used as a quarry to build Aroche's castle and the Hermitage of San Mamés, a 13th-century chapel with beautiful medieval frescos that sit next to the Roman ruins. There is a kids' playpark here.

→ Finca La Belleza, Ermita de San Mamés, Carretera Nacional 433 Sevilla-Lisboa,

16

15

17

At the end of the path, the hill falls away to startling views across the Valles de Carrasco and the Sierra de Huelva. It is undeniably a powerful place, as well as a rich mineral resource. Votive carvings of wildlife dating back to the Celtic period have been found here.

→ From Castañuelo take the HV-3115 S towards Aracena. After 2km park on the R where a dirt track leads through a metal gate (37.9243, -6.5651). Follow for 1km.

15 mins, 37.9268, -6.5753

CAVES & CASTLES

16 CASTILLO DE CORTEGANA

Built on a small hill, this 12th-century castle overlooks the narrow streets of Cortegana's white-washed *pueblo*. It is a rambling castle with shadowy corners and latticed windows looking across the serene woodland of the Sierra de Huelva.

→ From Cortegana, follow Calle castillo up to the castle.

10 mins, 37.9104, -6.8168

17 GRUTA DE LAS MARAVILLAS

One of Andalucía's most beautiful and largest cave systems is hidden under sleepy Aracena's ancient castle hill and main square. Also known as the Gruta de los Desnudos, Cave of the Naked Men, it has become a bit of a national joke as the stalactites dripping from the enormous caverns are absurdly phallic. But it is also worth visiting for its illuminated lakes which appear almost suspended in the underground galleries.

→ Calle Pozo de la Nieve, 21200 Aracena, 663 937 876, Aracena.es

1 min, 37.8914, -6.5649

18 CASTILLO DE SANTA OLALLA DEL CALA

This great hulk of a 13th-century castle crowns the small hill above Santa Olalla del Cala. Its horseshoe-arched gates and towers with storks' nests once presided over the Vía de la Plata, the silver trade route, and defended the northern flanks of the Kingdom of Seville, later defending against Portuguese attacks. It is a beautiful spot for a sunset, with views over to its neighbouring castle at El Real de la Jara in Seville province.

→ You can walk up to the castle from Santa Olalla town.

10 mins, 37.9055, -6.2346

km128, 21240, 959 140 201. Entrance is free but hours vary; closed Mon.

1 min, 37.9691, -6.9483

14 CALZADA ROMANA DE ALMONASTER LA REAL

This ancient, cobbled Roman trade route once connected Beja and Castro Marim in Portugal to Itálica and Seville in Andalucía. It crossed the Picos de Aroche, Cortegana and Almonaster la Real. Now you can wander down to its old cobbles on the riverbank by the barns and old tanneries on the outskirts of Almonaster. The 12km circular walk, Sendero a Calabazares, starts here and passes the tiny hamlets of Calabazares and La Escalada.

→ From the *ayuntamiento* at Almonaster follow Calle los Recueros until it crosses the river.

6 mins, 37.8707, -6.7850

15 RUINAS CELTAS DE CASTAÑUELO

Overgrown with rockroses, rosemary and lichen-covered cork trees, the woodland on this hilltop thins to reveal the foundations of a Celtic settlement that dates from around 400 to 500 BC. The hill also hides remains of a 2nd-millennium BC necropolis, known locally as 'El Santuarío'.

19 CASTAÑUELO

Darkly wooded hills rise up behind this tangle of sun-washed white streets. As most of these streets are pedestrianised, it feels like a window into centuries-old village life. In winter, small fires are lit in large pans on doorsteps and chimneys give off long plumes of woodsmoke. The bars are small and welcoming; a handful of peanuts passed over the bar is exactly that, scattered next to your beer.

→ You can follow a footpath from Corterrangel to the village. If you drive in, it's best to leave the car just outside the village.

5 mins, 37.9367, -6.5814 ▦🍴♀🏃⛰

20 ZUFRE

The narrow, winding white streets of this town, hidden in the hills and clouds above the sierra, testify to its Arabic roots; *xufre* is the Arabic for tributary river. Step down into the Plaza del Iglesia and it suddenly changes into Castillian brickwork with a 16th-century Italian-style loggia and a fountain that has supplied fresh water to travellers since Roman times. Vist in spring to see hundreds of swallows, house martins and orange blossoms. Come in late August for the Romería de Nuestra Señora del Puerto. The festival is famous for horse races that are run through the village's winding streets. At Easter, too, the village comes alive with religious processions.

→ There is free parking by the Plaza de Toros, from here it is about 300m to the central plaza.

5 mins, 37.8338, -6.3388 🍴♀▦✝⛵🏃⛰

21 MIRADOR PIEDRA UTRERA

A stony track leads through cork trees to this immense rock, a natural viewpoint. Climb to the top for views of the mountains and plains that surround the Cumbres de San Bartolomé. You can see the Arroyo del Sillo winding between the Huelva and Badajoz districts and the hills slowly merging into Portugal beyond.

→ From Cumbres de San Bartolomé take the road towards Cumbres de Enmedio for 1km and park on the roadside at signs for 'mirador'. Walk 200m down the track and the rock is on the L.

5 mins, 38.0815, -6.7268 ◼🅿🅿

22 MONASTERIO DE TENTUDÍA

The monastery sits on the border of Andalucía and Extremadura. The legend goes that the 13th-century captain Pelay Pérez, while losing a battle against the Arabs, implored the Virgin

for help, shouting, "Holy Mary, stop the day!" The miracle happened and the day drew out. Technically, the monastery is situated 1km into Extremadura, but it is a wonderful place to watch the long shadows of the hills stretch over Andalucía at sunset.

→ From Santa Olalla del Cala, take the A66 north for 21km until Monasterio, take exit 722, at the roundabout take the 4th exit and stay on the EX-103 for 8km, turn L at crossroads and continue 10km until the monastery. Parking.

1 min, 38.0545, -6.3383 ◼📷✝📧

23 MESÓN LA POSÁ

In the centre of the village, this 18th-century bar was a meeting point for smugglers and bandits; the most famous locally was Diego Corrientes, hanged in Seville in 1781. Its brick, stone and wood is over 300 years old and its restoration is true to its murky past. It is a great place to try a typical *revuelto de gurumelos* (Heavy Amidella mushroom), which grows in the sierra and is a good choice with *cerdo ibérico* (Iberian pig). Also try the *carrillera* (pigs cheeks), *morcilla lustre* (black pudding) or *guarrito frito* (fried pork).

→ Calle Botica, 1, 21390 Encinasola, 669 849 746
38.1355, -6.8718 ⬛⬛⬛⬛⬛

24 MESÓN MIGUEL TENORIO

A bar and restaurant in the old wine cellars of the 19th-century palace of Don Tenorio de Castilla. There is a shady terrace, a cool retreat from the sun-bleached white streets of Almonaster. Local, seasonal ingredients are used to make their traditional dishes.

→ Almendro, 2, 21350 Almonaster la Real, 959 736 054
37.8721, -6.7872 ⬛⬛

25 BODEGA LOS CURROS

'Save our Earth, it's the only planet with beer!' is scrawled in chalk behind the bar. A good choice of *onubense* wines are stacked in the walls of this welcoming bodega. Small plates, *montaditos* (open sandwiches) or tapas, will find their way from the bar to your barrel as you order drinks. Open Fri – Sun.

→ Calle Domingo Fal Conde, 11, 21220 Higuera de la Sierra, 659 649 546
37.8374, -6.4474 ⬛⬛

26 CABALGATA DE HIGUERA DE LA SIERRA

On Epiphany evening in 1918, three friends rode on horseback into Higuera de la Sierra dressed as Gaspar, Balthazar and Melchoir and throwing sweets to the children. The tradition caught on and now Higuera is home to the second oldest Cabalgata procession in Spain. On 5 January enormous trucks move slowly through the town carrying elaborate nativity scenes recreated with fantastic costumes and sets. Armfuls of sweets are thrown and balconies heave with families jostling to see their friends dressed as Mary, a star or a shepherd. With luck, you might catch a glimpse of a shadowy king on horseback. It is pretty hard not to get caught up in this festive excitement. Arrive early as the event is scheduled for 8pm but the roads are closed much earlier.

→ From Aracena head S on the N-433 for 15km and use the parking 500m outside Higuera. Bring reflective clothes and a torch for the walk into town.
10 mins, 37.8341, -6.4450 ⬛⬛⬛⬛

27 RESTAURANTE LA VENTANA

This rustic restaurant spills out onto the square in Zufre by its palm trees. It has a kids' climbing frame and views over the blue lake to the sierra beyond. Head inside if it's cold; the tables look out to these splendid views and there is a great choice of tapas, local meat dishes, *jamón* and wine.

→ Calle los Linares, 21210 Zufre, Huelva, 959 198 281
37.8327, -6.3400 ⬛⬛⬛⬛

28 JESÚS CERERO CARRASCO, FABRICA DE SALAZONES Y CARNES IBERICAS

A very good butcher if you're looking for meats to grill at home. There are great prices on the cured *jamón* here as they run the factory. The family also run a restaurant (open since 1940), Restaurante Primitivo in Santa Olalla.

→ Pol. Ind. C/ Los Cabezos, Nave 6, 21260 Santa Olalla del Cala, 616 138 831
37.9024, -6.2206

WILDER CAMPING

29 PUERTO PEÑAS

An excellent hideaway with yurts and wooden cabins. A cottage and hostel rooms are also available. Adventure activities are on offer, such as archery, climbing and kayaking. It is all sustainably run and the restaurant specialises in local *onubense* food and wine.

➜ Camino de los Rasos, 21240 Aroche, 959 109 209, Andevaloaventura.com
37.9446, -7.0574 🛡️🍴👤🏕️🅿️⛰️🐾

30 CAMPING RIBERA DEL CHANZA

A family-friendly campsite with lots of outdoor kids' crafts and workshops on the banks of the River Chanza and an easy stroll into Cortegana.

➜ Av. las Norias, 21230 Cortegana, 601 222 434, Campingdecortegana.es
37.9135, -6.8282 🚶👤⛺️🅿️🏕️🚶

COSY COTTAGES

31 FINCA MONTEFRÍO

This family-run, sustainable farm offers several idyllic cottages in the natural park. It has a pool and is close to many hiking routes. Well-behaved pets with prior permission are welcome as it is a working farm.

➜ Carretera Corte, 3, 21230 Cortegana, 666 756 875, Fincamontefrio.com
37.9423, -6.7977 🚶⛰️👤🅿️♻️🐾

32 CASA RURAL EL ALAMILLO

Surrounded by farmland and chestnut and walnut trees, these three ancient cottages have thick walls, chestnut beams and Arabic tiles. A short stroll leads into Galaroza and many footpaths lead into the natural park.

➜ Finca el Alamillo, Km 102, Nacional 433, 21291 Galaroza, 677 044 220, Casalamillo.es
37.9166, -6.7011 ⛰️🚶👤👤🅿️♻️🐾

33 MOLINO RÍO ALÁJA

Six cosy cottages along the banks of the river, with mountain views and a short stroll from the village of Alája. They run gastronomy, bird-watching and cycling holidays. Bike rental and guitar classes are on offer too.

➜ Finca Cabezo del Molino s/n, 21340 Alájar, 638 081 415, Molinorioalajar.com
37.8650, -6.6749 🅿️🚲🏊⛰️🚶👤🐾

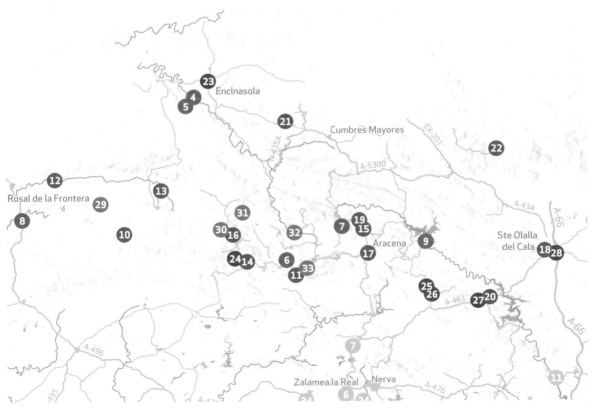

HUELVA COAST & DOÑANA

Our perfect weekend

→ **Watch** hundreds of pink flamingos preen and feed at the Parque Nacional de Doñana

→ **Listen** for birdsong under cork trees at the ancient burial site of Los Gabrieles, with views across the gentle hills of Sierra de Huelva

→ **Forage** for pearly white crowberries, *camariñas*, along the dunes at Acantilado del Asperillo

→ **Cycle** along the Vía Verde de Guadiana and scramble to find waterfalls at Arroyo del Infierno

→ **Plunge** from the grassy banks into the deep river water at Embalse del Calabazar from a rope swing

→ **Sling** up your hammock between pine trees and relax by the dunes of Playa San Miguel

→ **Wander** along the long, deserted beaches of Playa de Nuevo Umbría and skinny dip in its turquoise waves

→ **Hike** along the disused railway lines of the Río Tinto mining company, following the reddish ochres of the winding river

→ **Enjoy** the festivities and passion as pilgrims' horses kick up dust on their way to the sanctuary at El Rocío

The Huelva coast, with its long silver beaches, runs as far as the westernmost corner of Andalucía. Bordering Portugal, it is defined by two great rivers: the Guadiana to the west and the Guadalquivir to the east. From a bird's eye view, the Guadalquivir delta, as river meets sea, feeds into a fractal pattern of shallow streams, endlessly dividing like bright-green veins and capillaries. This is the Doñana National Park, over 500,000 hectares of protected wilderness whose ever-shifting dunes, sandbanks and marshland are home to over 300 species of birds. It is a glimmering haven for birds that migrate, flock or nest here, and every summer its marshes provide a habitat for hundreds of pink flamingos, storks, herons, glossy ibis and spoonbills. Its wilder corners are a breeding ground for the endangered Iberian lynx and are home to red deer, otters, a gamut of wildlife.

The shimmering marshlands are also a beautiful metaphor for the semi-mythical space it holds in history and the cultural imagination. The lost city of Tartessos is believed to have been located in Huelva, around the mouth of the Guadalquivir, where it thrived in the rich metal trade from the 9th century BC onwards. Ancient Greek texts refer to a great city here, and recently unearthed archaeological treasures – the golden hoard at El Carambolo, for example, with its intricate statue of the goddess Astarte, or the zoomorphic vessels La Joya – have shed a little light on its web of facts and fiction.

But for many there is another enigma attached to this misty haven: it is home to the Virgin of El Rocío, whose sanctuary annually hosts Andalucía's largest pilgrimage. Attracting over a million pilgrims, or *romeros*, from across Spain, the spiritual journey sees pilgrims plunge into the river with their horses at Vado de Quema as they approach the end of several nights' wild camping, feasting and dancing. In colourful flamenco dress and pulling garlanded bow top wagons, they resemble characters from a folk tale. Watched by many on the news, they move into Seville's Aljarafe, an area running from Aznalcóllar with its dazzling lakes, south along the green corridor of the Guadiamar river to the marshlands of Doñana. There is a dream-like quality to this brightly coloured procession as it moves through the wild, cracked-mud marshlands.

In this endlessly changing landscape, Doñana gives way to beautiful fossil dunes at Acantilado del Asperillo, with gullies and caves next to bright beaches. To the west is the sandy isthmus of la Flecha de Nueva Umbría and its deserted, white sands and warm, shallow water. But inland, before the Sierra de Aracena, lies a supernatural-looking landscape, the result of over two millennia of mining. Valleys with deep-red terraced fissures are crossed by the bright-green rivulets of the Río Tinto and the Río Odiel. Upon contact with the air, they change colour to become wide, meandering, blood-red rivers. Many of the mining railways have been converted into cycle paths, a good way to explore these rivers and lost ruins.

Recharge and refuel with the traditional seafood dishes of the Huelva coast; try the heaped plates of fresh seafood at the harbour in Lepe. Or you can opt for local specialities such as the *raya con Pimentón* (skate with paprika) if you are near Ayamonte or habas con choco (beans with cuttlefish). At Ardea Purpurea Lodge you can sleep under the old beams of thatched cottages, known as *chozas*, typically built by the fishermen and salineros working in the salt pans and marshlands.

SECRET BEACHES

1 ACANTILADO DEL ASPERILLO

A long, wide stretch of beach borders these incredible fossil dunes, whose layers of ochre, white, orange and grey tell a story some 15,000 years old. Formed by Atlantic sands washed out to sea by the Guadalquivir, these ancient dunes are continually changing due to the impact of the waves and rain and now reach up to 100m in height. Their stratified, fanciful undulations and geometric shapes are interrupted by several caves. *Camariña*, or Portuguese crowberries, cover this stretch of coastline and are known as the 'pearl of the dunes'. You can walk along a sandy trail to this natural viewing point out over a sea of pine trees, where there are great sunset views and ropes down the cliffs to the beach.

→ From Matalascañas take the A-494 towards Mazagón for 8km. At signs for Acantilado del Asperillo park in the layby on the L. For easier beach access continue 6km further to reach the Cuesta Maneli trail and follow along a 1.3km wooden walkway to the dunes, then wander back along the beach towards Matalascañas for quieter sands.

25 mins, 37.0408, -6.6309 🏖️🌊🐚📷🗺️💧🏛️📷

2 PLAYA DE LA FLECHA DE NUEVA UMBRÍA

This great spit of sand, some 12km long, also known as La Flecha del Rompido, hides some of the most beautiful virgin beaches. It is growing rapidly. Thanks to the accumulation of sand from the Piedras river, the west wind and the tides, it has grown 4km in the last 200 years. Its deserted beaches can be reached by ferry, but the 2km footpath from El Terrón passes tidal marshlands, home to Eurasian curlews and other waders, as well as a 16th-century watchtower, built to withstand Barbary pirate attacks, before reaching its long golden sands.

→ From El Terrón take the A-5055 towards La Antilla, and the beginning of the track is after 150m on the L.

30 mins, 37.2078, -7.1275 🏖️🐚🦅🌊🚶🏕️🚫🔆

3 PLAYA SAN MIGUEL

Just before the Río Piedras meets the sea it flows behind a protective arm of the sandy peninsula known as La Flecha because it resembles an arrow. Waves gently lap a protected sandy beach behind this flecha, perfect for children as it is quiet, shallow and warm. Sling your hammock up in the shade of pine trees just behind the dunes. A great hidden spot.

→ From El Rompido take the A-5052 for 2km towards El Portil and take the sandy track on the R at 37.2166, -7.0966
10 mins, 37.2154, -7.0956 🏊🏖️🌊

4 PLAYA EL PORTIL

A beautiful sandy beach with lots of shells and shallow swims, perfect for children. Come just after the summer solstice for the fiesta of San Juan, where bonfires are lit all along the beach and people feast, dance and swim late into the night.

→ From El Portil take the A-5052 for 2.5km and park opposite the Restaurante Rifeño.
2 mins, 37.2033, -7.0296 🏖️🏕️🍴

LAKES & LAGOONS

5 EMBALSE DEL CALABAZAR

Come on a cool evening and relax under the trees sheltering this calm, green lake. On clear nights, with a moonless sky, thousands of stars are reflected in the water and tiny crayfish, *cangrejo del río*, creep to the clear shallows. There is also a rope swing over the deeper part of the lake to the right of a rickety pier.

→ From Sotiel Coronada take the A-496 N for 1km and turn L onto the H-9019 for 700m,

then R onto a dirt track and continue to reach the concrete area by the lake.
1 min, 37.6096, -6.8647 🏊🍴ℹ️⛺

6 EMBALSE DE ZUMAJO

A hidden corner of the Zumajo reservoir with a freshwater bathing area, where you will share your swim with herons and kingfishers. This is a former reservoir of the British mines and now there is a hippy café and river club here with canoes, music, yoga and dance.

→ From Minas de Riotinto it's a 3km walk along quiet roads. Follow Calle Altozano out of town. At the crossroads follow the road curving R and continue on the track to the water.
40 mins, 37.6785, -6.5937 🏊🍴🛶

7 EMBALSE DE CAMPOFRÍO

The oldest dam in the province of Huelva and a great place for a cool dip in the heat of the summer. This small lake is just south of the mining village of Campofrío.

→ From Campofrío, take the A-461 for 1.7km towards Minas de Riotinto. Park on your L and follow the dirt track for 500m or so. There are paths down to the water.
10 mins, 37.7523, -6.5847 🏊❓

8 EMBALSE DE WALABONSO

A small but picturesque lake surrounded by pine trees and with good shady areas for picnics. It is named after Saint Walabonso who was martyred at nearby Niebla in the 9th century. There is easy entry for swims, a few stone BBQs and kids' swings. It can fill up with families on holidays and pilgrimages but is generally quiet.

→ From Niebla take the HU-3106 N towards Valverde del Camino for 12km. Turn L at signs for Camino Florestal and follow for 500m to reach the lake.

1 min, 37.4585, -6.7166 🏊🚶🏞🐕🦅🏕

RIVERS & WATERFALLS

9 PLAYA FLUVIAL SANLÚCAR DE GUADIANA

A short stroll from the small town of Sanlúcar del Guadiana, this grassy picnic park offers deep, green swims in the Guadiana river with views out to neighbouring Portugal. Don't miss the chance to zipline across the river to Portugal – if that's your thing. The jumping point is from the old castle of San Marcos. Call Limitezero – 670 313 933.

→ From Sanlúcar follow Avenida de Portugal to reach the river park.
5 mins, 37.4714, -7.4683 🚵🏕️🍴🏖️🏛️

10 CASCADA DEL ARROYO DEL INFIERNO

This hidden waterfall in the Arroyo del Infierno stream, just before the Guadiana river and the border with Portugal, is all but forgotten. The waterfall plunges over sharp rocks into a small pool, deep in woodland. The Vía Verde del Guadiana cycle route runs nearby.

→ Follow the Vía Verde del Guadiana from Puerto de La Laja for 1km to where a small dirt track leads down to the river. Follow your nose as access is uncertain.
30 mins, 37.5212, -7.4854 ❓📖🔦🚴

11 PUENTE DE LA CORONADA

The Río Odiel, with its striking mix of bright ochres, reds, azul blues and greens, passes under the arches of this 18th-century bridge. The impossible colours are a result of water draining through sulfide-rich earth and clay disturbed by centuries of mining. Start here for the 9km Ruta de los Molinos hiking trail, which follows the river through a landscape scoured with canyons, resembling a Wild West backdrop.

→ From Valverde del Camino take the A-496 towards Sotiel Coronada for 7km. Cross the river and turn R just after the white hermitage. Park here and follow the path round to the back of the bar for the beginning of the Ruta de los Molinos footpath and continue on the path down to the water and bridge.
5 mins, 37.5961, -6.8445 🚻🏞️🍴

12 RESTOS DEL MOLINO LA PATERA

One of the most picturesque corners of the Corredor Verde del Guadiamar, the green corridor along the river, is at this old water mill known as the duckhouse. In spring, after rain, the river cascades over the 2m-high dam and rushes on under shady woodland. Buzzards call overhead and approach quietly to see herons before they fly away. El Vado de Quema, the popular name for the ford in the river crossed by the annual pilgrimage to El Rocío, is found 3km downstream.

→ It is forbidden to drive in this area, unless authorised. The best walk is a 5km route from Área Recreativa Buitrago at 37.3050, -6.2597. Follow the footpath hugging the river S for 5km.
1 hr, 37.2693, -6.2615 🐦🚻📷🚶🚮

WILDLIFE WONDERS

13 DEHESA DE ABAJO

You can see hundreds of pink flamingos, storks and herons at Laguna de Rianzuela in the Dehesa de Abajo, which forms part of the Doñana wetlands. The dehesa is also one of the principal breeding grounds for the Iberian lynx and is a protected space. Behind the restaurant, which is open every day, you can wander 500m down to the bird hide for the best views. It also hosts the annual Doñana Birdfair.

→ Centro de Visitantes de la Dehesa de Abajo, Av. Isla Mayor, 89, 41130 La Puebla del Río, Sevilla, 954 186 500

5 mins, 37.2001, -6.1806 📺📧🍴

14 PARQUE NACIONAL DE DOÑANA

The vast expanse of the Doñana National Park comprises around 50,000 hectares of marshland, lagoons, pine groves, moving dunes and cliffs and is home to lynx, otters, boar and an immense array of birdlife. Much of it is roadless and access is restricted; the natural park surrounding it acts as a kind of bolster. To see some of this semi-mythical landscape contact the expert guide, José Manuel, at Doñana Nature who runs one of the few permitted tours.

→ Call 630 978 216, Donana-nature.com

37.0127, -6.4323 📺🚗🚐🏔️🌐

15 CAÑADA DE LOS PÁJAROS

A family-run bird sanctuary and breeding ground for around 200 species of native birds, many of which are endangered or under threat of extinction. A signed walkway circles the flamingo lagoon and leads through various habitats. Look out for friendly donkeys. A great place for kids.

→ Carretera de la Puebla del Río - Isla Mayor, km 8, 41130 La Puebla del Río, 955 772 184, Canadadelospajaros.com

2 mins, 37.2388, -6.1295 📺🍴🌐

ANCIENT & SACRED

16 TEJADA LA VIEJA

The remains of this late Bronze Age hilltop fort lies in the foothills of the Sierra de Tejada with views of Seville and Huelva provinces. Its wall dates to the 8th century BC and you can see the foundations of buildings abandoned in the 6th century BC. Built next to several mineral veins and a mining route, it is thought to have been a Tartessian settlement, later controlling the Phoenician metal trade.

17

→ You can gain access by booking a free, guided visit at Tejadalavieja.com or call 959 423 272

15 mins, 37.4972, -6.3621 ⊞🏍🖼⛰

17 PUENTE ROMANA NIEBLA

A nice place to pause by the copper-red vein of the Río Tinto before entering the beautiful walled town of Niebla with its medieval castle. This Roman bridge is over two thousand years old. Dedicated to the goddess Minerva, it was part of the Roman way linking Itálica and Seville, passing Itucci and Tejada la Vieja. Restored after heavy damage in the Civil War, it miraculously still stands, even under the weight of today's traffic.

→ Just off the A472, entering Niebla from the E.

1 min, 37.3652, -6.6729 ⊞🖼🎋

18 DOLMEN DE SOTO

One of Spain's largest subterranean burial mounds, thought to be around 5,000 years old. A long corridor leads into the circular mound formed of immense standing stones of quartzite, sandstone and limestone. Twenty capstones, some of which have engravings, form the roof of the passage. In

1924 eight ancient bodies were found buried with marine fossils, daggers and cups. At the spring and autumn equinoxes, the first light enters the passage and illuminates the interior chamber for several minutes; it is thought to represent rebirth.

→ Take Calle Sevilla from Trigueros, which passes Bar El Dolmen, follow signs for 8.5km. Closed Mon. All tours must be booked ahead, free or €2 for a guide. Call – 627 940 357, Giglon.com

2 mins, 37.3521, -6.7514 🏍🪝⊞✝

19 DÓLMEN DEL PUERTO DE LOS HUERTOS

A few stones standing like gaping teeth are all that remain on this hill overlooking the sierra and the treetops melting into the blue distance. Facing the sunrise in the east, it was built around 3,000 BC and grave goods of stone arrowheads, ceramic pots, prisms of quartz crystal, slate idols as well as many necklace beads of green stones have been unearthed here.

→ From Berrocal take the H-9026 towards El Madroño for 1km until you reach a green billboard for Berrocal on the L. Park here and walk down the dirt track for 50m.

5 mins, 37.6126, -6.5371 🏍✝📷🍴❓

16

19

20 DÓLMENES DE EL POZUELO

In a clearing on a small hill surrounded by dense eucalyptus forest are several enormous, ancient dolmens. These funerary structures date from 3000–2500 BC and are accessed by paths through tall grass and olive groves. You can stoop inside under some of the mighty stones, set here 5,000 years ago. In spring the air is heavy with the scent of rock roses. The Vía Verde de Riotinto passes nearby.

→ From Zalamea la Real take the N-435 S towards Valverde del Camino for 7.5km. Turn L at signs for El Pozuelo and continue for 3km through El Pozuelo village, following brown signs for Ruta Dolménica.

10 mins, 37.6039, -6.6632 🚲✝🏛◈✦🚴

21 DÓLMENES DE LOS GABRIELES

Surrounded by rockrose and rosemary, and overlooking the gentle hills of Sierra de Huelva, these dolmens rest in a wild and somehow unearthly place. Cork trees stretch burnt arms into a bare sky pierced only by birdsong. You can sense it was once a supernatural place, and one perhaps of pilgrimage, for the people who sank these stones deep into the earth around 2500 BC.

→ From Valverde del Camino take the A-493 for 1km. Turn L onto a dirt track at the sign

for Dolmen (37.5588, -6.7356) and park here. Walk down the track for 3km, following the wooden signs with sketched arrows. Various other dolmens are hidden on the hill.

45 mins, 37.5590, -6.7112 🚲✝🏛◈✦🚴

HIKING & BIKING

22 RÍO TINTO

This river is in the top five most dangerous places to swim in the world. The blood-red water with high acidic levels is the result of 5,000 years of mining pollution. Its extreme environment breeds organisms such as iron and sulfur-oxidising bacteria. Scientists at NASA believe the river's out-of-this-world conditions are similar to other worlds, such as Mars and Jupiter's moon Europa. A good way to see this technicolour river is by following the old railway track from Puente Gadea to the old Berrocal Station, soon to become a cycleway.

→ From Valverde del Camino take the A-493 S for 22km. Cross the bridge and park on the L.

5 mins, 37.4233, -6.6098 🚲🚶🏕

23 VÍA VERDE DE RIOTINTO

This 35km greenway cycle path starts in Valverde del Camino, passing Zalamea

la Real and the Dólmenes de El Pozuelo, ending in the town of Minas de Riotinto. Confusingly, it does have the same name as the old railway. You can walk along the Tinto river but this cycle path does not follow the blood-red river course; it runs through the beautiful green countryside. You can even start the cycle path earlier and take the Vía Verde de los Molinos de Agua in San Juan del Puerto, which runs 33km to Valverde del Camino.

→ From Valverde del Camino head N out of town towards Zalamea. After a few metres there is a camper van parking site at 37.5811, -6.7513 on the R. Park here and the cycle path is a few metres behind.

2.5 hrs, 37.5811, -6.7509 🚴🏻‍♂️🚶🏻‍♂️🚵

WILD RUINS

24 CEMENTERIO DE TRENES DE RIOTINTO

Several abandoned trains from the Río Tinto mining company are rusting next to the reddish river. The place has an eery atmosphere, as if their metal still rings with energy.

→ A small tourist train runs along the tracks here from Nerva. From Minas de Riotinto take the A-476 then the HU-6104 for 4km to Las

Delgadas. From here follow the HV-5015 for 3km downhill to reach a junction. The trains are on privately owned mining land, but you can easily see them through the trees, and the gates are often open.

5 mins, 37.6710, -6.5613 🔲🖼🏞

25 RESTOS DEL POBLADO DE LOS CABEZUDOS

The haunting ruins of this village with its church and shops were home to logging workers during the early 20th century. Queen Sofía once spent the night here on her way to El Rocío. Finally abandoned in the 1980s, its ruins are left open to the elements and storks nest in the belfry.

→ From Almonte take the HU-4200 south towards the coast. After 14km you will see the ruins on the R of the road. Park where you can and wander in.

1 min, 37.1761, -6.6226 🔲🖼🏞◈

FEASTS & FESTIVITIES

26 ROMERÍA DE EL ROCÍO

The Whitsun pilgrimage to El Rocío blends together elements of Seville's summer Feria and the Semana Santa, mixing the sacred and profane, to create one of the

LOCAL FOOD & WINE

28 CHIRINGUITO DER MATIAS

A great beach bar serving fresh fish, summer salads and rice dishes, located along the Punta Umbria beaches. Try the *chocos fritos* (fried cuttlefish) for which Huelva is famed, or the *acedías*, a small flat-bodied fish, similar to sole, and the *croquetas* are excellent. Well priced.

→ Carretera de Portil-Punta Umbría, Km 9, 21100 Punta Umbría, 607 086 411
37.2010, -7.0198

29 LA BELLA CASA REVUELTA

At this restaurant, right by Lepe's harbour, you can feast on the freshest fish cooked *onubense*-style. They serve heaped plates of *langostino* (king prawns), Huelva's famous *coquinas*, clams and cockles, *gambas blanco* (white prawns), as well as *choco* (cuttlefish), urchins, razor clams and tuna cured and cooked in many ways. It's a fish lover's heaven.

→ Bo. Puerto Terrón, 30, 21440 El Terrón, 959 380 261, Restaurantelabellaterron.com
37.2251, -7.1752

30 MESÓN EL TAMBORILERO

A little cathedral to the flavours of Huelva. Try the *corvina en salsa de almendra* (sea bass in almond sauce), *chocos con patatas* (cuttlefish with potatoes), *las alubias con almejas* (beans with clams), *los cocidos de verdura* (vegetable stew) or *la berenjena rellena* (stuffed aubergine). As for the wine, the staff also manage Almonte's wine museum, and they have a huge array of local wines to try. Homemade desserts. Good prices.

→ Av. de la Juventud, 2, 21730 Almonte, 959 406 955, Mesoneltamborilero.com
37.2652, -6.5178

WILD HIDEAWAYS

31 ARDEA PURPUREA LODGE

This peaceful retreat is named after the purple heron which can often be seen flying low over the surrounding Doñana wetlands. Several thatched cottages echo the traditional way farmers in the rice fields and marshland of nearby Dehesa de Abajo built their *chozas*, or huts. There is a pool and restaurant, and the annual pilgrimage of El Rocío, with its colourful wagons and decked horses, passes by the gates on its way to Vado del Quema. They offer several sustainable day trips, including horses and

most passionate festivals in Andalucía. Pilgrims travel along routes from across Spain, sleeping mostly outdoors and in bowtop wagons, dancing by campfires and exploding rockets all night. Women are dressed in colourful flamenco costumes and the men in cloth caps, with black-and-grey-striped trousers. The pilgrimage culminates on the Sunday at the procession of the Virgen Del Rocío, surrounded by the Doñana marshlands. Only the men from Almonte are allowed to carry her, and they defend this right viciously: jumping over railings, a surging, hysterical mass of sweaty bodies.

→ Calle el Real, 14, 21750 El Rocío
37.1308, -6.4851

27 LA GUINDILLA

Set a small way back from the Rocío pilgrim site, where there are many more bars to choose from, this restaurant is a great stop if you want to get a little piece of the Wild West experience. Just off the dusty road that leads into the sanctuary, waiters serve mounted riders with their orders as they pause on the road. There is a good, well-priced daily menu, *del día*, serving tasty dishes for a set price and views across the wetlands. During the festivities something close to anarchy rules in El Rocío; it's easy to lose your sense of time and social responsibility.

→ Av. de la Canaliega, 6A, 21750 Rocío, 959 442 030
37.1323, -6.4895

electric buggy, to see wildlife in the Doñana Natural Park.

→ Camino de los Labrados, 41850 Villamanrique de la Condesa, 955 755 479, Ardeapurpurea.com

37.2412, -6.2937 🅿️🚲🐴🍽️🚶🍴

32 KUKUTANA

A beautiful villa surrounded by the Doñana wetlands and located along the El Rocío pilgrim path. They offer birdwatching, horse riding and eco-tourism activities as well gastronomy and wine tours.

→ Camino del Rocío, 41849 Aznalcázar, 698 925 839, Kukutana.es

37.1775, -6.3116 🚲🍴♀️🏕️🐴

33 CAMPING DEHESA NUEVA

A basic, no-frills-attached camping ground under the shade of pine trees in the dehesa. There is a pool and a nice restaurant; wooden cabins are also an option.

→ Ctra. Aznalcázar, Km 3,200, 41849 Isla Mayor, 955 750 981, Campingdehesanueva.es

37.2773, -6.2345 🚲💀⛱️🍴

34 CASA RURAL EL ROMERITO

A 20-minute stroll down to the pretty village of Zalamea la Real, this charming cottage with gardens and terraces is a peaceful escape. Several hiking trails run nearby, and it is close to the Vía Verde de Riotinto. Sleeps 10. Pets welcome.

→ Diseminado Romerito, 70, 21640 Zalamea la Real, 665 554 231

37.6667, -6.6654 🚲🏔️🚶♿🐕

35 LOS MOLINOS

A number of small cottages and rooms are available at a guesthouse by the Guadiana river and the border with Portugal in the pretty village of Sanlúcar de Guadiana.

→ Calle Nueva, Sanlúcar de Guadiana, 608 558 803, Losmolinosturismorural.com

37.4706, -7.4668 🚲🚲🚶♿🏊

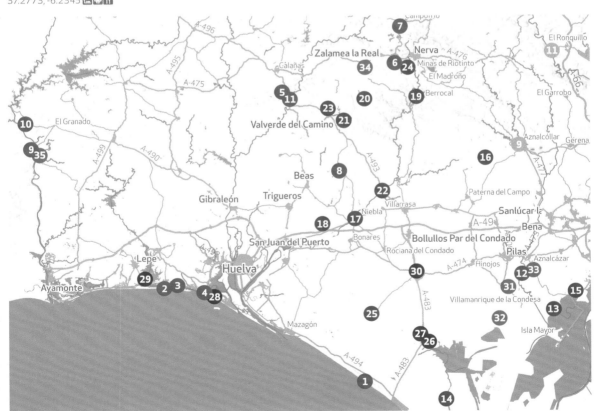

SIERRA NORTE DE SEVILLA

Our perfect weekend

→ **Climb** to the treetops and rattle along the rope bridges at Isla Margarita by the River Huéznar

→ **Cycle** along the disused railway line, the Vía Verde de la Sierra Norte, in springtime to see meadows popping with colourful flowers

→ **Wander** through dense, green woodland to reach the Cascadas del Huéznar waterfall

→ **Follow** footpaths through the Hornachuelos woodland and stumble across ruins of the 17th-century mill houses along the Rivera de Ciudadeja

→ **Clamber** down the river-smoothed rock pools at the Fluvial Majadallana river beach and dip into the cool river water

→ **Swim** out as the last rays catch the surface of the Embalse de José Torán lake and watch the sun set over the Sierra de Hornachuelos beyond

→ **Bed** down under the old beams at Cortijo El Berrocal and wake up to a day's horse trekking in the Cazalla hills

→ **Feast** on local tapas and wine before a siesta and swim at the river beach in San Nicolás del Puerto

The wild mountains just north of Seville stretch from the Roman mines and karstic rocks of Cerro del Hierro to the spherical granite boulders of El Pedroso and its border castles at El Real de la Jara. In between, you can find caves and waterfalls along the Huéznar river, fossilised jellyfish at Peña Escrita and over 170,000 hectares of cork oak, holm oak and olive trees. One of Andalucía's geoparks, it forms part of the immense Sierra Morena mountain range and is a popular destination for climbers of all levels. Winding through this wonderful scenery is an 18km cycle path and the long-distance GR48 footpath.

South of these mountains runs the Guadalquivir river, entering from the Córdoba province, at this point flowing wide and slow through the fertile plains. These endless, flat, green *campiñas* offer the famous Golden City no means of hiding from the beating sun. In the summer months, after the bitter oranges have flowered and fallen, Seville becomes what is commonly known as the 'oven of Spain'.

The oak forests and rivers of the Sierra Norte de Sevilla offer a beautiful escape from Seville's heat. If you visit in springtime, poppy fields and roadside wild flowers are bursting into colour. The hills here are gentle and the park is mostly *dehesa*: a mixture of pasture and woodland typical of the Sierra Morena, often used for rearing the famous black pigs. The main river, Rivera del Huéznar, is home to otters and trout, while a green tangle of elm, ash, alder, willow and hazel roots edge its banks. Well-signed footpaths and the 18km Vía Verde cycle route provide a great way to follow the river and stop off for cool swims.

At Cascadas del Huéznar, one of Andalucía's natural monuments, the river emerges from underground to form several waterfalls. Their deep, green bathing pools, sheltered by forest canopy, are idyllic places to swim. Nearby, the small town of San Nicolás del Puerto has eased the flow of the river to create a large pool under its Roman bridge. At the ancient mines of Cerro del Hierro, you can wander through a sculptural world of karstic needles, caves and chasms.

The Romans also left their mark at Santiponce: emperors Hadrian and Trajan were born at this monumental city, then known as Itálica. More recently, the ruined amphitheatre was the setting for a dragon scene in Game of Thrones and is a popular day trip from Seville. But you can discover deserted Roman ruins at Munigua, in the foothills of the Sierra Norte. And even more peaceful watermills can be found on the banks of the Guadalquivir at Molino de la Aceña.

At the end of the day, sling up a hammock at Camping la Fundición and watch the River Huéznar rush by, or retreat to the gardens and rustic haven at Casa Rural El Castaño. Refuel with grilled-game meats and stews by the grand fireplaces at Restaurante La Herradura and get ready for another day of cycling and swimming.

RIVERS & WATERFALLS

1 CATARATA LA MOLINETA

A beautiful picnic spot by a dam in the Rivera de Ciudadeja, deep in the Sierra de Hornachuelos. Tall holm oaks, cork oaks and wild olives provide ample shade. While it is green all year round, water is present only in the winter and spring. Follow the path upstream 200m to find the ruins of a 17th-century flour mill. The way lies along the old livestock route to Constantina, in some places known as the 'tunnel' as it becomes a holloway. Several footpaths pass by, including the Geo-Ruta Las Chorreras, which follows the Ciudadeja river.

→ From Las Navas de la Concepción take the A-3301 and after 400m park at signs for 'Complejo Polideportivo'. Follow the footpath signs for the Vereda de Constantina Camino del Tunel trail for 1.9km and before it turns R into an olive grove, continue for 100m down to the dam.

30 mins, 37.9160, -5.4787 🏕🏞⛰

2 CASCADAS BARRANCO RISCO BLANCO

A beautiful series of very wild waterfalls in ravines that fill pools in a narrow canyon. Limestone cliffs tower overhead and griffon vultures circle. It is best to go with a guide as the footpath starts in Almadén de la Plata and permission must be sought from the Delegación Provincial de Sevilla de Medio Ambiente as a few gates need to be unlocked.

→ Contact Montañaviva.es for canyoning here and at various other sites, 626 720 720

1 hr, 37.7949, -5.9690 🏊🏞🐦❓

3 FLUVIAL MAJADALLANA RIVER BEACH

The Siete Arroyos river has carved several beautiful, natural pools in the flowing limestone upriver from La Ermita de la Virgen de Aguas Santas and Villaverde del Río. There is access to water with ducks behind the Ermita, but upriver it opens out to more dramatic rocks, green pools and a 6m waterfall known as la Última Olla. In May there is an annual pilgrimage to the Ermita to celebrate the small statue of the virgin, hidden in the walls during eight centuries of Arab rule and discovered after the Christian conquest.

→ Entering Villaverde del Río from the direction of Alcalá del Río, cross the river and take the third exit at the roundabout. Follow signs for Parque Fluvial de Majadallana for 3km along the river. Pass the Ermita and there is a signed parking area. Walk upriver for 1km to find several pools.

15 mins, 37.6276, -5.8862 🏊🏞⛰🐦

4 PLAYA DE SAN NICOLÁS DEL PUERTO

The Los Parrales river has been dammed as it runs under the old Roman bridge in San Nicolás and offers long swims in its deep, glassy water. A couple of bars and cafés, popular with locals and bikers, line its banks. It is a great balance of town and nature but come off-season for a quieter swim. The Vía Verde passes by.

→ By the old bridge on C. Galidón in the centre of the village, head down through the town towards the river; you can't miss it.

1 min, 37.9964, -5.6521 🅱🏊🚴🍴🚶

5 CASCADAS DEL HUÉZNAR

Gnarled roots edge the river banks and the Huéznar eddies around mossy green stones. You'll hear the cascades as you approach. Follow the path downstream to the tallest waterfall and deepest pool. Come at dusk for sun-warmed water and a magical stillness.

→ Park at Camping El Martinete and follow the path 200m up and to the right for the first cascada. Then follow the path for another 100m, crossing the river at the old factory, and follow the path downhill to the pool under the waterfall.

15 mins, 37.9934, -5.6680 🏊🏞🐦🅿🚶

6 ÁREA RECREATIVA ISLA MARGARITA

Rope bridges, ziplines, galleries and cabins are suspended in the forest canopy above the River Huéznar. Located along the Vía Verde, this great natural adventure park offers a deeper section of the river, perfect for a dip.

→ Ctra Cazalla San Nicolás del Puerto, km 8, 41370 Cazalla de la Sierra, Aventurasierramorena.es

1 min, 37.9338, -5.6956

LAKES & MOUNTAINS

7 EMBALSE DEL GERGAL

A small track leads down through woodland to the quiet banks of the reservoir, with shallow entry for a swim in the calm water. For the more adventurous, the 14km signed Guillena trail passes by, a picturesque way to see the Cala and Huelva rivers, as well as deserted railway stations, tunnels, refugios for a wild camp and even prehistoric ruins. It can be cycled or done on horseback.

→ From Guillena take the SE-187 towards Las Pajanosas. After 3km turn R at signs for the Guillena trail and follow the dirt track for 2.5km to reach parking and the bike rental cabin. Call 607 744 289 for bike rental, Bicisrutadelagua.com

10 mins, 37.5726, -6.0571

8 PLAYA EL ALMENDRO, EMBALSE DE JOSÉ TORÁN

Gradual pebbly entry to the water at this reservoir beach, with plenty of space for stargazing and views across to the Sierra de Hornachuelos. Arrive at the end of the day for swims in silky light and sun-warmed water.

→ From Puebla de los Infantes take the road for 6km towards Lora del Rio, just after the restaurante turn R down to the reservoir. There is a parking area but not usually busy.

1 min, 37.7646, -5.4549

9 LAGOS DE AZNALCÓLLAR

Grassy banks lead down to this huge, shining reservoir with rope swings, trees for jumping and deep, cool water perfect for longer swims. It is a green haven, even in summer when the surrounding plains of Seville are baked dry in the heat. It is popular with kids, campervan owners and dog owners, but follow the path and you will always find a quiet corner to take a swim.

→ From Aznalcóllar continue out of town past the Residency and follow the SE-530 for 1km. After the curve where you can see the lake, take the first R on to a stony track and follow it for 100m to the parking. Follow the path over the bridge and then R to grassy area for swim.

2 mins, 37.5261, -6.2824 ⬛🍴🏊

10 PANTANO EL PINTADO

This reservoir straddles both the Extremadura and Andalucía regions and is fed by the rivers Viar, Arroyo del Moro and Benalija. Here on the Andalusian side there are some picnic tables and easy access to the clear water.

→ From Cazalla de la Sierra, take the SE-179 towards El Real de la Jara for 20km. Cross the dam and after 200m, turn R on to the dirt track. Park where you can.

1 min, 37.9871, -5.9547 ⬛

11 EMBALSE DE LA MINILLA

A rocky beach leads down to the Minilla reservoir, which supplies Seville with drinking water. The warm water makes for a beautiful swim on a sunny evening as the light catches the pine trees.

→ From El Ronquillo take the C-421 W for 4km and stop at the parking area on the left.

1 min, 37.7165, -6.2115 ⬛🎋

12 LOS LAGOS DEL SERRANO

A huge expanse of calm water reflects the pine woodland at this reservoir. The banks are gravel but further back from the water there is grass and shade under the trees.

→ From the main road of El Ronquillo, take the road that runs down alongside Bar Casa Paco, under the bridge, and follow for 7km past the camping ground to reach the reservoir.

1 min, 37.7116, -6.1118 ⬛🚻

13 EMBALSE DE HUESNA

Acres of rolling hills studded with wide cork oaks lead down to this deep-blue reservoir. Cattle graze and come to drink at the edges of the lake, and you can follow a track to the water.

→ From El Pedroso take the road towards Constantina. After 4.5km turn R at signs for Hueznaventura. Follow for 3.5km and then turn R on SE-197. Follow road to the hotel and park. Walk 1km down the dirt track.

15 mins, 37.8042, -5.7128 ⬛➕⛰❓

14 EMBALSE DE RETORTILLO

Several tracks lead down through the undergrowth from the old roadside to the edge of this reservoir in the Sierra de Hornachuelos. A mix of strawberry trees, oaks and myrtle fringe its banks and the water is green but clear.

→ From La Puebla de los Infantes take the road N towards Las Navas for 7km. Turn R at the fork and continue for about 1.5km to a gap in the trees and park.

2 mins, 37.8424, -5.3671 ⬛🐾

15 CASTILLO EL REAL DE LA JARA

Run along the ramparts of this 13th-century castle, which has incredible views of the Sierra Norte. Built as part of the belt of fortifications to defend Seville from Nasrid and then Portuguese attacks, the castle had complete control over the Vía de la Plata, the old silver trading route, now a footpath that passes nearby.

→ Park in the main square of El Real de la Jara by the Ayuntamiento (there is a fountain with a great stag sculpture). Follow Calle Colon to cross Calle Real and take the cobbled street opposite (marked with a Santiago shell) up to the castle.

15 mins, 37.9531, -6.1544 🖼🎋🚶

16 MOLINO DE LA ACEÑA

Overlooked by the church of San Juan Bautista and a wildflower meadow are the ruins of this late-medieval watermill on the banks of the Guadalquivir. Just outside Seville, it is a great spot for a picnic by the long reeds. Even in August there is usually a little water for a dip with a lot of clay below. The mill was built by Mudejar builders in the 15th century on the remains of a much older one. You can see starred half barrel vaulting and ashlar brickwork as well as the millstones, which were abandoned in the late 20th century. Church bells toll the hour nearby.

→ From Carmona, enter Alcolea del Río on the SE-4104. At the roundabout take the second exit and follow the riverside for 400m to a dirt track that leads downhill to the river bank. Park and walk to the mill.

1 min, 37.6154, -5.6736 ⬛🏛🎋🏚

17 LA PIEDRAS NEGRAS

A scattering of smooth, black basaltic rocks emerges from the grassy banks of the Guadalquivir as it passes by the beautiful town of Peñaflor. They lie just next to what was once the ancient Roman city of Celti. This is a good place for a stroll or a picnic, but the currents are probably too strong for a swim.

→ From the Ayuntamiento in Peñaflor, follow the narrow pedestrian road opposite down under the tunnel and to the river. Turn R and walk about 600m to reach the stones.

5 mins, 37.7039, -5.3509 🎋

9

11

12

13

21

18 PIEDRA ESCRITA DE CONSTANTINA

Believed for centuries to be prehistoric engravings, even the marks of aliens, these trace fossils are in fact some of the largest and rarest examples of ancient jellyfish. More than 550 million years ago the jellyfish were washed up and buried on a beach after a storm, and their amazing circles, some up to 88cm wide, can be seen in this rock today. At this ancient site, often called the Sistine Chapel of Paleontology, you can see the waves and ripples from this lost world.

→ This site lies in the private grounds of Finca el Revuelo and is currently only open to guests. There are a couple of houses available in its 1,500 hectares as well as a museum of carriages. Fincaelrevuelo.es

1 hr, 37.874, -5.4800 🏖️⊞🚲❓

19 ENCLAVE ARQUEOLÓGICO DE MUNIGUA

The remains of a Roman city called Munigua are hidden in the foothills of the Sierra Morena. Drawn here by the iron and copper mines that had been used by the Turdetani tribes since 2000 BC, the Romans settled here from the 1st to 3rd century AD. You can see the remains of houses, a street, thermal baths and a temple dedicated to Fortuna and Hercules. An earthquake in the 3rd century AD marked the start of its decline.

→ Open 10am – 2pm, closed Mon/Tue, 955 929 152, munigua.aaiicc@juntadeandalucia.es. On private farmland but access is free and accessible on foot or bike along a 2.5km footpath from the parking. You must email beforehand to secure a visit. Working farm, close gates after you and stay on path.

30 mins, 37.713, -5.7405 🏖️🚶🏔️🖼️

20 CUEVA DE LOS COVACHOS

These limestone caverns, with their impressive rock formations, are the second biggest in Sevilla province and hide over a thousand Neolithic cave paintings and engravings related to fertility rites. Mysterious carvings dating from the 18th century sparked a legend that a dark passage connects the caves to the nearby village Almadén de la Plata. The caves are gated off today to protect its ancient bat colony but you still sit at the cave mouth and look out to incredible views.

→ From Almadén de la Plata follow the footpath from its old bullring out of town. After 1km, at the dusty crossroads, head straight on over and continue for 400m. The cave is on your R.

20 min, 37.8821, -6.0813 🏖️🚶🏔️

16

16

CLIMBING & CYCLING

21 CERRO DEL HIERRO

The presence of iron in the earth means this land has been mined from Roman times until the last century. This activity, and ensuing erosion, has left an amazing scape of limestone gullies and karst needles, corridors and chasms, great for climbers. The old railway line that transported minerals to Seville is now a cycle route, the Sierra Norte Greenway. A 2km-long signed Cerro del Hierro trail, leading through tunnels and caves, begins and ends at the Casa de los Ingleses, the house of the engineers and miners who came from Scotland in the 19th century. A branch of the GR-48 and Vía Verde passes by. The nearby Restaurante La Mina is a great place to refuel after the hike.

→ Parking and the beginning of the signed trail are located 500m S of Cerro de Hierro village.
15 mins, 37.9502, -5.6206 🏃🚴🌳⛰

22 VÍA VERDE DE LA SIERRA NORTE DE SEVILLA

An 18km cycleway along the old railway line that took minerals from the iron mines at Cerro del Hierro to the railway station at Cazalla-Constantina. It follows the pretty banks of the River Huéznar and offers several opportunities for a cool dip along the way. Cycle rental is available at Bicicletasverdevia.com

→ Ctra A-455 Km 8, 41370 Cazalla de la Sierra, 955 490 104
1.5 hrs, 37.9318, -5.7050 🚴⛰🏊

RURAL RESTAURANTS

23 RESTAURANTE LAS PALOMAS

A popular restaurant with lots of outdoor tables on the terrace overlooking the José Torán reservoir and mountains beyond. All the dishes are excellent but they specialise in carne de caza or slow-cooked wild boar, venison and partridge. Dogs are welcome and there are also a few apartments available.

→ SE-6102, Km 16, 41479 La Puebla de los Infantes, 955 956 063, Las-palomas.com
37.7637, -5.4474 🍴🍽🍷🐾

24 RESTAURANTE LA HERRADURA

A hunters' restaurant in the heart of the Sierra Norte with large fireplaces for winter and a terrace for summer. The speciality is grilled Iberian pork and game. It is a great place to refuel with typical Andalusian food after swimming in the nearby El Pintado reservoir.

→ SE-179, 41370 Cazalla de la Sierra, 654 357 774
37.9803, -5.9528 🍴🍷⛰🏊🍽

25 PAJARTILLO BAR

A small courtyard brightly painted with bullfighting murals; its vines provide shade for a beer and tapas. The restaurant is dark and cool with traditional old furnishings. Come here to escape the busier tourist cafés outside the entrance of the Roman ruins of Itálica. Try the pollo frito (fried chicken), tomate aliñados (seasoned tomatoes), olives and queso viejo (aged cheese).

→ Plaza Pajartillo, 3, 41970 Santiponce, detapasconchencho.es, 955 996 443
37.4395, -6.0403 🚴🍷🍴

26 CAFÉ BAR EL CARMEN

A small bar at the end of the main street in Cazalla de la Sierra. Tables and chairs in the sun, usually with a charcoal grill on the go. Locals sit out on long afternoons sipping sweet anis liqueur, Cazalla El Clavel, for which the town is known. A tip from one local, Manolo, is to mix a dash of the sweet and dry liqueurs in one cup. Cash only.

→ Plaza del Carmen, 41370 Cazalla de la Sierra, 666 339 681
37.9358, -5.7593 🍴🍷

27 RESTAURANTE LA CANTINA

Along some wilder roads and hidden deep in the Sierra by the Gergal reservoir, this is a great place to escape to for lunch. There is a charcoal grill on the go and the house specialises in game. Popular dishes include carrillada en salsa (ibérico pig's cheeks), venado (venison) and salmorejo, a cold tomato soup garnished with rabbit meat in this region, rather than jamón (ham). The Guillena Ruta del Agua passes by.

→ Camino de la Ruta del Agua, 41210 Sevilla, 661 702 615
37.6381, -6.0716 🍴🍷⛰🏃

RUSTIC RETREATS

28 CORTIJO EL BERROCAL

Several traditional Andalusian cottages with heavy walls, old beams and hammocks slung under lemon trees in the garden. This is a genuine hideaway and Francisco, the owner and self-proclaimed bandolero of the Sierra, stables his horses behind the houses and runs horse trails around the foothills of the Sierra Norte. Dogs are welcome; a pack of about seven and several cats lounge around the farm and pool.

→ Cortijo El Berrocal Ctra. Real de la Jara Km 1, 41370 Cazalla de la Sierra, 661 475 377, Turismoelberrocal.es
37.9286, -5.7684 ⛰🍴🍷🐾

29 CAMPING LA FUNDICIÓN

A green and peaceful caravan-friendly camping park by the River Huéznar. There are kids' rope swings in the trees, and a wooden walkway over the Huéznar river leads straight on to the Vía Verde cycle path.

→ SE-7101, 41370 Cazalla de la Sierra, 955 280 027, Campinglafundicion.es
37.9394, -5.6849 🚴🚵🚶

30 PARAÍSO DEL HUÉZNAR

Five rural guest houses on the banks of the Huéznar river with access to bike rental, footpaths, a treetop adventure park and the Vía Verde cycle path. The houses are of varying size with open fireplaces and dark wooden beams.

→ A-455 Km 8, 41370 Cazalla de la Sierra, 955 490 104, Paraisodelhueznar.com
37.9317, -5.7049 🚶🚲🚵🚴🏊📷

31 CASA RURAL EL CASTAÑO

Several rural cottages in the old farmstead with horses, chickens and ducks roaming the gardens and a biological pool. There is also a 3km footpath through the grounds, where the owners have carefully rigged up a treetop climbing park.

→ Antigua Carretera de Cazalla, 3.5, 41360 El Pedroso, 669 057 571, Casaruralsierradesevilla.com
37.8611, -5.7902 🏊🚶🚲🏠

32 MONASTERIO LA CARTUJA DE CAZALLA

Inside this restored Carthusian monastery there are several beautiful guestrooms, many of them once used by visiting laymen in the 15th century. The monastery is open for artist residences, and stargazing nights are offered in the gardens.

→ C. de Anis Cazalla 3, 41370 Cazalla de la Sierra, 951 193 446, Lacartujadecazalla.com
37.9523, -5.7287 🏠🍴🖼📷

29

29

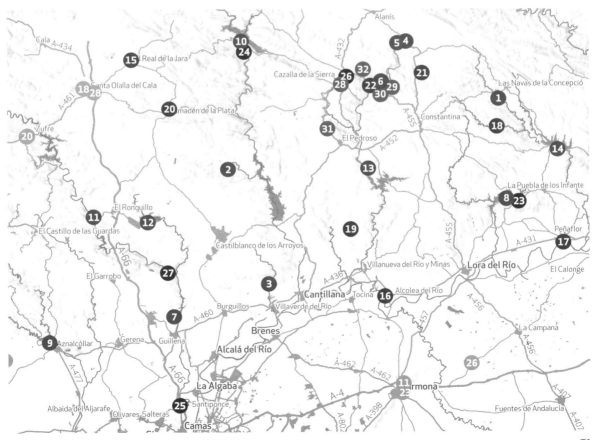

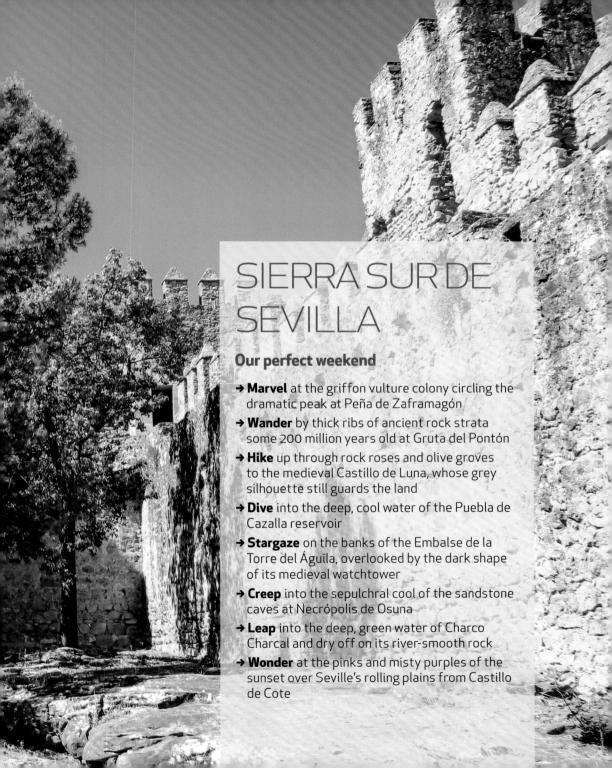

SIERRA SUR DE SEVILLA

Our perfect weekend

→ **Marvel** at the griffon vulture colony circling the dramatic peak at Peña de Zaframagón

→ **Wander** by thick ribs of ancient rock strata some 200 million years old at Gruta del Pontón

→ **Hike** up through rock roses and olive groves to the medieval Castillo de Luna, whose grey silhouette still guards the land

→ **Dive** into the deep, cool water of the Puebla de Cazalla reservoir

→ **Stargaze** on the banks of the Embalse de la Torre del Águila, overlooked by the dark shape of its medieval watchtower

→ **Creep** into the sepulchral cool of the sandstone caves at Necrópolis de Osuna

→ **Leap** into the deep, green water of Charco Charcal and dry off on its river-smooth rock

→ **Wonder** at the pinks and misty purples of the sunset over Seville's rolling plains from Castillo de Cote

Head south from Seville and plunge yourself into a different space and rhythm. To the east, endless, sunburnt fields and olive groves give way to dusty, orange plains around the ancient towns of Osuna and Carmona. Miles of dead-straight Roman roads pass *cortijos* or a *hacienda* with its faded grandeur peeling in the sun, storks nesting in belltowers and palm trees. But don't be fooled; in a moment the scenery can shift, and a fork in the road will lead you up into the Sierra Sur de Sevilla or down to a hidden watery oasis.

Like the Sierras Subbéticas a way to the east and Serranía de Ronda to the south, the Sierra Sur de Sevilla forms part of the massive limestone Baetica Cordillera mountain range. Myrtle, rosemary, cork oaks, wild olive and rockrose hide watchtowers and forgotten castles known as *La Banda Morisca*, a 13th-century frontier between the Muslim kingdom of Granada and that of Christian Seville. At Pruna you can hike up to one of these legendary castles perched on a rocky hill where the land falls away like a map of itself beneath. At Castillo de Luna buzzards soar over its ruined keep, and prehistoric arrowheads are often found in the River Corbones coursing below. The landscape becomes more rugged to the south; great fingers of rock reach up 1130m at El Peñón de Algámitas, Seville's highest peak, where vultures circle.

A neighbouring vulture colony circles over the dramatic peak at Peña de Zaframagón, which borders the Sierra de Cádiz, running into the Serranía de Ronda. This wild and untamed landscape hides ancient dolmens, gorges and Arabic ruins and is best seen from the 36km cycle route that follows an old train line, zigzagging along the provincial border.

One of Seville's green oases can be found at Torre del Águila. In the evening, golden light reflected by its lake catches the stone of the ancient watchtower. An evocative place, it's easy to see how folk tales have sprung up from this eroded landscape and attached themselves to its peculiar corners. They say it was at Gruta del Pontón that the famous bandit, El Tempranillo, negotiated his pardon with Ferdinand VII. At Charco Charcal folk leap into green bathing pools so deep, it is said, that an entire horse and carriage once fell in and was lost.

The pilgrim trail, the Camino de Santiago, runs through much of the Sierra Sur. One of its branches, the Camino de Antequera, arrives at Alcalá de Guadaíra, with its cycle path that follows the line of the old Bakers' Train from Carmona. Two hundred years ago it was known as Alcalá de los Panaderos (of the bakers), and mill houses still line the River Guadalquivir, which once supplied Seville with its bread. It was a buzzing industry with the women, *sobadoras*, kneading the bread and the men, *horneros*, using long wooden bread shovels to move it into the oven. At Mesón de Chaparrete, deep in the Sierra Sur, you can see an old bread oven and try the crusty, wood-smoked bread.

Come at the end of summer to enjoy local festivities at the *ferias de septiembre*. Flamenco dresses whirl, horses kick up dust and delicious fare is passed around. Its gastronomy is based on an abundance of good olive oil, wine and local produce from *las huertas*, or small-scale farms. At Algámitas you can try *la porra algamiteña*, a variant on a cool *salmorejo* with orange and tuna, or *alboronía* at Carmona, a ratatouille-style dish with medieval Muslim–Andalucían roots.

Stargaze at Camping El Peñón and wake up under the wild, wooded peaks or bed down in one of the rustic country houses near Pruna, ready for adventures.

RIVERS & MILLS

1 MOLINO DE LAS ACEÑAS

A popular spot for a picnic on the banks of the Guadaíra river by this late medieval mill. Follow the footpath downriver to discover a number of semi-mythical watermills and their weirs which once famously supplied Seville with its bread. The ruins date from the 17th and 20th centuries, but records speak of mills here in the 12th century and even earlier. The Vía Verde de los Alcores cycle path starts nearby. It can get busy on weekends as the park is close to town.

→ The walk starts on Avenida Tren de los Panaderos in Alcalá de Guadaíra just down from the castle and the Roman bridge. Take the path down to the river and follow for 2km, passing several mills.
30 mins, 37.3236, -5.8351 🚻🚴🚶

2 ARROYO DEL BÚHO

The 'stream of the owl', as it's known in the town, is also called Arroyo de Salado, or salty stream. This is owing to a saline spring located in a tributary a few hundred metres upstream that joins the freshwater. The stream has smoothed its bedrock into a series of tiny cascades and they say the water is curative.

Locals fill up water bottles to heal skin afflictions. Come after rain to see it at its best.

→ Coming into Pedrera from the S on the A-353 park near Bar El Paso. Opposite is sign for 'Baño del Búho'. Follow the road for 120m to a small track on the R; this will take you over the AVE railway line. This is the old droving way, Vereda de Hortelanos. Follow for 900m until you cross a dry stream. Carry on for 300m to a crosstracks, take the R and continue for 50m to reach the octagonal viewing platform on your L. Follow the stream down to the pools for 1km.
30 mins, 37.2110, -4.9230 🏞️❓🚻

LAKES & LAGOONS

3 LAGUNA DEL GOSQUE

A beautiful lake and wetland, home to pink flamingos who move between here and Fuente de Piedra, it is bordered by olive groves and vineyards. The annual pilgrimage, or romería, from Martín de la Jara used to come here before it moved to Los Cucus, so there is still a lot of sand on one side of the lake where pilgrims would swim, as well as picnic tables before the footpath down to the bird hide.

→ From Martín de la Jara take the A-353 towards Pedrera for 3km. Take the L turning

by the pylon, which leads through olive groves, quickly becoming a dusty white track. Follow for 600m to reach the picnic park and follow the footpath to the bird hide. Continue on the white track for a further 1km keeping L for access, although uncertain, to the sand area.
15 mins, 37.1321, -4.9434 🚹🏞️🚰❓

4 EMBALSE DE LA TORRE DEL ÁGUILA

This secluded oasis is green even in the summer months when the sun beats down on the arid plains south of Seville. Pine and carob trees shade a picnic area which runs down to muddy clay banks for easy swim entry. In summer the lake stays as warm as a bath well into the night hours and is canopied by stars. The silhouette of a 14th-century watchtower guards its hill and once communicated with the nearby towers of Boyo and Lopera. In 1348 it would have been armed with 25 men, as the area was under constant attack from Muslim Ronda. Beneath all this are the remains of the ancient Roman city of Siarum, such a quiet place for such a busy history.

→ From El Palmar de Troya, follow signs for Embalse de la Torre del Águila on the SE-9015 to a small flat bridge on the L. Cross this and

goes that in 1579 a woman carrying her sick child made a desperate journey to Alameda hospital. The Holy Virgin kicked up a storm and appeared to the woman, hewing her a path through the sheer rock. The nearby hermitage of Fuensanta was built in the years afterwards and is the site of the negotiations between the bandit El Tempranillo and Ferdinand VII. You can follow the woman's journey along the 9km footpath linking Badalatosa to the Ermita de Nuestra Señora de la Fuensanta or follow the footpath from the gruta to the Mirador del Meandro del Río Genil for great views over the river.

→ Park at the Ermita de Nuestra Señora de la Fuensanta. Follow the track downhill from the parking. The track forks into three; take the middle path through the olive groves and keep L, curving down to the river. After the bridge, follow the steps down to the L to reach the stream and grotto.
15 mins, 37.2837, -4.6842 🧍‍♂️🏊‍♀️✝️🏞️

7 CHARCO CHARCAL
In the foothills of the Sierra de Peñagua, and looking up to its striking marlstone cliffs known as Tajo de la Serena, lies this small but surprisingly deep pool. Legend says that centuries ago a horse and cart fell into the pool. It was so deep they were never found. Now it's a perfect hidden spot for a dip or a picnic. The walk here passes under the vertical limestone of the Peñagua cliffs, as well as passing by the ruins of a 1st-century AD Roman settlement called Flavium Villonensis.

→ From La Puebla de Cazalla follow Avenida Fuenlonguilla (SE-457) out of town for 8km to the junction. There is a small parking area next to the trail sign at this junction, park here. Continue on foot straight over the junction on the track and follow green and white signs to reach the Charco. The circular trail is 12.8km in total and about 5km to the pool. There is a tiny detour to the pool, on your L.
1.5 hrs, 37.1451, -5.3523 🏞️⛰️🧗‍♂️🏊‍♀️🚶‍♂️

8 ARROYO DE LAS MUJERES
Just to the south of the sun-bleached village of Villanueva de San Juan lies this stream, once the source of the village's drinking water. It owes its name to the women who would come to wash clothes here. Once it would have been a busy social route but now the footpath is used mostly by livestock en route to the watering place. On either side the cliffs of Los Tajos tower, formed by centuries of erosion.

→ The footpath is signed from Camino de Algámitas in Villanueva de San Juan, 2km
30 mins, 37.0384, -5.1771 🏊‍♀️🚶‍♂️⛰️🏞️❓

continue for 1.3km. Turn R and follow palm trees down to water. Parking
1 min, 37.0496, -5.7460 🏊‍♀️⛺🅿️🚻🍽️📷

5 EMBALSE DE LA PUEBLA DE CAZALLA
There is shallow beach access to this glimmering turquoise lake after following the track along its high banks. Thyme and rockrose grow along the stony sides, and the beach area is more popular for fishing than swimming. In summer the water is alive with trout, bass, pike, carp and barbels.

→ From La Puebla de Cazalla head towards the A-92 to Osuna. Before joining the A-92, turn R on to the untarmacked road, the SE-452, and follow this for 15km downhill to the dam. Don't cross over. Park before the dam and follow the path to the L for 500m down to the water's edge.
10 mins, 37.1270, -5.2366 🏊‍♀️⛺

CAVES & GORGES

6 GRUTA DEL PONTÓN
This ribbed tunnel was carved over millennia by the slow-moving groundwater of the Pontón stream. Hidden between two hills in the Sierra Cabrera, the cavern can be accessed by some stone steps. The legend

9 TAJOS DE MOGAREJO

A thick forest of carob, palm, rosemary and rockrose hides this deep gorge carved by the Salado de Morón stream. With sides reaching heights of 30m, the stream is set apart from its low-level surroundings by its strange geology. Over time, its calcarenite limestone has been eaten away by the river, forming cavities and hollows resembling honeycomb called tafoni. You can wander by a 17th-century bridge, old flour mills and abandoned quarries.

→ From El Coronil follow the A-375 towards Montellano for 6km. Park opposite the petrol station with all the flags at km28. Follow the path with the Arroyo Salado de Morón on your R for 3.5km to the old bridge.

50 mins, 37.0350, -5.5830 🏃🧍🏔✉

ANCIENT & SACRED

10 ÁREA RECREATIVA CHAPARRO DE LA VEGA

This monumental holm oak is over two hundred years old and is known locally as 'el chaparro'. Pilgrims meet under its ample shade, which is over 30m wide, every year for the spring pilgrimage to the nearby chapel of Nuestra Señora de Fátima in mid-May. Deep in the Sierra Sur, its picnic area has great views of the limestone peaks of Zaframagón and their vultures. The Vía Verde de la Sierra cycle path passes nearby.

→ Park at Estacíon de Coripe, walk behind the station house and continue for 1.2km along the Vía Verde, taking the L at the fork.

15 mins, 36.9580, -5.4269 🚲🅰🌳

11 CUEVA DE LA BATIDA

These ancient caves in the dusty plains outside Carmona were hollowed out by Romans quarrying into the sandstone and used up until the 15th century. The track winds through agave and cacti to the immense entrance offering a dark, cool respite on a hot day. The 5km signed trail here from Carmona passes the remains of the Via Augusta, a Roman bridge and a Mudejar hermitage to San Mateo.

→ From the Puerta de Sevilla in Carmona take the fourth exit on A-380 S for 280m. Turn L just after the bollards and park. Signed 5km footpath begins here.

1 hr, 37.4854, -5.6336 🚲🏔🚶🏕🧍🛖

12 NECRÓPOLIS DE OSUNA

These ancient burial caves, hollowed into the sandstone, lie just outside Osuna along the Cañada Real, the old cattle drovers' road to Granada. It is a dusty track, now rarely used, and the caves, even in summer's beating heat, are deathly cool. The most recent caves are Visigothic and the oldest possibly pre-Roman, each with various anthropomorphic tombs carved inside. This is only a small part of what is yet to be excavated. Follow the road uphill back to the crossroads for the Roman theatre and the famous *canteras*, or beautiful Roman quarries, with monumental carvings, now used as a concert space.

→ From Osuna follow pink signs for Zona Arqueológico to reach the dusty crossroads at the edge of town. Continue straight over and follow signs for 'Necropolis', along the dirt track for 550m. Parking at crossroads or just after caves.

1 min, 37.2405, -5.0913 🚲🧍✝◈

HIKING & BIKING

13 VÍA VERDE DE LA SIERRA

This 36.5km greenway runs along the old Jerez–Almargen railway line and winds through some of the most spectacular and untouched countryside in Andalucía. Crossing through the northern hills of the Sierra de Cádiz and into the Seville province, it links Olvera to Puerto Serrano and crosses

the municipalities of Coripe, Montellano, El Coronil and Pruna. The way runs through dark tunnels, over viaducts and passes the magnificent natural monument of Peñón de Zaframagón: a gigantic rocky crag, home to the largest nesting colony of griffon vultures in western Andalucía. With an altitude of 584m, the crag is composed of hard limestone which has been cut through by a gorge known as El Estrechón, carved by the River Guadalporcún. Pack some binoculars in your backpack to see the vultures circling its peak. The best views can be seen from the viaduct near the Interpretation Centre and small café. The route passes the Alberquilla Megalithic area as well as Junta de los Rios and many Roman and Arabic remains.

→ A good place to start if you don't want to cycle the whole route is at the old station house, now a restaurant and hostel, at Estación de Coripe (great tapas and raciones). Bike rental from José – call 679 613 069, Irippobikes.es, see Viasverdes.com.
4 hrs, 36.9640, -5.4304 🚶🚲🐎🛤🥾🍴🦽

14 VÍA VERDE DE LOS ALCORES

This 25km cycle route, once the line of the Bakers' Train, runs from Carmona to Alcalá de Guadaíra. It took the bakers and their wheat to the flour mills at Alcalá. It is a good way to see the castles at Mairena del Alcor, Gandul and Alcalá de Guadaíra, as well as the Chalcolithic necropolis and dolmens of Gandul, although these are now located on military ground.

→ The route starts just next to the Hidalgo RV dealer on the outskirts of Alcalá. See Viasverdes.com.
2.5 hrs, 37.3284, -5.8050 🚶♿🚲🚻🏞

15 CAMINOS DE SANTIAGO

Several branches of the long-distance pilgrim path, Camino de Santiago, cross the Sierra Sur. You can follow the Camino de la Frontera, the Vía Serrana, the Via Augusta or the Camino de Antequera through its sierras and villages. A good 13km walk starts from Pruna and takes you to Algámitas along the Camino de la Frontera, with views of the Sierra de Tablón, hillside chapels and white villages.

→ Follow Calle Cruces and then the yellow arrows out of Pruna. From more information about the Camino routes, see Turismosevilla.org.
3.5 hrs, 36.9757, -5.2177 🚶✝🏞🚻

16 CASTILLO DE LAS AGUZADERAS

This magnificent castle goes almost unnoticed from the road as it is built, unusually, in a dip in the land. It once defended an important water source, unfortunately very recently lost. The heavy stone walls, some 3m thick in places, with turrets and ramparts, remain strong and upright and are home to baby owls. Built during the Al-Andalus reign in the 14th century, but probably resting on older foundations, it takes its current name from the wild boar that sharpened, or *aguzaban*, their tusks on its rock. At night, a shadowy soldier is said to haunt the parapets, waiting for his lover.

→ From El Coronil take the road S towards Puerto Serrano for 2.5km. The castle is signed on your R. Follow down for parking on your R.
1 min, 37.0523, -5.6261 🚻🚻◈

17 CASTILLO DE COTE

This picturesque keep crowns its wooded hill with views over the endless rolling fields of the Seville countryside. Along with the watchtowers of Lopera, Bollo and Águila, and the castles of Morón and El Coronil at Aguzaderas, it formed part of La Banda Morisca, a belt of

watchtowers. Built during the 10th-century rule of the Córdoban Caliphate, it was handed over to Fernando III in 1240, who ordered the construction of the gothic vaulting that remains today. Four curved apses join to form its strange shape, with dark recesses and ribbed vaulting. A shadowy door and staircase lead up to the best 360-degree views in the province.

→ From Montellano follow purple signs out of town for Castillo de Cote. Take the A-8127 for about 3km to reach the information board for the castle on the L at the start of a dirt track. Park here and walk uphill as the tracks are in bad condition. Take the first L and walk uphill through four hairpin bends in the track to reach the signed start of the footpath at the fifth bend.

40 mins, 36.9970, -5.5269 ⊞◨▲◈

18 EL CASTILLO DE HIERRO, PRUNA
This famously impregnable castle, perched on a rocky summit, was part of La Banda Morisca, the defensive castles built between the Muslim eastern territory and the Christian west. A beautiful winding path climbs up this small, steep hill thick with wildflowers,

passing picnic tables and secret tunnels to reach the ruined keep and *aljibe*, or water cisterns. From here are magnificent views out to neighbouring Castillo de Olvera, raised in relief against the low, green countryside. The castle overlooks the River Sanguino, and according to legend the Christians were unable to capture the castle, so they tied flaming torches to the horns of goats who fled up the hill, terrified, and burnt the castle, its inhabitants jumping to their deaths in the 'bloody' or Sanguino river below.

→ From Pruna take the A-363 towards Olvera. After 1km, and just after the petrol station, there is a tiny parking area on the R, and the walk is signed uphill from the drinking fountain.

20 mins, 36.9665, -5.2318 ⊞⏚◨◨⭐◈

19 CASTILLO DE LUNA
The enigmatic ruins of this ancient castle crown the sun-scorched grassy knoll rising up from the low hills of the Sierra Sur Sevillana. You'll have to cross the Río Corbones to get here and the way is steep, but you'll be rewarded with excellent views. It is a peaceful spot with a riotous history.

The first fortification was built here by the pre-Roman tribes, the Turdetano people, in the 5th century BC, and it was later used by the Romans. Under Muslim rule it was an *alcazaba*, or Moorish fortification, becoming part of La Banda Morisca in the 12th century, the belt of Christian-occupied watchtowers, as they moved upon Al-Andalus territory.

→ From La Puebla de Cazalla take the SE-458 S towards Villanueva de San Juan for 7km. Turn L onto the dirt track just before the junction and signs to Olvera. Park here and follow the bumpy dirt track to the R for 800m. Wade over or cross the river on the palette bridge and follow the footpath 1km up to the castle.

45 mins, 37.1688, -5.2852 ▲✚◨◨◉◈

SUNSET HILLTOPS

20 PICO DEL TERRIL
The two highest peaks in the district of Seville are El Terril (1,129m) and Peñón de Algámitas (1,121m). Separated by the Zamorano pass, they lie within the limestone massif of Sierra del Tablón. This gentle 3km footpath winds up the southern slope of El Terril to beautiful views of blue hills melting into the horizon.

Come at sunset, or the purple hour, for stunning colours.

→ From Pruna take the SE-462 towards Algámitas for 4km to reach parking on the L. The footpath is signed with a rock a few metres further along the road to the R.

50 mins, 36.9963, -5.2045 🏃🏔🏖

FEASTS AND FERIAS

21 BAR NENO

A great stop for a couple of tapas and a beer; the *bacalao* (fried cod) is excellent, as is the *chipirones fritos* (fried baby squid). From the end of the road you have a great view of the castle at Morón de la Frontera. The bar owner, Antonio Menacho, sings flamenco; have a look on YouTube.

→ Av. del Pantano, 156, 41530 Morón de la Frontera

37.1328, -5.4489 ⊞🍴🍷

22 MESÓN EL CHAPARRETE

Follow the old road, which climbs up into the Sierra de Peñaguas, and you'll find this great hunters' refuge and rustic restaurant. In winter the chimney and log fires provide a warm welcome and Antonio, or 'El Veneno', keeps pigs, chickens and several dogs that roam freely. He makes fresh cheeses, chorizo, jamón and honey on-site, as well as regular rounds of the local bread in the wood oven: a doughy loaf with a thick crust; each bite tastes of woodsmoke. Rooms are available.

→ SE-458, 41540 La Puebla de Cazalla, 625 037 992

37.1112, -5.2928 ⊞🍴🍷🏔🏖

23 MOLINO DE LA ROMERA, CARMONA

Located in the ancient town of Carmona, this restaurant is in a renovated, 15th-century olive oil mill. Tables and chairs are set out under its porticos or in the cool of its courtyard under vines. They specialise in charcoal-grilled meats.

→ Calle Sor Angela de la Cruz, 8, 41410 Carmona, 954 142 000

37.4710, -5.6352 ⊞🍴🍷

24 RESTAURANTE VENTA EL POTAJE

A good roadside *venta* with flowers, barrels and dark, wooden beams. There is usually a set menu with several dishes to choose from, such as the restaurant's famous *el potaje* (stew), *el arroz con conejo* (rice with rabbit) and *el arroz con perdiz* (rice with partridge).

→ Coripe, Carretera, 0, Km 2, 41770 Montellano, 954 875 041

36.9831, -5.5496 ⊞🍴🍷

25 LAS FERIAS DE SEPTIEMBRE

Outside of Andalucía, the colourful festivities, or *ferias*, in the rural towns of the Seville province are less well known than the capital's Feria de Sevilla. This is unduly so, because at these ferias you can enjoy concerts, flamenco dances, horses and *casetas*, or booths, which are invite-only in Seville, but which outside of Seville are open to all to enjoy the celebrations. At Lebrija, for example, usually the week around September 8th, you can try the traditional celebratory dishes of *puchera, el ajo Lebrijano* and *caldos de Lebrija* (broth) surrounded by musicians and dancers. There are ferias in Utrera, Los Palacios, Morón de la Frontera, El Coronil, Arahal, El Cuervo, La Puebla de Cazalla and Las Cabezas de San Juan and Écija.

→ C. de los Tanguillos, 11, 41740 Lebrija

36.9265, -6.0848 ⊞🍴🍷

RUSTIC RETREATS

26 HACIENDA SAN JOSÉ

Palm trees shade this restored 19th-century olive oil hacienda located just outside Carmona. It offers several apartments and has maintained all its traditional touches: decorative tiles, ochre paint and cobbled courtyards.

→ Ctra. de Carmona, Km 5, 41410 La Campana, 651 607 382, Hacienda-sanjose. business.site

37.5188, -5.5112 ⊞🍴🍷🏖

27 CAMPING EL PEÑÓN, ALGÁMITAS

The 55 hectares of woodland provide ample camping ground on the hillside beneath El Peñón, the highest peak in the Seville province. At 1,130m the marly limestone is home to vultures and eagles which whirl over the campsite below. Several activities are on offer here, including rock climbing, archery and horse riding. There is a restaurant as well as wooden cabins and a few stone cottages.

→ Crta. Algámitas-Pruna, Km 3.5, Algámitas, 955 855 300, Algamitasaventura.es

37.0191, -5.1750 🍴🏖🅱

28 FINCA DE LAS ENCARNACIONES BAJAS

A beautiful country house with five bedrooms, a terrace and a pool, located deep in the Sierra Sur de Sevilla. There are amazing views over the rolling hills, high ceilings and pets are welcome. Sleeps 12.

→ 41530 Morón de la Frontera, 692 265 379

37.0569, -5.2864 ⊞🐾🏖

29 CASA CAMPO EL MAYORAZGO

A rustic country house with a pool, terraces and a chimney for log fires in the winter. Vineyards provide shade over the terrace and barbeque in the summer. A great hideaway with two bedrooms. Sleeps six.

→ 41530 Morón de la Frontera, 662 388 301

37.0548, -5.2564 ⊞🏖🏔

30 CASA RURAL EL VENTORILLO

A couple of beautiful rural houses perfect for families. They both have great views over the Sierra Sur de Sevilla, a pool, barbeques and shady terraces. Located just outside Pruna, the smaller house sleeps up to 12 and the larger sleeps 24.

→ Carretera A363, 41530 Morón de la Frontera, 633 810 075

37.0492, -5.2908 ⊞🏖🏔

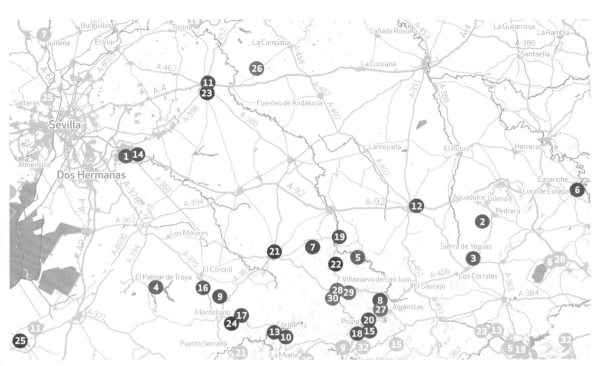

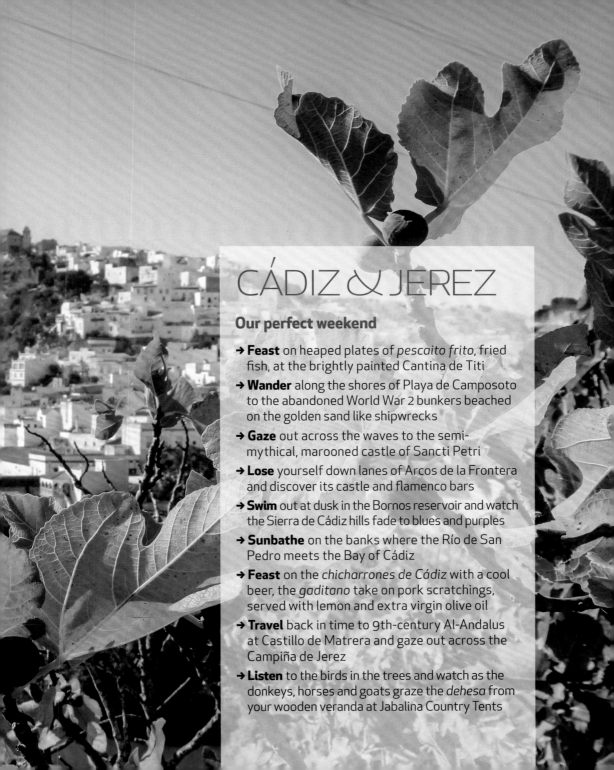

CÁDIZ & JEREZ

Our perfect weekend

→ **Feast** on heaped plates of *pescaito frito*, fried fish, at the brightly painted Cantina de Titi

→ **Wander** along the shores of Playa de Camposoto to the abandoned World War 2 bunkers beached on the golden sand like shipwrecks

→ **Gaze** out across the waves to the semi-mythical, marooned castle of Sancti Petri

→ **Lose** yourself down lanes of Arcos de la Frontera and discover its castle and flamenco bars

→ **Swim** out at dusk in the Bornos reservoir and watch the Sierra de Cádiz hills fade to blues and purples

→ **Sunbathe** on the banks where the Río de San Pedro meets the Bay of Cádiz

→ **Feast** on the *chicharrones de Cádiz* with a cool beer, the *gaditano* take on pork scratchings, served with lemon and extra virgin olive oil

→ **Travel** back in time to 9th-century Al-Andalus at Castillo de Matrera and gaze out across the Campiña de Jerez

→ **Listen** to the birds in the trees and watch as the donkeys, horses and goats graze the *dehesa* from your wooden veranda at Jabalina Country Tents

The Campiña de Jerez with its pastures and endless vineyards is bordered to the north by the River Guadalquivir, which runs to its mouth in Sanlúcar de Barrameda. To the south, curling under Jerez de la Frontera, is the green Guadalete which meanders to the Bay of Cádiz. The name of the river is of Arabic origin meaning 'river of forgetfulness', an apt name for a river running by what is known as the 'sherry triangle': an area of land between Jerez de la Frontera, Sanlúcar de Barrameda and El Puerto de Santa María that produces the famous *vinos de Jerez*.

The character of Jerez, known to the Romans as Xeres but corrupted to Sherrish under Muslim rule, is best expressed by its holy trinity: horses, flamenco and sherry. While the annual horse fair or wine-treading by the cathedral are both popular, stepping out of the city for a horseback trek through pine woodland or camping out under the stars in the *dehesa* is a great way to get back to the rural roots of these *Jerezano* traditions.

Coming south, the Bay of Cádiz shares in the sherry and flamenco legacy but its horse fair is exchanged for a wild springtime *carnaval* and a culture inextricably tangled with the sea. One of the oldest cities in Europe, founded on an archipelago by the sea-faring Phoenicians and connected to the mainland by an isthmus, Cádiz has a vibrant history of many layers. Phoenician sarcophagi lay under the mud that became Columbus' shipyard. The rich history and faded elegance of Cádiz surface time and again in its wilder ruins and hilltop villages across the province.

At Bornos, an ancient *pueblo blanco* with views of the distant blue Sierra de Cádiz, you can wander down to swim in its lake or hike up to the hilltop Roman ruins at Carissa Aurelia. Arcos de la Frontera is particularly dramatic, its white houses crowning a steep ravine, an excellent place to explore a maze of streets with many bars for flamenco and *finos*. Its name, like that of Jerez de la Frontera, refers to the ancient frontier with the Nasrid kingdom of Granada. Along with nearby Medina-Sidonia, the Islamic influence can be seen in its ancient entrance gates and hidden patios.

You can escape from Cádiz to quieter beaches at Rota, where long stone fish traps, once used by the Phoenicians, reach into the calm sea; or to Punta del Boquerón, where a wooden walkway leads through dunes and flowering marshland to ruined artillery houses. This line of defence played a crucial part in Cádiz's resistance when all the rest of Spain fell to Napoleon. The only defences now are the barricades of wild cacti and armies of crabs at low tide. From here you can kayak out to the marooned castle of Sancti Petri, a temple to the Phoenician god Melqart and later a Roman sanctuary to Hercules. Hannibal and Julius Caesar are said to have made pilgrimages to this sacred site.

At the end of a day's adventures, you can continue exploring the Cádiz province through its wines from La Tierra de Cádiz and its delicious local fare. You can choose drier sherries, *fino*, *palo cortado*, *oloroso*, *amontillado* or the sweeter *Pedro Ximénez* and *moscatels*, not forgetting the dry *Manzanilla* from Sanlúcar. Typically, the *bodegas*, or wineries, line the dusty roadside. A great bodega to visit is Primitivo Collantes: the air is heavy with the smell of old barrels and the earth is damp beneath your feet, the 'angel's share' lingering in the air as light pours through high windows. As evening comes, sip a *vino de Jerez* and stargaze from the vineyards surrounding the 19th-century bodega La Bendita Locura.

(3)

SECRET BEACHES

1 PLAYA DE LEVANTE

A short walk from the busier Valdelagrana beach lies this peaceful, secluded area by the protected marshland of Los Toruños Natural Park. A haven for birds, such as curlews, sandpipers, plover, herons and terns, the Caño de Casarón snakes through the flowering marsh to a quiet sandy beach with views to Cádiz city. The way to the beach makes for a great cycle but, as its name suggests, it is open to the strong levante wind. For bike hire call 956 910 479.

→ From Cádiz take the CA-35 then the CA-32 towards El Puerto del Santa María. Just after crossing the San Pedro river, turn L on to Av. del Mar where after 700m you'll see parking. Here enter the high white gateway 'Puerta del Toruño' and cycle or walk the boardwalk, taking the first or second R. Continue 2km to reach the beach.

30 mins, 36.5719, -6.2146 🏖🚣♿

2 CORRALES DE ROTA

These Phoenician fishing traps point like a long, stony finger into the sea. You can swim alongside them and there are normally a few fishermen perched on the very end. The beach is narrow here but the tide levels hardly change. Backed by thick pine woodland, this beach is where for centuries people have harvested La Almadraba, the tuna migration. 'Almadraba' is the Andalusi (Arabic spoken in Al-Andalus) for the ancient technique of laying traps in the migration path of tuna. It is a peaceful place just south of the busier Rota beaches and the American naval base.

→ From Rota follow the Av. de la Diputación and park behind the Navarro Flores football stadium, by the campervans to the side of Restaurante El Picadero. Follow the boardwalk S and R to the beach.

5 mins, 36.6323, -6.3924 🏖⊞🍴✦

3 PLAYA CANINA CAMPOSOTO

Long stretches of golden sands reach along the west face of the Punta del Boquerón peninsula. As they are only accessible by foot, they become quieter the further you walk and dogs are welcome. A couple of bunkers built to withstand Republican attacks in the civil war sit half-sunken in the sand, facing out to sea, while the enigmatic Sancti Petri island lies beyond.

→ From Cádiz follow the CA-33 S for 11km and take exit 7. At the roundabout take the first exit and continue straight for 3km. At the third roundabout take the first exit and drive past the first parking area and continue as far down the Punta del Boquerón as you can. Walk further along boardwalks or the beach to reach the dog area near the bunkers.

15 mins, 36.4043, -6.2187 🏖🌐🚶♿🏖🚫

4 CASTILLO DE SANCTI PETRI

The southern tip of the Punta del Boquerón peninsula with its golden sand and crystalline water looks out to the semi-mythical marooned castle of Sancti Petri, a fortified stronghold dating back to the 13th century. It was here the Phoenicians built a temple to their god Melqart in the 1st century BC; later, the Romans dedicated it to Hercules. Both Hannibal and Julius Ceasar stopped here to make offerings to their gods. They say Ceasar wept here by the statue of Alexander the Great, feeling he had accomplished so little at the same age.

→ You can kayak to this island. Call Novojet for kayak rental and trips to Sancti Petri – 956 494 932.

1 hr, 36.3890, -6.2137 🏖🌐♿🚣

5 BATERÍA DE URRUTIA

The ruins of this 18th-century coastal artillery are hidden at the end of the Punta

del Boquerón peninsula. Along with further deteriorated ruins in the marshland and the island fortress of Castillo de Sancti Petri nearby, it once formed a defensive line protecting San Fernando from Napoleon during the Peninsular War. Its grey stone crenellations rise out of a thick barrier of flowering cactus. When the tide is out, wander down to the Caño de Sancti Petri beach to find armies of crabs guarding the coast.

→ Follow the Sendero Punta del Boquerón wooden walkway, which begins at the parking area for Camposoto (36.4181, -6.2239), for 2.5km, with the marshes on one side and the dune systems on the other. A small track enters the ruin at the end of the walk.
30 mins, 36.3991, -6.2122 🖼️📷🚶🐾⊞◈

RIVERS & LAKES

6 PLAYA RÍO DE SAN PEDRO

This narrow stretch of sandy beach is located where the mouth of the San Pedro river meets the Bay of Cádiz. A short drive from the busier beaches in Cádiz, this peaceful shore has views of La Pepa bridge in the distance. The water is shallow and warm and there are several hidden spots to siesta in the shade of pine woodland.

Popular with families, fishermen and birdlife, the tidal pools in the sand are perfect for paddling. Be careful with the tides if swimming further out.

→ Park at the Chiringuito Katanga (36.5262, -6.2198) and cross the footbridge to the R. You can either walk along the path behind the University of Cádiz for 5 mins then turn L on to the beach or slip down the side of the bridge and wander up the beach that way.
10 mins, 36.5289, -6.2169 🏊🏖️

7 EMBALSE DE GUADALCACÍN

A narrow asphalt way used by fishermen leads right down and into the reservoir here. It also makes a great launch spot for wild swims in the deep, cool water. Watch out for submerged trees and branches.

→ From San José del Valle take the A-2201 towards Algar. After 9.8km there is a small way on the L. Park and follow it down to the water.
5 mins, 36.6401, -5.7127 🏊🏞️

8 EMBALSE DE ARCOS DE LA FRONTERA

A wide, blue expanse of water just outside the beautiful *pueblo blanco* of Arcos de la Frontera. Although this spot can get very busy in summer, it is worth coming off-season for a dip or walking a little way from

the imported sand area to the reedy banks for a quieter swim.

→ From Arcos follow the road for 5.5km around to El Santiscal on the other side of the reservoir. Park where you can near the beach bar Taberna de los Vientos.

1 min, 36.7675, -5.7840

9 RÍO GUADALETE

In the 19th century workers from Jerez would cool off at this point in the river, a few hundred metres downstream from the beautiful late-Gothic monastery of La Cartuja. A colourful longship is sometimes moored up, and in 2019 a Roman watermill was excavated here, with a tunnel to the monastery. In a strange case of history repeating itself, a relief of the Roman goddess Ceres was found in the brickwork of the Roman mill, oddly echoing the Virgen de la Merced, the Patron of Jerez, whose image was found in the brick kilns.

→ From Jerez de la Frontera take Av. Medina Sidonia S towards the La Cartuja. Take the first exit at the roundabout, the A-2002, for Cádiz and follow for 550m to reach a few restaurants. Park where you can and walk down past the archaeological site to the river.

5 mins, 36.6534, -6.1038

10 EMBALSE DE BORNOS

Natural pools along the banks of the Bornos reservoir are a stroll away from the pretty, historic town of the same name. It is a haven for fish and birdlife and perfect for an evening dip as the swallows wheel overhead and the Sierra de Grazalema fades to soft blues on the horizon. See Bornos Activo entry for kayak rental.

→ From Bornos follow Av. de la Diputación down to the reservoir and park. Follow the curve of road down past the boathouse to the water.

1 min, 36.8076, -5.7423

11 BALSA DE MELENDO

This artificial lake near Lebrija is surrounded by pine, broom, oleander and carob woodland and is a haven for birdlife. There is a 13km cycle track around the lake and canoes for hire. Call Club de Piragüismo Tarfia for canoe rental – 650 725 282.

→ Take the A-8150 out of Lebrija towards the Poligono Industrial Las Marismas. After 1.7km turn sharp R and the road doubles back before turning L to the lake.

5 mins, 36.9541, -6.0481

HILLTOP VILLAGES

12 MEDINA-SIDONIA

One of the oldest towns in Europe. Come in the evening to see the golden stone of this *pueblo blanco*'s ancient walls, horseshoe arches and intricate facades light up in the sun. Medina means 'city' in Arabic and Sidonia refers to 'Sidon' in Lebanon, referencing its ancient Phoenician connection. It was home to Duke Alonso Pérez de Guzmán, who led the Spanish Armada against England. It was also home to the Red Duchess, Luisa Isabel Álvarez de Toledo y Maura, named so for her life-long anti-Franco, left-wing activism.

➔ Parking is signed to the L on the CA-203 entering from the S.

15 mins, 36.4568, -5.9250 ⊞ ⎮⎮ ⬚ ⬤ ⎘ ⬤ ◻ ⬤

13 BORNOS

With over 30,000 years of history, this beautiful *pueblo blanco* on the banks of the Bornos reservoir is a wonderful place to explore. Its jewel is possibly the Castillo-Palacio de los Ribera with its early medieval Islamic origins. Its beautiful cloisters and fountains lead to Gothic doorways and the Garden of Sighs with a 16th-century loggia, grottoes and gargoyles. The stones are steeped in tales of legends and hauntings. Follow the staircase upstairs for incredible views across the town and lake to the blue hues of the Sierra de Cádiz. Come to Bornos for its *carnaval* celebrations, *Semana Santa* or Corpus Christi.

➔ Parking can be found along the CA-402 into town, just after the petrol station. Park here and walk in.

15 mins, 36.8152, -5.7435 ⊞ ⎮⎮ ⬚ ⬤ ⬤ ◻ ⬤

14 ARCOS DE LA FRONTERA

Named several times as the most beautiful village in Spain, this *pueblo blanco* crowns the sheer cliffs of La Peña rising proudly above the wide Guadalete river curling below. It sits on the remains of a Roman city and under Muslim rule it was known as Medina Ar-kosch. Explore its flowering white streets leading to incredible views and narrow corners opening out to its Basílica de Santa María, medieval castle and churches.

➔ From Jerez take the A-382a into the town. Parking is signed on the R 600m after the townhall.

15 mins, 36.7485, -5.8067 ⊞ ⎮⎮ ⬚ ⬤ ⬤ ◻ ⬤

15 CUEVAS-CANTERAS DE LA SIERRA DE SAN CRISTÓBAL

The sea once reached as far inland as these ancient sandstone quarries hidden deep in the undergrowth near the ruined Phoenician settlement of Doña Blanca. An ancient, worn footpath, seemingly cracked under the weight of heavy dragged stone leads through wildflowers to these man-made caves with views of Jerez and Cádiz to either side. The landscape seems to hold the memory of the lost sea as the flowers and broom recreate the feeling of walking through dunes. The stone taken from the deep chambers and dark recesses here, called *piedra ostionera* locally, was used to build the cathedrals of Sevilla, Cádiz and Jerez. What is left feels like an inverse, underground cathedral. It is a great place to explore, and popular with scramble bikers, but take care of small drops if visiting with kids.

→ From Laguna de Torrox in Jerez de la Frontera, take Av. del Reino Unido steadily uphill, away from Jerez, for 1km. As the last suburban road petters away continue straight on as the road turns into a footpath, passing a flytipping area, follow this straight on for another 3km until C. Tempranillo, the main street of the rural, ramshackle hamlet of Sierra San Cristobal. Follow this R and uphill for 500m, turn L on to Caballo Negro and follow down until a roundabout. Head straight over this, take the way marked 'Calle Caballo Negro 14' and follow to where the dirt tracks start. The footpath is unsigned but a rough 3km loop passes the quarries, follow to the R and keep the 'military zone' low boundary wall to your L.

1.5 hrs, 36.6366, -6.1837 🚶♿Ⓥ🚲🚵

16 CASTILLO DE MATRERA

This 9th-century Islamic castle on a small hill outside Villamartin was built by Umar Ibn Hafsún to defend Iptuci, the largest city in the Cora de Ronda and one of the taifas that emerged as the Caliphate of Córboda began to crumble during the 10th century. The site is a national monument and recently underwent a controversial restoration which has been described as 'absolutely terrible' while also winning prestigious architectural awards. The *Guardian* described it as being neo-brutalist but as having restored 'the clout its Moorish creators originally intended'.

→ From El Bosque take the A-373 towards Villamartin. After 9km turn R and follow signs for El Santuario. Park here. There are some decorative tiles illustrating the route at the

23

18

20

19

21

beginning of the track leading uphill. It is a 4km circular path which passes the castle.
60 mins, 36.8073, -5.5657 🏕️🏞️⊞

17 CASTILLO DE TORRECERA

The ruined mortar walls of this 12th-century watchtower survey beautiful views over the low Guadalete valley and towards the Sierra de Grazalema. It has a visual connection with Torre Estrella in Medina-Sidonia a well as the towers in Sierra de San Cristóbal and Gibalbín, the castles of Arcos and Jerez. It once guarded Jerez and its trade route against Christian attacks from the north as well as attacks from North African troops. The aqueduct, which supplied fresh water to Cádiz from Tempul, ran nearby. Ancient stone idols, 5000 years old, were found here and can be seen in the museum at Jerez.

→ This site is accessed by footpaths through private land. From Torrecera take the CA-3110 towards La Ina for 1.2km. Turn L at signs for Finca Torrecera. If the gate is shut, park and continue on foot for 1km to the bodega, the current landowner, and follow signs up to the castle.
25 mins, 36.5943, -5.9531 ⊞☎️❓

ANCIENT & SACRED

18 CARISSA AURELIA

At the end of a long, dusty track, and surrounded by open plains, lie the remains of what was once a terraced city and necropolis dating back to Iberian and early Roman times. Although very little remains of the city, the road, with its ancient cart ruts, is a peaceful spot with beautiful views of the Sierra de Grazalema and the white houses of Espera and Fatetar Castle rising above. From the remains of early Christian burial niches, a 1.5km footpath will take you to further ruins, chambers and tombs dating back to the 2nd century BC. An underground passage once connected all these sites.

→ Leave Bornos on the CA-402 and at the junction with the petrol station, head straight over the A road, following signs to Espera. Follow for 2km to reach an unpaved road on the R. Park here and walk uphill along the track for 2km, keeping L at the first fork. After 2km turn R and follow the track for 3km to reach the first tombs.
1.5 hrs, 36.8668, -5.7302 🏊🚶🚲

19 DOLMEN DE ALBARITE

This monumental passage tomb, some 23m long and protected by a huge geometric roof, sits as incongruously as a spaceship in these tomato fields outside Villamartin.

Its huge stones were once decorated with ochre suns, moons, figures and engravings of weapons. It is hard to make out the forms now, as it is around 6,000 years old, one of the oldest in the Iberian Peninsula. The remains of two individuals were found with grave goods which included a stone necklace, amber beads and a giant smoky quartz crystal of about 20cm high, which you can see in the first room as you enter Museo de Cádiz today.

→ Access is fenced off due to conservation but Albanta Educación run guided tours, call – 615 159 798. See Albantaeducacion.com for more creative kids workshops.
15 mins, 36.8160, -5.6366 🏞️⚙️◈❓

20 SALINAS DE IPTUCI

These bright white salt pans appear like virgin snow in the middle of the green Sierra de Cádiz. A small, salty spring that rushes from the depths of the earth is one of a handful that emerge across Andalucía, the result of salt deposits from the ancient sea of Tethys some 250 million years ago. The Phoenicians harvested the salt, followed later by the Romans who built the city of Iptuci on a nearby hill. You can visit the salt farm today and see the traditional harvesting of the *fleur de sal*, salt flakes or coarse salt.

→ Call 639 467 512 for a guided tour. Restaurante Los Molinos, 100m up the road, has a salty pool supplied by the same spring.
5 mins, 36.7500, -5.5462 🏠🍴🍴

21 NECRÓPOLIS DE FUENTE DE RAMOS

A series of Bronze Age tombs carved into the rock that were used for burial up until the 12th century. A 4km circular walk leaves from Puerto Serrano and passes the hermitage of Santa María Magdalena, which is a popular picnic spot with great views.

→ The route is unsigned but begins at the end of Calle Blas Infante. Follow it all the way out of Puerto Serrano.
25 mins, 36.9186, -5.5263 ⚙️🏞️

CULTURE & TRADITIONS

22 CÁDIZ EXPERIENCES

Surfing, gastronomy and alternative historical routes can be explored with this great local guide. Much of Cádiz's remarkable history is hidden behind a door, in private patios and watchtowers and down secret streets. Letícia is a local *gaditana* who leads English-speaking tours off the well-worn routes. You can also take a day

out surfing at the local beaches or enjoying gastronomy tours. Better still, mix it all up and surf then feast on the best *pescaito frito* and *chicharrones de Cádiz*.

→ Pl. San Antonio, 1, 11001 Cádiz, 623 177 191, Cadizexperiences.com
36.5347, -6.2990 1sYe67€2

23 ALCANTARA ECUESTRE

Spend a day horse riding in the beautiful Jerez countryside. The equestrian arts are rooted deep in the culture and life of Jerez, and if you want to discover more about the passion Jerezanos have for their horses then Alfonso is your man. Riding since he was three, he is an authority and horses are very much a part of his *alma*, or soul.

→ Carretera Cortes, Km 10 Cañada Albadalejos – Cuartillos, 11593 Jerez de la Frontera, 670 891 558, Alcantaraecuestre.com
36.6855, -5.9971 z€

SHERRY & FLAMENCO

24 TABERNA JÓVENES FLAMENCOS

A dark, family-run tavern with glossy oak barrels and seating spilling out into the sun. Inside, the walls are covered with signed pictures of local and visiting flamenco artists, old bullfights and holy week icons. Further inside is the *cueva*, built into the old town wall and now used for flamenco nights. A great selection of tapas and vino de Jerez is on offer.

→ Calle Dean Espinosa, 11, 11630 Arcos de la Frontera, 657 133 552
36.7487, -5.8074 ⚙️🍴🍴

FARMS & VINEYARDS

25 PRIMITIVO COLLANTES

This 19th-century bodega creates excellent sherries, Olorosos, Amontillados, Finos, Creams, Moscateles and white wines, all from the Uva Rey, an ancient grape endemic in Chiclana. In the late 20th century this grape was almost lost but is now protected and cultivated here. Call ahead for a tour and tasting at the winery or you can drop in to purchase wines.

→ Calle Arroyuelo, 15, 11130 Chiclana de la Frontera, 956 400 150, Bodegasprimitivocollantes.es
36.4214, -6.1506 ⚙️🍴

FRESH SEAFOOD

26 VENTA LA COMPUERTA DEL ALBUR

This restaurant, located by the meanders just before the meeting of the mouth of the

Guadalquivir and the sea, is worth every pothole in the road to get there. A downbeat place, the landlord is welcoming and there are excellent Jerez wines. You can try a classic dish of *las anguilas* (eels) when they are in season, and the *camarones al ajillo* (shrimp in garlic) are heavenly.

→ 11549 Sanlúcar de Barrameda, 956 237 233 36.8995, -6.2941 🖼️🍴🍷🏊⛰️

27 VENTA EL ALBARO

No frills and no need for them at this roadside restaurant by the River Guadalete which offers real home-cooked traditional dishes, grandma-style. Try the *berza con pringá* (cabbage cooked with slow-roast pork), eaten with crusty bread to pull away the meat; *garbanzos con cola de toro* (chickpeas and bull's tail), *pochas con chorizo* (beans with chorizo) or *un guiso del día* (stew of the day).

→ Hijuela del Pantanal, 5, 11406 Jerez de la Frontera, 956 156 421, Ventaelalbero.com 36.6546, -6.1044 🖼️🍴🍷⛰️

28 CANTINA DE TITI

This brightly painted beach bar stands on wooden legs and the tide rushes in below the decking. It looks out towards the Bay of Cádiz and La Pepa bridge from a tiny harbour with a few rickety sheds. The bar started out in 1934 as a place for the fishermen to enjoy a glass after returning from sea. Now run by the grandchildren, it is also known as El Bartolo, after Bartolomé who inherited it from Titi. Popular with singers, writers and artists over the years, the bar has a photo of one of San Fernando's most famous sons, the flamenco singer Camarón de la Isla, in pride of place. Try the *papas aliñas* (potatoes drenched in oil), *boquerones* (fried whitebait) with a heaped plate of fried green peppers or the *ortiguillas* (fried snakelocks sea anemone). All the grilled fish is fresh, of course, and you can choose the *choco* (cuttlefish) with or without ink.

→ 11110 Playa De La Caseria, 11100 San Fernando, 686 734 966
36.4852, -6.2013 🖼️🍴🍷🏊🚗

29 RESTAURANTE SALINAS DE CHICLANA

The team behind this restaurant is dedicated to the conservation of the ancient Cádiz salt marshes, farmed for their salt since prehistory and providing an important habitat for birdlife. Their passion is for food and well-being. You can explore the salt marshes and enjoy incredible views. Soak at their salt-pan spa and then feast on wonderful dishes made from local produce. Try *garbanzos con algas* (seaweed

and chickpeas), *langostín* from Chiclana, *croquetas de dorada* (sea bream croquettes) and huge rice dishes. There are figs with Moscatel wine for pudding or *helado de camarones* (prawn ice-cream) for the brave.

→ Salinas de la Chiclana, 11130 Chiclana de la Frontera, 667 664 844, Salinasdechiclana.es 36.4392, -6.1643 🖼️🍴🍷

30 VENTORILLO EL CHATO

A fantastic restaurant along the Via Augusta facing the long, golden sands of the isthmus joining Cádiz to the mainland. This is the place to try an array of fresh seafood and typical Cádiz dishes. Try the *tortillitas de camarones* (prawn fritters) or red tuna with vino de Jerez and *tocino de cielo* for dessert. There is an apocryphal story that King Alfonso XIII stopped here en route to Cádiz. Just as he ordered a glass of sherry, the *levante* wind kicked up and the innkeeper, thinking quickly, covered (*tapado*) the glass of sherry with a thin slice of jamón to protect the wine from filling with sand. The king loved it and ordered another, and so was born the tradition of tapas, at this humble bar in Cádiz.

→ Av. Via Augusta Julia, 11011 Cádiz, 956 250 025, Ventorrilloelchato.com 36.4801, -6.2624 🖼️🍴🍷🏊🚗

WILDER CAMPING

31 BORNOS ACTIVO

Six wooden cabins in a small, private camping ground on the banks of the Bornos reservoir. The sunsets behind the distant blue hills of the Sierra de Grazalema are spectacular and on summer evenings the calm water stays warm for swims. Francisco, the owner of Bornos Activo, has over 20 years' experience teaching parapenting and runs courses here. Kayaks are also available. See Lijarsur.es for more details. Dogs are welcome.

→ Av. de la Diputación, 34, 11640 Bornos, Cádiz, 617 490 500, Bornosactivo.com 36.8095, -5.7398 🏊🚗⛰️🐕

RUSTIC HAVENS

32 JABALINA TIENDAS

Several luxurious safari tents are hidden in the pine forest of the Dehesa de las Yeguas, in the heart of the Bahía de Cádiz Natural Park, and a few kilometres from the best beaches. The 100 hectares belonging to a 19th-century *cortijo* were used for rearing *toros bravos* and horses for the nearby Jerez bullfights. Now Amparo and Cosima keep a

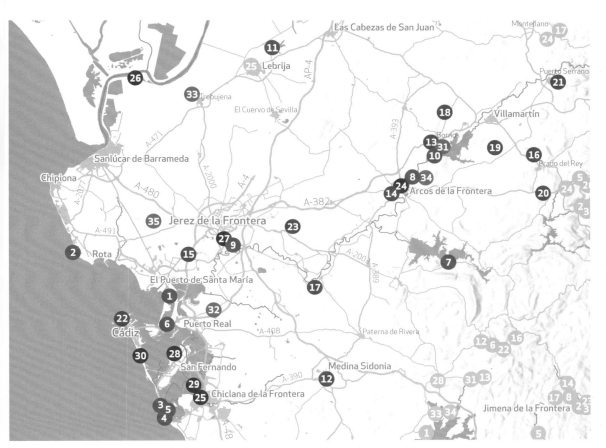

menagerie of rescue donkeys, horses, goats and cats. The *plaza de tientas*, a smaller bullring once used for testing young bulls' bravery before fights, remains along with the old weight system and corral from Seville, now overgrown with rockrose and wild thyme. Enjoy fresh dips in the old *alverca*, now converted into a pool.

→ Carretera del Portal CA-3113 Km 3,3 Buzón 31, 11510, Cádiz, 687 272 514, Jabalina.es
36.5535, -6.1337 🌿🔧🏞️🔲🎯

33 CASA MARTINETE

A great place to stay for birding, this guesthouse on a country estate outside Trebujena is surrounded by vineyards and just 5km from the Doñana National Park. The estate is an oasis of tranquillity, with almond, carob, fig and pomegranate trees and the best sunset over Doñana. The owner, Juan Martín, runs birding tours and visits to the ancient salt marshes, wineries and vineyards. He has won awards for his work

in conservation and eco-tourism and has a team of nature experts ready to explore Cádiz with you.

→ Carretera de Trebujena al río Guadalquivir, Km 1,5, 11560 Trebujena, Cádiz, 687 959 256, Martinete.eu
36.8785, -6.1900 🌿🐦🔲🍴🔦🎯🐾🔄

34 HACIENDA EL SANTISCAL

A high-end, sustainably run hotel just outside Arcos de la Frontera, surrounded by gardens and with views of the Sierra de Grazalema and the Arcos lake. A peaceful retreat, the hotel occupies what was once a noble 15th-century house.

→ Av. del Santiscal, 173, 11638 El Santiscal, Cádiz, 956 708 313, Santiscal.com
36.7665, -5.7689 🔲🔦📷🍴🔦🌿

35 LA BENDITA LOCURA

A beautiful 19th-century *cortijo* set deep in the Jerez countryside and surrounded by vineyards. It produces ecological wine, and

the seasonal smells of wine production fill the old house. There are three luxurious suites named after each grape variety and they offer dinner with stargazing, vino de Jerez tasting and pairing, food and falconry or wine harvest activities.

→ Av. el Tejar, Km 2, 11500 El Puerto de Sta María, 670 512 230, Labenditalocura.com
36.6849, -6.2495 🔲🔦📷🍴🌿🔲

CÁDIZ & COSTA DE LA LUZ

Our perfect weekend

→ **Gaze** out across the glimmering, blue Strait of Gibraltar to Jebel Musa mountain on the coast of Morocco

→ **Marvel** as late summer skies fill with griffon vultures making migration over the strait

→ **Wander** the golden beaches of Bolonia and keep an eye out for the somewhat surreal herd of local Retinta cows who also like to sunbathe

→ **Look** out for whales and dolphins from salty, splashed decks sailing out from Tarifa

→ **Tumble** down the enormous dune systems at Playa de Bolonia and at Valdevaqueros

→ **Surf** the waves and feel the wind in your hair at the long golden sands of Playa de Los Lances

→ **Listen** to cowbells as livestock graze the green hillside below Silla del Papa, the highest point of the Sierra de Plata

→ **Watch** the sun set into the ocean in gold, greens and pinks from the Calas de Roche

→ **Dine** on the delicious wild red tuna caught in the seasonal *Almadraba* migrations or enjoy a heaped plate of pescaito frito by the sea

The golden sands of La Costa de la Luz continue south from Cádiz to Tarifa, at the southernmost tip of continental Europe. Its hills look out over the Strait of Gibraltar to the blue silhouette of the mountain of Jebel Musa on the Moroccan coastline, a mere 14km away. Together with the nearby Rock of Gibraltar, they form the gateway to the Mediterranean and the legendary Pillars of Hercules. Green hills dotted with white villages give way to a coastline of yellow sands, cliffs and caves. This area is a flyway for colourful birdlife migrating to Africa.

Birds are not the only ones to migrate; this strait has witnessed several millennia of human migration. It was on a calm morning in ad 711 that Tariq ibn-Ziyad, governor of Tangier, sailed over hidden among busy merchant vessels, ushering in the era of Al-Andalus, eight centuries of Islamic rule. He renamed the limestone mountain *Jabal Tariq*, meaning Tariq's rock or Gibraltar.

Waves of settlers came to Cádiz long before Tariq and continued to arrive long after. The Phoenician longships which touched the sand in the 12th century BC were hardly the first visitors. Hundreds of ancient sites testify to earlier cultures. In the hills behind Bolonia is Peña Sacra de Ranchiles, a sacrificial altar carved in a prominent rock by *turdetanos*, ancient pre-Roman tribes. Wander from here to gaze at Cueva del Moro, a cave facing out to Africa, with carvings over 20,000 years old. Down at Playa de Bolonia are the ruins of a Roman city, Baelo Claudia. A statue of Emperor Trajan faces the sea among columns that hold up only sky.

This sea witnessed a golden age of piracy in the 16th century, and a line of coastal watchtowers were built to defend the coast from marauding Barbary pirates. Follow old paths up from Playa de la Hierbabuena to these towers that still guard the coast. Later, they saw bombardment of the Spanish and French navies who met with Admiral Nelson off the Cape of Trafalgar. The cliffs and coves which once rang with canon fire are now eerily quiet. At low tide you can wander from freshwater springs, tumbling down cliffs between Los Caños de Meca and Barbate, to rock pools and nudist-friendly coves.

Within hiking distance is Silla del Papa, highest point of the Sierra del Plata, and reputedly where Sertorious rallied his rebel army against Rome. On clear days at these high places, the limestone peaks of two almost-touching continents come into breathtakingly sharp focus. Many of the ancient *pueblos blancos*, strategically crowning hills, share these views. Wander to the springs and Roman aqueducts at Santa Lucía outside Vejer de la Frontera; their panoramic views remind us how easily Andalucía became a melting pot of cultures.

Be warned, strong winds can tear across this beautiful landscape. The infamous easterly wind, the *levante*, was thought to inspire madness and now fuels the lunacy of surfers that flock to the beaches. Valdevaqueros is often filled with kite surfers, while Los Caños de Meca and El Palmar have become a surfing mecca.

Seek refuge from wild winds at Cádiz's numerous beach bars, where you can taste the ocean on your plate. *Atún rojo salvaje de la Almadraba* is the wild tuna caught in the seasonal migrations, and around Barbate its preparation - cured, seared or tartare - is an art form. Or you can feast on plates of *papas aliñás*, potatoes drenched in olive oil, or try a *cartucho de pescaito frito*, fried cuttlefish, whitebait, or sherry-marinated *cazón en adobo* (dogfish) to eat on the beach.

At the end of the day, bed down in one of Finca Suerte Tierra's luxurious yurts. At dusk you can wander up to where the lights of Tangier glimmer over the strait.

SURF & SAIL

1 PUENTE ROMANO, PLAYA DE LOS LANCES

While the nearby Roman ruins of Baelo Claudia are more popular, this ruined bridge crossing the Jara river offers a quieter insight into the once busy Roman trade route between Africa and Europe. The small wetland here forms part of the Paraje Natural Playa de los Lances. Home to Audouin's gulls, terns, sandpipers and plovers, the wetland has a couple of bird hides along the wooden walkway. The Camino de Santiago passes nearby.

➔ From Tarifa follow the E-5 N for 1km. Turn L at signs for Paraje Natural and park. Head down towards the beach and just before the cattle grid there is a footpath to your R. Follow this to the bridge.

5 mins, 36.0382, -5.6258 🏊🐟🏄👣

2 DUNA DE VALDEVAQUEROS

A 4km stretch of virgin, sandy beach with an immense sand dune and views across the bright blue Strait of Gibraltar to the crags of Jebel Musa. The beach is one of Europe's best kitesurfing spots so it can get busy. Head up to the top of this dune to try some sand surfing.

➔ From Valdevaqueros take the N-340 N for 1.5km, turn L at brown sign for Punta Paloma and continue for 1km. Park on roadside and walk down.

5 mins, 36.0682, -5.6977 🏊🏄

SECRET BEACHES

3 PISCINAS NATURALES DE BOLONIA

Dramatic fingers of rocks reach into the sea to create natural pools at this nudist-friendly spot. Filled by the tide and warmed by the sun, the pools are known as the baths of Claudio in reference to the 1st-century BC Emperor Claudius, uncle of the scandalous, sex-crazed Caligula, who gave the city its title. They make a great place for a crystal-clear dip. Bring a snorkel to discover the tiny crabs, pebbles, seaweed and beautiful shells.

➔ Park at Bolonia and follow the beach to the E for 3 km. If the tide is in, you can follow a small path with runs behind the dunes and woodland.

45 mins, 36.0685, -5.7399 🏊🐟⛺👣🚫

4 PLAYA DE BOLONIA

The bleached bones of a Roman amphitheatre at the old city of Baelo Claudia frame a brilliant-blue sea. Following the earthquakes and tsunami that took place between the 3rd and 6th centuries AD, the theatre and

its temples to Isis, Jupiter, Juno and Minerva were abandoned, only to be rediscovered relatively recently. This long, sandy beach is now world-famous for its windsurfing and its friendly, if somewhat surreal, herd of Retinta cows, which often come from nearby pastures to wander along the sand. Don't miss the chance to run up and tumble down the huge dunes on the west side. From the dunes, follow the coastal path for 200m to reach great places for snorkelling and quieter spots when it is busier in summer. Entry to Baelo Claudia is ticketed and worth it.

→ From Tarifa take the E5 towards Cádiz for 14km. Turn L on to CA-8202 at brown signs for Bolonia and continue over the hills to the large beach parking.

15 mins, 36.0885, -5.7781

HIDDEN COVES

5 PLAYA DEL CAÑUELO

This secret sandy cove is reached following a beautiful footpath through ancient rocks, juniper, pine and mastic trees. Views of Playa de Bolonia with its dunes and Playa de los Alemanes fall away to either side. At the end of the footpath is Faro de Camarinal, a 16th century beacon that once defended the coast from Berber pirates. This is a good sunset spot from where you can spy the cove's golden sands with the striking limestone crest of Cerro de Bartolo rising behind. Cañuelo is a quieter, nudist-friendly haven when the neighbouring beaches are busier in summer.

→ See directions to Playa de Bolonia and continue on 500m to the Baelo Claudia musuem. Continue uphill with the sea on your L and after 2km you will pass military zone signs and Piedra Sacra on L, carry on uphill for 700m until a small parking bay. From here the footpath Sendero Faro Camarinal is signed. Follow this for 1.5km and 100m before the lighthouse turn L onto a woodland path down to the cove.

30 mins, 36.0881, -5.8048

6 PLAYA DE LA CORTINA

A short stroll along the beach from Los Caños de Meca lie these emptier sandy beaches under the immense Barbate cliffs. Freshwater springs tumble down over the cliffs and there are several hidden caves. It is a great area for rockpooling, but be careful as the tide comes in very quickly and there are not many paths directly up. It's odd to think that this quiet, naturist-friendly cove would have once looked out upon pirate attacks and the battle at nearby Cabo de Trafalgar.

→ From Los Caños de Meca, walk E along the coast. After clambering over the rocks and

passing some beautiful secluded coves you will see the falls on your L above the cave. ONLY attempt this walk when the tide is going out, otherwise you may get stuck.

30 mins, 36.1793, -5.9913 🏖🌊🐾📷🚿🚻🌀

7 PLAYA DE LOS ALEMANES

This small cove with its fine golden sands and crystalline water is bordered by the lush woodland of the Sierra de la Plata. To the south you can see the coast of Tangier. On its northern side are the ruins of a bunker built in the 1940s to defend against Allied attacks. The popular belief is that the name of this cove refers to the Nazi Germans, who sought Franco's protection after World War 2.

→ There is parking at Parking Faro Camarinal (36.0940, -5.8096); the beach is a short walk down.

10 mins, 36.0994, -5.8167 🏖🐚🌊🐾

8 PLAYA DE LA HIERBABUENA

At this sheltered, sandy cove the sea is often warm and crystal clear. It is bordered by the woodland of the Parque Natural de la Breña y Marismas del Barbate and a footpath, the Sendero Torre del Tajo, takes you up on to the Barbate cliffs to its 16th-century watchtower, which was used during pirate

attacks. You can follow the footpath onto Playa de la Cortina and Los Caños de Meca, 5km away.

→ The beach is within walking distance of Barbate. Leave Barbate in the direction of Los Caños de Meca, and behind the harbour at the roundabout there is parking. Follow the track down to the beach.

10 mins, 36.1863, -5.9371 🏖🐚🌊🐾

9 CALA DEL GUADALMESÍ

A 16th-century watchtower built to defend against Barbary pirates stands guard over this small, pebbly cove at the river mouth. All along this stretch of coast run tracks to numerous coves with crystal-clear rockpools and views out to Jebel Musa. The jagged rocks forming these long, lineal rockpools are known as 'the flysch' and were formed by plate movements in the cretaceous period. The Camino de Santiago passes here, following the disused coastal road to Tarifa.

→ From Tarifa take the N-340 towards Algeciras for 4.5km. Pass km89 and after 800m take the dirt road on the R and follow without deviating for 5km to reach the coast. You will pass many 'Military No Access' signs but these are now defunct, and

a small community lives near the Torre de Guadalmesí. Popular dog-walking area.
10 mins, 36.0369, -5.5205 🏖️🌊⛰️🏕️

10 CALAS DE ROCHE

Sandy tracks lead under pine trees and greenery hiding snakes, butterflies and lizards down to several small coves, including Cala del Pato and Cala Enebro. The turquoise sea contrasts with the brilliant orange of the ostioneria cliffs, a porous type of limestone made by ancient seashells. This is the millennia-old rock used to build many of the buildings in Cádiz, including the cathedral. Here you can see the oysters crumbling out of the stone. Great rockpooling; nudist and dog friendly.

→ Park along the road leading up to the lighthouse on Cabo Roche. Follow the wooden walkway or tracks down to the coves.
5 mins, 36.3043, -6.1469 🏖️🌊🐚🦞🏕️

11 CALA DEL ACEITE

When the strong easterly winds of the *levante* are kicking up in Cádiz, this beach offers a sheltered respite. It can get busy in summer, but you can follow the signed footpaths 500m south along the clifftops to Cala Puntalejo or Cala de los Pitones. Nudist friendly and usually a little van community in winter months.

→ From Cádiz take the CA-33 then the A-48 S to exit 15 onto the N-340. Take the first exit at the roundabout for 'Urb. Roche' and continue for 3.7km. Turn L on to Av. Europa and follow for another 3.5km, passing the lighthouse at Cabo de Roche, to a sharp R onto a sand track. Follow for 700m to reach beach parking.
1 min, 36.297, -6.1318 🏖️🌊◈⛰️

WILDLIFE WONDERS

12 FIRMM – WHALE WATCHING

A small team of marine biologists dedicated to the research and protection of whales and dolphins. They offer day trips out in small boats and if you're lucky you might catch sight of these amazing mammals.

→ Calle Alcalde Juan Núñez, 10, L-1, 11380 Tarifa, 956 627 008, Firmm.org/en/
1 min, 36.0109, -5.6047 🚗📱🏖️

13 INGLORIOUS BUSTARDS

The birdlife of Andalucía, mid-flyway between continents, is some of the richest in Europe. Simon and Niki's expertise and passion for the incredible birdlife makes it a great day for rookies and avid birders alike. Whether you're interested in bustards, eagles, flamingos

or the migration of thousands of griffon vultures crossing the strait to Africa, a day trip or longer adventure could take you to wild islands, ancient sites, salt marshes, sierras or straits.

→ C. Guzmán el Bueno, 1, 11391 Facinas, 665 945 992, Ingloriousbustards.com
1 min, 36.1429, -5.6986 🦅🌐🚶🌿🐾🏞️🚗♿

14 ENTRE RAMAS

A treetop playground with rope swings, ziplines and tight ropes in the pine woodland just outside Conil de la Frontera.

→ Carretera Urb Roche, 11149 Conil de la Frontera, 633 698 334, Entreramasaventura.com
1 min, 36.3207, -6.1396 🚗💶

SUNSET HILLTOPS

15 BATTERÍA D9, EL VIGÍA

Here you can see hidden bunkers built in 1940 to defend the Strait of Gibraltar. The guns were salvaged from the *Jaime I*, a Spanish dreadnought built in the early 20th century and used by Republican forces in the civil war. She was wrecked by an accidental explosion in June 1937, and her guns were salvaged and laid at various coastal batteries after the war. Great views of the strait.

→ From the Lidl in Tarifa head onto the N-340. At the roundabout take the first exit towards Algeciras. After 400m take a R on to the dirt track and continue for 2km to reach the Observatorio del Estrecho. Park here and walk up keeping L.

10 mins, 36.0193, -5.5806 ⊞⛰🚶🚶⊡

ANCIENT & SACRED

16 SILLA DEL PAPA

From the limestone ridges along the highest point of the Sierra del Plata you have panoramic views of Africa, Europe, the Mediterranean sea and the Atlantic ocean. One side falls away to the Atlantic coast and the other looks across the Strait of Gibraltar to the African coast, its hills disappearing into the blue behind the Jebel Musa massif. There are pre-Roman steps and carvings in the rock here. It's thought to be the place known as Mons Belleia, where in 80 BC Sertorius rallied the Lusitanian tribes in his rebellion against the Roman Senate. Beautiful cork oaks provide shade, and you can look down on the griffon vultures circling below.

→ On the N-340 at km71, take the CA-8202 road to Bolonia. Carry on past the ruins and after about 2.5km turn R at signs for Quesaria. Park here and walk uphill. After the Quesaria take the second L and continue uphill for another 1.5km. There is a hole in the fence you can climb through. Wander on 500m to the peak.

80 mins, 36.1243, -5.7643 🆅⛰🏠🐂🍴⊡✝

17 PEÑA SACRA DE RANCHILES

These ancient steps cut into rock are said to be pre-Roman and were possibly used as a sacrificial altar for sky burials similar to sites in Portugal. The rock is surrounded by scrubland with panoramic views of the sea and the Sierra de la Plata. Along with nearby Silla del Papa, it has been considered a possible site where Sertorius rallied his rebel army against Rome. A magical spot for sunset, follow the road uphill and onwards for Cueva del Moro and its vulture colony. Looking out to Africa, the cave hides paintings over 20,000 years old, and can be glimpsed from the quiet roadside below, but has no access currently.

→ From Bolonia beach continue past the museum of Baelo Claudia on the CA-8202. After 2.5km park where you can before the military zone signs. The rock is on private land to the L but a footpath, accessible through a hole in the fence, leads 50m from the road to the site. For Cueva de Moro continue along the road uphill for 2km.

5 mins, 36.0949, -5.7890 🐂⛰✝🏠🦅🚶🏃

18 ERMITA DE SAN AMBROSIO

The ruins of this small chapel by a stream can be safely dated to around the 15th century but many say it dates back to at least the 7th century. Ancient inscriptions mention its consecration in the year 644, as some martyrs' relics were deposited in a column. Storks nest in its roof and the Torre del Tajo footpath starts nearby.

→ From Los Caños de Meca take the A-2233 towards El Palmar for 3km. At the roundabout take the first exit signed to Ermita de San Ambrosio. Follow signs for another 3km.

5 mins, 36.2148, -6.0026 ⊞✚✠†⚑⚐

19 TUMBAS ATROPOMORFAS DE BETIS

Ancient anthropomorphic graves carved into rock beneath the limestone crags of Cerro de Bartolo and circling vulture colonies above. A spring runs nearby while goldfinches and black redstarts dart between the scrub and boulders. It's a peaceful place with stunning views of the Sierra de Enmedio towering overhead. The exact age of the tombs is a mystery; they have been considered to be Phoenician, Visigothic, Roman and Muslim. Follow the footpath signed from Betis to discover more of the Cerro de Bartolo, a popular climbing spot.

→ From Tarifa take the N-340 N for 11km towards Cádiz. Turn L at sign for Betis and continue for 3km to Betis. Parking on the L and the rock is signed in the fields on the R.

5 mins, 36.0928, -5.7183 🧗‍♀️⛰†⚐🚶

20 ACUEDUCTO ROMANO DE SANTA LUCÍA

Just north of Vejer de la Frontera are La Muela springs. The Romans saw their value and built aqueducts to supply nearby fields and orchards and they were later remodelled during Muslim rule. An easy 5.5km circular footpath takes you from the small hamlet with some great restaurants to the cascades and aqueducts. It passes 15th-century mills and carries on to beautiful views of Vejer and the north African coastline behind.

→ From Vejer de la Frontera take the N-340 towards Cádiz for 1.5km. Turn R at a small white sign for Santa Lucía and follow the narrow tarmac road for 1km to a parking area after the restaurants.

1.5 hrs, 36.2697, -5.9777 🚶‍♀️🧗‍♀️⛺📖†⚐

FARMS & VINEYARDS

21 QUESERÍA EL CABRERO DE BOLONIA

A family-run goat farm that produces the famous Sierra de Cádiz Payoyo cheese. The best time to visit if you want to see the goats with their milk is from January to July. They offer guided tours,

depending on the number of guests and the timing. Call to see if you can drop by.

→ El Realillo, 20, 11391 Playa de Bolonia, 650 421 774, Elcabrerodebolonia.blogspot.com

36.1089, -5.7657 ⊞🍴⚐⛰🚶🥾

22 SANCHA PÉREZ BODEGA ALMAZARA

This earthy, joyous bodega and *almazara*, or olive farm, is a family-run enterprise producing organic wines as well as olive oil. They run activities, tours and tastings where you can visit the ancient groves and vineyards, learn about their sustainable ways of farming, and sample the cream of the crop. A happy sanctuary.

→ Camino de los Moledores, s/n, 11150 Vejer de la Frontera, 670686849, Sanchaperez.com

36.2692, -6.0458 ⊞🍴⚐⛰🚶

LOCAL FOOD

23 PEÑA EL ATÚN

This relaxed restaurant in Barbate is the *peña*, or club house, for the fishermen here. It specialises in *Atún Rojo Salvaje de la Almadraba*, the wild red tuna caught in its seasonal migration between April and June. Well priced.

→ C. Ancha, 39, 11160 Barbate, Cádiz, 956 432 319, Elatun.es

36.1932, -5.9204 ⊞🍴⚐

24 RESTAURANTE EL MIRLO

A popular seafood restaurant with incredible views out over the Dunas de Valdevaqueros to the Moroccan coast. A small footpath leads down to the quiet Punta Paloma beach.

→ Punta Paloma, 11380 Tarifa, 956 685 100

36.0647, -5.7231 🏖⚐⊞🍴⚐

25 EL TROPEZÓN

A great stop on the way to Bolonia beaches where you can feast on local *retinto* beef, fresh seafood and hearty sharing dishes. Chairs and tables spill out into a garden surrounded by farmland and looks up to Cerro de Bartolo and green hills sweeping down to Bolonia beach.

→ 11391 Bolonia, 653455996, El-tropezon-desde-1984.webnode.es

36.1003, -5.7330 ⊞🍴⚐⛰

YURTS & CAMPING

26 FINCA SUERTE TIERRA

This sustainable and family-run finca is the perfect hideaway in the sleepy hills of Tarifa. Sling up a hammock or bed down in a beautiful yurt with only the sound of

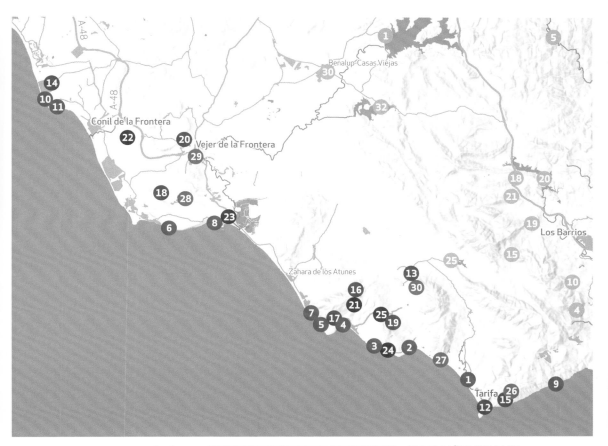

cowbells in the evening. There are fresh eggs for breakfast, donkeys in the neighbouring field and a number of footpaths leading through the hills to several secret beaches.

→ Unnamed Road, 11380 Tarifa, 626 538 423, Yurtstarifa.com
36.0278, -5.5736

27 CAMPING TORRE DE LA PEÑA

The campsites along this stretch of the coast towards Tarifa can get busy with noisy nightlife revellers, but this campsite has two areas divided by the main road: one side right by the sea and the other side up in the pine woodland next to the 12th-century watchtower. Camping in the woodland area is sleepy and peaceful. The side by the sea has a great bar and restaurant with decking like the prow of a ship, splashed by salty waves.

→ N-340, Km 78, 11380 Tarifa, 956 684 903, Campingtp.com
36.0568, -5.6595

RUSTIC RETREATS

28 HOTEL EL PALOMAR DE LA BREÑA

A beautiful hotel in an 18th-century hacienda surrounded by La Breña y Marismas de Barbate and by several footpaths. The ruins of the world's largest dovecote, with 7,770 terracotta nests, are on the grounds. The pigeons were used as messengers during the 18th century and their guano supplied the manufacture of gunpowder used by ships in Trafalgar.

→ Pago de La Porquera, 11160 San Ambrosio, Barbate, 956 435 003, Palomardelabrena.com
36.2099, -5.9732

29 CASA RURAL ANTIQUA

This tiny but charming house is located just down from the castle in the white-washed *pueblo blanco* of Vejer de la Frontera. It has thick walls and a patio, and part of the house and the cellar is built into the ancient bedrock.

→ C. Canalejas, 20, 11150 Vejer de la Frontera
36.2528, -5.9629

30 LOS BAÑOS DE LA LUZ

A wellness retreat with several cosy rooms located in an old stone guesthouse. There are also various wild camping options in the grounds, from a geo-dome to log cabins by the bio pool.

→ Calle Saladaviciosa, 4, 11391 Facinas, 956 687 703, Banosdeluz.com
36.1287, -5.6919

26

LOS ALCORNOCALES

Our perfect weekend

→ **Ruminate** in the hills at La Casa de Piedra, a 6th-century chapel carved into hillside rock

→ **Hike** through the twisted cork oaks of the Ojén valley to Cueva de Bacinete, the site of hundreds of ancient cave paintings

→ **Plunge** into the silvery pools, home to tiny frogs, at the old flour mill of Molino San Francisco

→ **Swim** out from grassy banks of the Guadiaro river and watch as dragonflies dance over the surface

→ **Scramble** up and slip into smooth river pools in the deep gorge of Cañón de las Buitreras

→ **Discover** hundreds of monarch butterflies in the woodland along the Guadarranque river

→ **Listen** out for the ghost of Gabriel Moreno Pantisco, a 19th-century smuggler and brigadier, at La Garganta del Capitán

→ **Seek** refuge behind the old castle walls at Castillo de Castellar de la Frontera and feast on locally reared Retinto beef

→ **Bed** down to the hoot of the night owl at Reserva Ecológica Las Lomillas on the banks of the Barbate reservoir

The weathered peaks of the Parque Natural de Los Alcornocales are the last coastal bastion before sea winds sweep in from the ancient port of Algeciras, bringing with them humidity and a thick cloak of fog that settles over its dark forest. These brooding mists and an abundance of rain have resulted in a network of rivers which flow into the Mediterranean and the Atlantic. Over the ages, they have carved one of the most extraordinary of Andalucía's landscapes, the so-called *canutos*: long, deep ravines sheltering living remnants of a lost world, a laurisilva forest.

Twenty million years ago, much of Europe was covered in laurisilva, a unique mass of oaks, rhododendron, alder, holly, laurel, bracken and many types of ferns, moss and lichen. The *canutos* provide a constant climate of rainfall and humidity for this subtropical forest to survive, trapped in time. This eroded rock has also preserved pockets of our human history, and it is a little-known fact that Cádiz is the most bountiful region for cave art in Spain. The sandstone caves of the Gamero gorge are home to paintings of what might be the oldest representations of sailing boats in the Mediterranean. And at Cueva de Bacinete there are paintings of humans and animals that range in age over several millennia, suggesting these valleys were ancient places of human passage.

Climbing up to villages such as Jimena de la Frontera, with its proud sandstone castle glowing in the sunlight, you can survey vast swathes of woodland. Los Alcornocales means 'the cork oak groves', and it is one of the largest in the world. At over 168,000 hectares, it reaches north from its coastal area as far as the Sierra de Cádiz. Its thick forest canopy of cork provides shelter for ibex, roe deer, genets, badgers and mongoose, and eleven species of bats live in its caves. Look out for herds of black pigs; they are looking for acorns, and will steal sandwiches.

The wide, green Hozgarganta river sweeps through this woodland, passing under Jimena castle with great places for a swim by the ruins of its 18th-century royal artillery factory. Up at its 7th-century castle, carved in the living rock, are several niches known as *Los Baños de la Reina Mora*: the baths of a long-forgotten Muslim queen. And at Pico del Aljibe, the highest point of Los Alcornocales, and a beautiful spot for sunset, lie other niches filled with rainwater, where Queen Isabel I of Castile was said to have bathed after battle. There are river swims fit for a queen at the waterfall along the Río de la Miel with its deep, milky pool.

Mossy stone huts, forest clearings and ruined villages stand testament to the dispersed communities who once lived in these hills. The gall oaks provided a rich source of charcoal which was used to heat homes until the 1960s. Follow the footpath along Canuto de Risco Blanco to pass these clearings (*alfanje*), with their old charcoal ovens and small thatched huts known as *moriscos*: the homes of shepherds and charcoal burners. Further north, the abandoned village of La Sauceda was once a notorious hideout for 19th-century bandits but saw the last resistance of Cádiz against Fascism in the 20th century. Its empty chapel and school are now overgrown, but stand as a monument to the bravery of its people.

The traditional cuisine of these forests is seasonal, and often the best option is to order the dishes chalked up on the board. Try the asparagus, artichokes, snails or *cabrillas* and many types of mushrooms that grow here. Several peaceful retreats are hidden away in Los Alcornocales; you can camp in tipis on the banks of the Celemín reservoir at Wakana or listen for night owls at Finca Las Lomillas on the shores of the Barbate reservoir.

3

LAKES & LAGOONS

1 EMBALSE DE BARBATE

A silvery reservoir, surrounded by low hills, with shallow entry as the sandstone from the Sierra del Alijbe resurfaces before sloping down to the water. To the east of these banks are the remains of a necropolis dating back to around 2000 BC; you can only just make out the hollows in the stone. The meeting place of three rivers, this would have been a fertile farming area for prehistoric Cádiz.

→ From Benalup-Casas Viejas drive 5.5km N on the A-2228 towards Alcalá de los Gazules. Turn R at signs for Presa de Barbate, follow for 2km and park on roadside. Wander down to the banks through olive groves.
5 mins, 36.3818, -5.7412 🏕️🚲

WATERFALLS & DEEP POOLS

2 MOLINO DE SAN FRANCISCO

A ruined watermill by the Cañuelo stream before it joins the River Hozgarganta, deep in cork oak woodland. Monumental boulders slope into its silver plunge pool. Despite being a ruin, the tall mill house retains its imposing grandeur. It was one of eight flour mills that supplied Jimena during the 18th century. The footpath here is a wonderful way to see some magnificently twisted cork oaks, namesakes of the Alcornocales.

→ See directions to La Real Fábrica de Artillería and cross the bridge over the river to a grassy area on the R. A 1.5km footpath follows the Hozgarganta river upstream. Follow this, turning L at the Cañuelo confluence, and the mill pool is located 500m or so upstream.
30 mins, 36.4279, -5.4669 🚶🚌♿✝️🏄🚗🧍🏠

3 LA REAL FÁBRICA DE ARTILLERÍA

The ruins of this artillery factory, abandoned in 1788, flank the north banks of the Hozgarganta river. It is a very picturesque spot and wild cork oaks, olive, heather and myrtle climb the rocky hill to Jimena castle, and the river forms deep green pools along the valley. Cannonballs were made here using iron ore from the nearby mines at San Pablo de Buceite. The bellows of the furnaces were powered by the water channels, which remain parallel to the river. The ammunition was used against the British during the Great Siege of Gibraltar (1779–83). The surrounding woodland and the small Chinchilla Natural Area here provide shelter for a mix of wildlife, including otters, frogs and rich birdlife.

→ Enter Jimena de la Frontera on the A-405 and turn L on to Av los Desportes. After 600m, turn L on to Calle Pasada de Alcalá and continue until the end; don't cross the river but turn sharp R then first L onto a dirt track. After 50m there is a small parking area before the river. Follow the old water channel upstream for 500m to deeper pools behind a dam.
15 mins, 36.4275, -5.4549 ♿🚗

4 RÍO DE LA MIEL

Milky blue pools along the Río Miel (honey river) are bordered by woodland and a tangle of roots. Follow the footpath upstream, winding around boulders and old mill houses, to find the deepest pool for a plunge under the freezing waterfall.

→ From Tarifa take the N-340 for 17km towards Algeciras. Turn L at the first roundabout (colourful painted trees) and follow for 2km, straight through the industrial park. Turn R then first L, and after 200m park near signs for the Sendero Río de la Miel (36.1172, -5.4769). Follow the track 2.5km to the river.
45 mins, 36.1118, -5.4989 🚶🧍🏔️🚗

5 CHORREÓN DE LAS NARANJAS

A high waterfall plummets over grey limestone to fill a wide but shallow pool in the woodland. A magical sight, it is formed by two branches of the Zapata stream before it meets the Guarranque river. The 6km trail here is one of the most beautiful ways to see the Alcornocales, and on misty days it has a dreamlike quality.

→ From the Fábrica de Bombas at Jimena de la Frontera, cross the bridge and take the road in the direction of Pasada de Alcalá. After 200m take the R fork and follow the paved but narrow road for 1.2km. Park at Lomas de Cámara. The track starts on your R and is barred by a small green gate between the rocks. You can climb over; part of the route is on private land but there is a right of way. Continue for 6km, following signs.

2 hrs, 36.3866, -5.5394

GORGES & RIVERS

6 GARGANTA DE PUERTO OSCURO

The name translates as Dark Harbour gorge. Running between the granite and limestone peaks of El Picacho and Pico del Aljibe, it forms a couple of dark plunge pools pierced by shafts of sunlight filtering through the alder woodland. It is best to visit after the winter rains. The Sendero Pico del Aljibe runs by.

→ From Alcalá de los Gazules take the A-375 N for 14km to Área Recreativa El Picacho. Park here and follow the footpath on the R to the lagoon. Pass the lagoon and continue 1km to the old bread ovens. At the crossroads turn R and continue for 700m. Turn L and follow the road uphill for 1km until you hear the river on your L.

1.5 hrs, 36.5163, -5.6278

7 PRESA EL COLMENAR

At this bend in the Guadiaro river, just before the dam, the river widens and deepens offering some longer swims. Grassy banks make for easy entry and dragonflies hover over the water in summer. Follow the footpaths into the wild woodland and ancient cork forest and pass the dam for more river swims.

→ Park where you can in El Colmenar. From the town square near the train station follow Calle Cerillo downhill for 300m. Take a sharp R and follow the track for 300m. Pass the horse arena and continue to the riverbank on the L.

10 mins, 36.5386, -5.3927

8 GARGANTA DE GAMERO

A cool, blue pool under a waterfall at the bottom of the Gamero gorge before it meets the Hozgarganta river. It is hidden deep in the wild olive and cork oak woodland and a little way downstream from Cueva de la Laja Alta (see entry).

→ Access is a little uncertain but follow the footpath along the Hozgarganta for 4km, starting at the Real Fábrica de Artillería outside Jimena. Where the Garganta de Gamero meets the Hozgarganta river, follow it for about 300m to reach the pools.
1 hr, 36.4425, -5.4841 🏊🥾🏞️❓

9 CAÑÓN DE LAS BUITRERAS

This spectacular canyon is named after the vultures nesting in its high sides, but it is also known as La Catedral de Barrancos, the Cathedral of Cliffs. The Guadiaro river is the slow sculptor of its siphons, walkways, caves and wonderful deep pools. Look out for otters in its wilder corners. The forest is a mix of oaks, juniper, mastic and carob, but one palm tree, the *palmetto*, stands out as Europe's only indigenous palm tree. For canyoning call Sport Mountain – 664 444 855, Sportmountain.es.

→ The 4km way is signed from Calle Buitreras in El Colmenar.
1.5 hrs, 36.5582, -5.3681 📱🏊🥾📷⛺🚶🏞️♨️

10 GARGANTA DEL CAPITÁN

A circular footpath of 5.8km takes you to the river, passing thick laurisilva forest with ferns, alders, ash, cork and gall oaks. The path passes Bronze Age tombs cut into sandstone, the ruined flour mills of San José and the cattle and goatherds of the neighbouring farmland. The river was haunted by the ghost of Gabriel Moreno Pantisco, known as El Capitán, a brigadier and later smuggler who fought agaist Napoleon's troops in Gibraltar and Fernando VII's absolutist reign during the early 19th century. Shot and buried in a mass grave in Algeciras, he is said to have haunted the river near the mills here until a priest ordered a cross to be carved on a rock for him by the river. They say on a new moon his spirit still searches for unwary travellers.

→ Entering Algeciras on the A7, take exit 107A. At the roundabout take Av. Europa, lined by palm trees, and follow this road. Head straight over the next four roundabouts. Turn L at the fifth roundabout on to CA-P-2311 and follow for 1km to reach parking on your R. Park and walk over a

113

11

14

15

cattlegrid to the beginning of the trail. Close gates for livestock.

45 mins, 36.1401, -5.5053 🚶⛲🏕🛏🚴🏊♿🎪

11 RÍO GUADARRANQUE

The Guadarranque river runs beneath the ancient hilltop town of Castillo de Castellar and is now home to Europe's largest breeding colony of monarch butterflies. A 5.5km footpath, the Sendero de la Mariposa Monarca, runs alongside the shallow river from the Venta la Cantina to the Restaurante La Jarandilla, with numerous spots for a picnic along the way.

➔ From Castillo de Castellar take the road S for 2.5km and park after Restaurante La Jarandilla on your R. Follow the path down to the river on the R of the information board and walk downstream.

5 mins, 36.3099, -5.4469 ♻➰🐟

ANCIENT WOODLAND

12 LAGUNA EL PICACHO

In the autumn and winter months, after some rain, this is a beautiful, secluded lagoon surrounded by a rich woodland of wild olive, gall oaks, cork oaks, heather and rock roses. The lagoon is a haven for birdlife and the woodland is a great place to picnic. There is

a small, circular footpath around the lagoon and picnic tables.

➔ From Alcalá de los Gazules take the A-375 N for 14km to reach signs for Área Recreativa El Picacho. Park on the roadside and head R for the lagoon and woodland.

2 mins, 36.5211, -5.6484 🐦🏕🚶

13 SENDERO RUTA DE LOS MOLINOS

This signed, short 2km walk follows the old cattle-droving track of Vereda Patriste, which links Alcalá with Jimena and which was also used by charcoal makers and millers. It follows the course of the Montero stream as it becomes the Rocinejo river, passing vestiges of millstones and water channels. It will take you under Mirador de Los Tallones, towers of limestone where vultures nest, and through a rugged gorge. A little detour takes you to the Garganta del Espino stream.

➔ The way is signed from Venta Patrite (see entry). Turn R on the first bend on the A-375 out of Alcalá and continue to the end of the tarmac. Park here.

35 mins, 36.4676, -5.6412 🥾🛏🚶♿

14 ÁREA RECREATIVA LOS ACEBUCHES

A rambling picnic area under the wild olive, cork oak and carob trees with many hidden corners and a children's play area. There are picnic tables, drinking fountains and a stream rushing down to the deep forests of the Hozgarganta valley below. A friendly family of black pigs lives here, so don't be surprised if they come close; goats and donkeys graze here too.

→ From Jimena de la Frontera take the C-3331 N. After 7km turn sharp L.
1 min, 36.4627, -5.4900 🏛️🍴♻️🥾

15 SENDERO CANUTO DE RISCO BLANCO

This 5km circular walk takes you deep into the rich laurisilva forest: an ancient woodland and one of the last vestiges of a subtropical climate dating back to the Tertiary Era. Ferns grow under the laurel and gall oak, shaggy with moss and lichens. The footpath takes you along the Canuto del Risco Blanco, passing woodland clearings, known as *alfanje*, and charcoal ovens. It passes several of the *morisco* huts. To pass the Tiradero stream, take the walk in conjunction with the 2.6km circular trail of Arroyo de San Carlos del Tiradero. Due to visitor quotas, you can only visit in an authorised vehicle; call the Forest Guard in Alcalá – 856 587 508

→ From Facinas take the CA-221 E into the Alcornocales. After 15km the walks are signed by a layby.
1.5 hrs, 36.1656, -5.5794 🧗🛏️🚴🍴💧❓

16 LA SAUCEDA

Due to its remoteness the village was used as a refuge for Muslims fleeing Christian rule after the Morisco Rebellion of 1570. It was later a refuge for bandits in the 19th century; it then saw the last resistance of Cádiz against Fascism. But Francoist troops stormed the village in 1936, taking residents to a nearby camp in El Marrufo for execution. What remains are the ruins of the town, its chapel, school and cemetery, now overgrown, but a testament to the bravery of these people. The footpath follows the stream to a beautiful pond shaded by oak trees.

→ From Jimena de la Frontera take the C333-1 for 24km towards Algar. Park up on your R. Enter the garden up the steps to the L. Close the gate as the donkey is not tethered and very inquisitive.
5 mins, 36.5283, -5.5861 🏊‍♀️🔆🧍‍♂️🏛️🍴✖️

PREHISTORIC CAVES

17 CUEVA DE LAJA ALTA

In the wild oak woodland of the Gamero gorge, it is easy to forget that the sea is just 30km to the south. But sheltered under a massive sandstone rock lie these caves, eroded by sea winds charging inland. The rock is covered in red and ochre daubs, representing naval scenes, with figures, masts and possibly bundles of twisted plant stems. They date back to around 3000 to 4000 BC, making them the oldest representations of sailing boats in the Mediterranean. The same wind that formed these caves and brought the boats is now blurring the paintings; they need protection.

→ Access is uncertain, and it is best to go with a guide. Call Arqueoroutes – 617 838 194. You can follow a small footpath up the gorge from where it meets the Hozgarganta river, just north of Jimena.
1 hr, 36.4405, -5.5109 🧗🚴🏊‍♀️⛰️🧍‍♂️💧

18 CASAS CUEVAS EL PALANCAR

The fringes of the Alcornocales woodland run into wild heaths known as *las herrizas*, Mediterranean scrubland. From the reddish earth grow hardy, medicinal plants, such as rockrose, heather, hawthorn, crocuses and gorse. The wind whips over from the strait, forming striking shapes and shelters in the numerous sandstone outcrops. A couple of cave houses look out across this scene;

easy to imagine yourself back in Neolithic times. It is essential to obtain permission to enter the caves from the landowners two weeks in advance – call 956 622 700. Or call Arqueoroutes – 617 838 194 for a guide.

→ From Los Barrios take the A-381 N. Take exit 77 and drive over the bridge. Turn L at the first fork and R at the second. Continue for 3.5km to signs for the sendero on your R with a stile.

25 mins, 36.1979, -5.5568 ♿✿⚠🚶❓

STRANGE ROCKS

20 PIEDRA CRÁNEO DE DINOSAURIO

Looped and weathered sandstone resembling a dinosaur's skull lies at the edge of the reservoir and makes a good jumping rock.

→ This footpath starts 400m down the road from Casas Cuevas El Palancar and is joined by the same circular footpath. Follow the path along the banks for 3.5km to reach the skull rock and swims.

1 hr, 36.2441, -5.5438 ♿🏊🚶

21 LA MONTERA DEL TORERO

This strangely weathered limestone rock, resembling a bullfighter's hat, emerges from a sea of cork woodland. Its huge scape and honeycomb texture is a type of tafoni and has earned the epithet *montera*, the hat of the *torero*, bullfighter. The part that represents the skull of the bullfighter is hollow and forms a small cave. Folk have described the honeycomb texture of the limestone cavity as the convolutions of the bullfighter's brain. It's a fitting image for hills that for centuries have been the breeding ground for the *toros bravos*, fighting bulls.

→ Head N from Los Barrios on the C-440a for 12km. There is parking to the R.

5 mins, 36.2249, -5.5825 ⚠️📷🏞️

SACRED SITES

22 PICO DEL ALJIBE

The highest point of Los Alcornocales sits at 1,100m above sea level and surveys a dense sea of cork oaks. On clear days you can see north to the Serranía de Ronda and south to Gibraltar, Ceuta and Morocco. There is a hollow in the sandstone rock, which is probably an early medieval grave. It collects water and, according to legend, in the final stages of the Christian conquest of Andalucía, Queen Isabela took a bath here. It has been known as *la Pilita de la Reina*, or the Queen's Bathtub, ever since. About 1km to the south is a standing

used by shepherds until the 20th century, their ceilings are scorched black from woodsmoke. There are no cave paintings but that is not to say these shelters were not inhabited in prehistory. The footpath passes an anthropomorphic rock tomb, typical of the first human settlers here, as well as a ferruginous spring and *morisco* huts.

→ From Los Barrios head N on the C-440a and join the A-381 in the direction of Acalá de los Gazules. After 7km take exit 73 and continue, with the motorway on the L, for 1.5km. There is parking for three cars on the R up a small track. Park at the gate/information board and follow the circular 3km footpath for 1.5km to reach the cave houses.

20 mins, 36.2435, -5.5779 ♿⛺🏞️🔄🏞️

19 CUEVA DE BACINETE

A series of limestone boulders form a corridor through cork oak woodland leading to several caves. They contain hundreds of schematic figures of humans and animals ranging between 3000 and 7000 years old. Possibly a communal meeting place for the different tribes that once populated the hills, it lies along a natural passage, the Ojén valley, connecting La Janda with the Bay of Algeciras. As you walk along, it is

menhir. Look out for vultures, eagles and peregrine falcons.

→ The 7km footpath Sendero Pico del Aljibe starts at El Picacho Área Recreativa (36.5220, -5.6501) and winds past Garganta de Puerto Oscuro (see entry).
2 hrs, 36.5102, -5.6079 ⚶🏕🏔

23 CASTILLO DE JIMENA DE LA FRONTERA

A beautiful 7th-century castle sits proudly on the rocky hill above Jimena de la Frontera. Its distinct circular, sandstone keep can be seen for miles around. Much of the castle stems from the medieval period and Roman carvings can be seen at the entrance gate. It was built with bricks looted from a previous Roman settlement. On the west side of the hill there are carved sandstone baths said to be the bathing spot of a legendary Moorish queen. From here there are beautiful views across Los Alcornocales Natural Park.

→ Open 9am – 8pm, free entry, parking below. Calle Misericordia, 16D, 11330 Jimena de la Frontera
36.4327, -5.4553 e*q

24 LA CASA DE PIEDRA

Surrounded by farmland, this wild chapel was hand-hollowed into its sandstone boulder around the sixth century AD. An early Christian sanctuary, it was most likely used by the Mozárabes: clandestine Christians living under Muslim rule. It still feels hidden away today, its intricately carved columns covered by an enormous fig tree. During more recent centuries it was used as a winery and for making olive oil; the remains of the press can be seen inside the chapel's alcoves. It now lies along the Camino de Santiago and the GR245.

→ Park at 36.6062, -5.3339 along the A-373 and walk 200m down the old stone path to the house on your R.
5 mins, 36.6062, -5.3339 ⚶✝🎏🏔🚶

25 TORRE VÍGIA TORREGROSA

This 13th-century watchtower sits squatly on the small hill above the sparkling Almodóvar reservoir. Its heavy walls are over 2m thick and it is at least twice the size of neighbouring watchtowers, earning its name 'the fat tower'. It would have controlled access to the Ojén valley which communicated with the Bay of Algeciras and along which ran the old Roman road from Carteia, the Vía Heraclea. Hidden in woodland, the footpath here passes some ancient rock tombs before winding down to the water's edge. The GR7 footpath runs by.

→ From Facinas take the CA-221 towards Los Alcornocales for 6km. Park where you can. Opposite the hotel is a gate leading to the footpath with the rock tombs to the R.
5 mins, 36.1573, -5.6516 🔲🈳🏕🏊⛳🏃🕇🏇❓

RURAL RESTAURANTS

26 EL ALJIBE, CASTILLO DEL CASTELLAR
A popular restaurant in Castellar. This medieval Muslim hamlet is encircled by a fortress wall and crowned by an imposing castle. The only access is on foot. Once inside the respite can be found on its battlements, with sweeping views to Gibraltar, and in this restaurant with its cavernous system of rooms serving dishes of local Retinto beef and hearty stews.
→ Calle Rosario, 3, 11350 Castellar de la Frontera, 956 693 150, Tugasa.com
36.318, -5.4532 🍴🍷🏠🔲

27 BAR ESPAÑA, JIMENA DE LA FRONTERA
Uphill and set apart from the more popular bars in the main plaza, this dark, narrow bar opens out to a small balcony with incredible views at the back. Great local food.
→ Calle Sevilla, 82, 11330 Jimena de la Frontera, 625 568 030
36.4351, -5.4536 🍴🍷🏠

28 BAR JAMÓN, ALCALÁ DE LOS GAZULES
There is nothing immediately striking about this typical Andaluz bar. What is extraordinary are the tapas. Try the *boquerones rellenos* (stuffed anchovies): these are the chef's invention using local ingredients and Jerez wine.
→ 11180 Alcalá de los Gazules, 699 031 902
36.4600, -5.7244 🍴🍷

29 VENTA PATRITE
A rustic restaurant serving great Andalucían dishes and tapas. Try the *refrito de espárragos majados* (seasonal asparagus). Next door to Camping de los Gazules.
→ Ribera de Patrite, Km 4,200, 11180 Alcalá de los Gazules, 956 420 127
36.4638, -5.6641 🍴🍷🔲

30 COCINA DE ISA
A restaurant with seating spilling outside around oak barrels. There is a good choice of local cheese; try the *queso viejo* (matured cheese preserved in olive oil). Various inventive and seasonal tapas made with local produce on offer.
→ Calle San Juan, 12, 11190 Benalup-Casas Viejas, 661 382 330
36.3431, -5.8095 🍴🍷

31 CAMPING LOS GAZULES
A lovely campsite deep in the Alcornocales woodland with wooden bungalows, rivers nearby, a restaurant, a pool and a picnic area by some climbing frames. Horse riding routes nearby.
→ Carretera de Patrite, Km 4, 11180 Alcalá de los Gazules, 956 420 486, Campinglosgazules.com
36.4635, -5.6649 🏊🏃🏇🏕🐕🛶

32 WAKANA LAKE GLAMPING
Indian tipis, Mongolian yurts and several bell tents are pitched on the banks of the Celemín reservoir at this sustainable retreat. Sling up your hammock under cork trees or enjoy some outdoor activities, such as kayaking, ziplining, paddlesurfing or archery. Horses graze nearby.
→ A-2226, KM6, 11190 Benalup-Casas Viejas, 687 929 459, Wakana.es
36.3101, -5.7431 🛶🏕🍴🛶🏇🛶

RUSTIC RETREATS

33 RESERVA ECOLÓGICA LAS LOMILLAS
A beautiful old farmhouse in an idyllic spot on the banks of the Barbate reservoir with views out to the Sierra del Aljibe and the pretty *pueblo blanco* of Alcalá de los Gazules on the shores beyond. The Barbate reservoir is a stopping point for migratory birds crossing the Strait of Gibraltar. There is a small birdhouse and at night you can hear owls. Sleeps 8.
→ Alcalá de los Gazules, 11180, 662 323 311, Laslomillas.es
36.4105, -5.7258 🏊🏃🏠🦅🏇🛶🐕🐕

34 HACIENDA DEL AGUA
A rural farmhouse surrounded by wild olive trees and cork oaks. The rooms look out across the Barbate reservoir, with paths leading to good swim spots. Wander to the bird hide and riding stables or borrow a bicycle to explore further.
→ Finca Hacienda del Agua, 11180 Alcalá de los Gazules, 679 418 668
36.4138, -5.6996 🔲🦅🛶🚴🏇🛶🐕

35 CASA RURAL AHORA
Rooms and apartments are available in this rustic guesthouse which offers slow food and a spa with mud baths, a jacuzzi and a sauna. Located in the pretty white-washed village of El Colmenar, the guesthouse has several footpaths leading through Los Alcornocales Natural Park nearby.
→ Calle Lepanto Finca la Vega, 29490 El Colmenar, 696 720 889, Casaruralahora.com
36.5371, -5.3894 🍴🍷🏃🛁🏊🛶🚴🐕

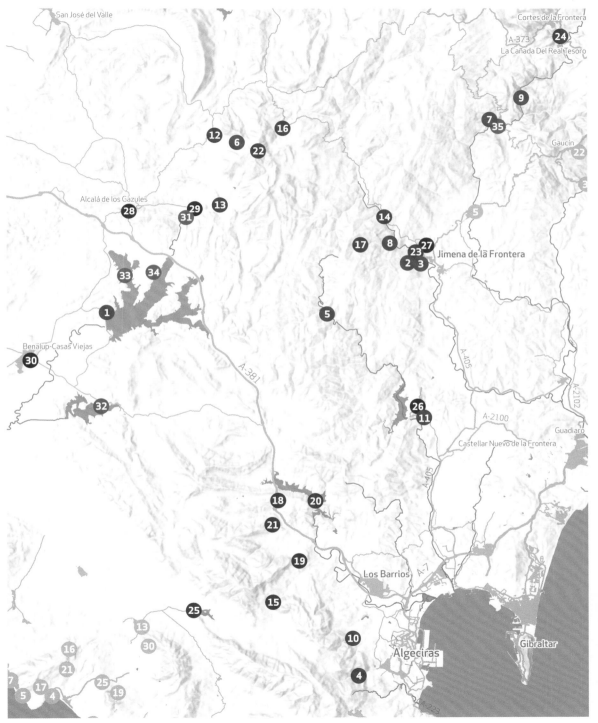

SIERRA DE GRAZALEMA

Our perfect weekend

→ **Sit** in the shade of the 1000-year-old olive tree at the Roman hillfort of Ocuri

→ **Wander** into Zahara de la Sierra in the evening light to see its castle flash gold above its bright white village and still blue lake

→ **Lean** into the wind at Cueva de las Dos Puertas and watch birds over ancient *pinsapo* woodland

→ **Journey** back in time and follow the Roman road from Ubrique through olive groves to Benaocaz

→ **Feast** on *payoyo* cheese from the milk of the local breed of goats that graze across these mountains

→ **Breathe** in the aromatic hillside scents at Dolmen del Gigante

→ **Canter** out into the Sierra de Líbar from Tambor del Llano and feel the spirit of the *bandoleros*

→ **Climb** up to the 13th-century Nasrid castle of Aznalmara and take in views of the Sierra de Cádiz

→ **Seek** refuge in a local restaurant and try *potaje de tagarninas*, made with blood sausage

→ **Bed** down in a cottage in Villaluenga del Rosario ready for a morning hike in the surrounding hills

The wild limestone peaks of the Sierra de Grazalema, in the south-eastern corner of the Sierra de Cádiz, are crowned by some of Andalucía's most beautiful *pueblos blancos*. These white-washed villages stand bright against lush countryside watered by the highest rainfall in Spain. The rain filters into rivers and streams such as the Bocaleones, the green glinting pools of the Tavizna or the forest canopied Majaceite. Seasonal streams meander through the karstic plateaus of the Sierra de Líbar, marking the border with the Serranía de Ronda. While the wide and deep Guadalete forms a lake at Zahara de la Sierra, a beautiful village as white as a snowdrift under its ancient castle.

The Bocaleones stream has carved one of the most impressive gorges in Andalucía, La Garganta Verde. With sides more than 400m high, it offers canyoning and hidden caves with long stalactites. The gorge is a refuge for nesting griffon vultures; look up to see them wheeling overhead.

Sculptural stone continues into the Sierra de Líbar, where chasms, caves, and crevasses surround the wide plains (*poljes*) of Llanos del Apeo and Llanos del Republicano. The Arroyo de los Álamos flows through both these plains, passing great holm oaks and grazing cattle, black pigs and *payoyo* goats. It then drains through the *polje* into enormous caverns with depths of up to 1,100m. When Nationalist troops seized Ronda during the civil war, the caves at Sima del Republicano gave refuge to loyal Republicans. You can follow the GR7 footpath through these historic hills.

These rugged and sparsely populated hills provided many hiding places for bandits and resistance against 19th-century French occupation. Up behind Tambor del Llano guesthouse is the ruined farmhouse where María Jerónima Francés from Cádiz, wife to El Tempranillo, met her death in childbirth during an attack from the Migueletes (king's soldiers who fought against banditry). Overseeing all these fugitive stories are the eery ruins of medieval border castles, which have stood and watched these dramas unfold.

You can hike up to these evocative ruins at Castillo de Aznalmara, which guarded the Tavizna river pass, or to the eroded stone towers of Castillo del Moral on Malaver hill. In the 15th century, neighbouring Serranía de Ronda was the last bastion of the Kingdom of Granada before Christian territory. Climb up to the castle at Olvera, the Christian side of the *Banda Morisca* frontier, or ruins along the Islamic side at Setenil, Grazalema, Zahara de la Sierra, Aznalmara, and Moral.

The *pueblos blancos* can get busy, but their wilder archaeological heritage is beautiful and much less visited. You can follow a stretch of Roman road linking Ubrique to Benaocaz, treading over ancient cart ruts, or watch the sunset from the Roman hilltop fort at Ocuri. From Benamahoma, follow the River Majaceite through woodland to nearby El Bosque. Or hike through *pinsapo* pines, a living Ice Age relic, at Grazalema to hidden chapels and panoramic mountain views.

Cool off from these adventures in the Embalse Zahara-El Gastor, where many inlets give easy entry to clear water. Or sit in the sunshine in El Bosque and enjoy tapas with a glass of wine from bodega El Algarrobo. The vineyards suffered the phylloxera blight in the 19th century, but native grapes are slowly recovering. You can try an exquisite white wine made from the *perruno* grape at Bodega Ambrosio in Olvera. As evening draws in, head to La Molina, just outside Setenil de las Bodegas, and listen to the River Trejo babbling by their woodland retreat.

LAKES & RIVERS

1 EMBALSE DE ZAHARA-EL GASTOR

A good entry point for a swim in the lake under Zahara de la Sierra. The scrubland slopes gently down to the shores from the shade of pine trees. There is beautiful stargazing at night and plenty of level space to pitch a tent under the trees. La Playita de los Arroyomolinos is nearby, which is occasionally open. Call Villaluenga Aventura at the Zona Recreativa on the opposite bank for kayak hire – 653 986 009.

➝ From Zahara de la Sierra, take the A-2300 S for 6km to a sign, 'A.R.A Arroyomolinos', on the R. Here turn L into the parking. Follow the track down to the water.

2 mins, 36.8188, -5.3757 🏊🏕️

FOREST RIVERS

2 CHARCO LA BOMBA

A small, rustic dam in the River Tavizna outside the Charco la Bomba, a little bar that opens occasionally. Follow the river upstream, where there are chickens in the hedgerows, for quieter pools filled with hundreds of barbel fish.

➝ From El Bosque take the A-373 towards Ubrique. Turn L after 5km onto the track running parallel and pass houses following the road L and out of the hamlet for 2km. Park where you can near the river and cross the bridge to the pool.

5 mins, 36.7320, -5.4730 🏊🏖️🥤🍴

3 RÍO TAVIZNA

Further down the road from Charco la Bomba are more forest pools along the Tavizna. Canopied by green, sun-dappled shade, even in August, the Río Tavizna sparkles past one of the last surviving millhouses, a private home complete with its own chapel and bell, to fill shallow pools. The El Pontón footpath leads up to Castillo Aznalmara from here.

➝ From El Bosque take the A-373 towards Ubrique. Turn L after 5km onto the track running parallel and pass houses following the road L and out of the hamlet for 2km. Park near La Bomba and walk 400m to cross the little bridge and walk upstream on the left-hand side along a footpath to pools.

5 mins, 36.7319, -5.4647 🚶🏊🥤

4 ARROYO DE CAMPOBUCHES

You can follow this tributary of the River Campobuches, also known as the Guadares, downstream until it joins the river and forms some deeper pools. The footpath passes small limestone gorges, the last of the foothills of the Sierra de Líbar, and livestock grazing under cork oak woodland. The largest of the oak trees is known as 'Chaparro de las Ánimas', 'Oak of the Souls'. Look up for vultures gliding overhead.

➝ From Grazalema take the A-372 towards Ronda for 3km. Turn L at signs for Ronda and R at restaurant Mesón los Alamillos. Continue on track for 2km. Park at 36.7438, -5.3336 and head downstream for 2km.

30 mins, 36.7585, -5.3113 🚶🏊🥤🐶🏞️

5 RÍO MAJACEITE

A small cascade called Cascada Honda is about halfway along the Río Majaceite, between the mountain villages of El Bosque and Benamahoma. A footpath follows the river passing many ways down to the river and connecting the two *pueblos blancos*.

➝ From El Bosque park along the Camino de los Pescadores and begin the 2km walk at 36.7617, -5.5064.

30 mins, 36.7718, -5.4807 🚶🥤🍴♿🏖️🌳

WILD WATERFALLS

6 CASCADA DEL MÍTANO

A little footpath leads up from Benaocaz through green farmland and cork, oak and wild olive woodland, rising up to rocky views across the Sierra de Grazalema and the peaks of Sierra Alta, La Silla and El Higuerón. The cascade falls in a horsetail shape over smooth, dark rock, but it is seasonal so best to visit after rains.

→ The footpath is not signed but there is an 8km circular route starting behind Posada El Parral in Benaocaz. It is 2.7km to the waterfall, which you will hear before you see it.

45 mins, 36.7186, -5.4067 🚶📖🔍📷📖

7 EL CHORRERO DE VILLALUENGA

A deeply hidden waterfall surrounded by the karstic landscape of the Sierra de Líbar. There is only water here after heavy rain, when the footpaths and cattle tracks are at their muddiest. The way passes the Llanos del Republicano, named after the Republicans who hid in the hills and caves here during the civil war, when Nationalist troops seized nearby villages. The 6.5km Llanos del Republicano trail runs nearby along part of the GR7 long-distance path.

→ The way is unsigned and difficult. From Villaluenga del Rosario take Calle Albarrada for 1km to reach the parking. At the fork take the R turning and follow the path, keeping R then straight on for 2.2km. At the crossroads turn sharp R and continue for another 2km to the waterfall. For more detailed info see the wikiloc walk and use maps.

45 mins, 36.6633, -5.3773 🗺🚶🔍📷📖📖

8 LA GARGANTA VERDE

This walk winds slowly down the 400m-high sides of La Garganta Verde canyon. The stony track is a bit of a scramble at points, but it passes ledges in the limestone rock where griffon vultures nest. In spring look out for young vultures learning to fly; they soar startlingly close sometimes. Deep in the canyon itself, carved by the Arroyo de Bocaleones, are a number of sparkling, clear pools. Once you reach the canyon, scramble over the river boulders 250m to your right to find la Cueva de la Ermita (the Hermit's Cave): a church-like overhang in the rock with almost sepulchral stalactites. The river is often dry in summer but for canyoning routes further down call – Experienciaoutdoor.com, 609 585 934. Permission must be obtained via Centro de Visitantes in El Bosque, 956 709 733.

All trails that require a permit are closed between June and October due to fire risk.

→ From Grazalema, take the A-372 towards Benamahoma. After 1.5 km, turn R and take the CA-9104 towards Zahara de la Sierra. After 10km turn L at signs for Sendero La Garganta Verde (36.8082, -5.3922). Park here. Follow the linear track 2.5km down to the river and continue 250m R to the cave.

105 mins, 36.8150, -5.4046 🏔🔽🏞🏕👣🚶🏃❓

BORDER CASTLES

9 CASTILLO DE OLVERA

The 12th-century castle of Olvera with its wind-lashed turrets crowns the white town; its striking silhouette can be seen from all around the sierra. Olvera was once a notorious bandits' lair: *mata tu hombre y vete a Olvera*, "kill your man and flee to Olvera" went the saying. This reputation probably came about during the repopulation of Olvera with convicts after its medieval Muslim population was expelled. From its battlements you can see the Serranía de Ronda and Castillo del Hierro at Pruna, a neighbouring *Banda Morisca* castle.

→ The castle is a short but steep walk up from Calle Llana to Plaza de la Iglesia where it is signed on the R. €2 entry.

10 mins, 36.9357, -5.2680 ✝🏞🖼💶🔄

10 CASTILLO DEL AZNALMARA

The ruins of this once proud 13th-century Nasrid castle crown the hill and can be seen from all around. From a distance, it retains its original imposing appearance, guarding the River Tavizna and the natural pass into the Sierra de Cádiz. A steep, almost vertical, hill leads up to the thick walls and ancient battlements.

→ See directions to Charco La Bomba and park there. Walk 400m to cross the little bridge and walk upstream on the right-hand side along the footpath, passing behind the old mill houses and bell tower. Continue for 1km to a large gall oak where the path turns R and uphill to the castle.

45 mins, 36.7294, -5.4663 🖼🏞✝🏃❓🏔🌿

11 CASTILLO DEL MORAL

From a distance the eroded mortar of this ruined castle appears to be the natural weathered rock of Cerro de Malaver. It is, in fact, the remains of a Nasrid castle that once defended the late medieval border between the Nasrid Muslim and Christian kingdoms. Its neighbouring watchtowers and castles built along Nasrid defences included those

at Gaucîn, Grazalema, Setenil and Ardales. Narrow steps with a wooden handrail lead up its slippery, ancient rock to incredible views.

→ The 2.5km footpath here is unsigned but follows a straight course. From the *ayuntamiento* in Montecorto, follow Calle Nacimiento for 120m to reach a path on the R.

45 mins, 36.8326, -5.2927

PUEBLOS BLANCOS

12 SETENIL DE LAS BODEGAS

A unique and striking *pueblo blanco* that hasn't so much as been built above its rocky pinnacle but which has grown out of the network of caves in the cliffs above the River Trejo. Rising above it all is the ruined castle, probably dating back to 12th-century Almohad rule. The town's name refers to the flourishing bodegas or wineries of the 15th century, but the caves probably also kept Roman wines cool. You can follow a good 3km, linear footpath by the old flour mills and olive oil mills along the Arroyo de los Molinos stream.

→ Parking is available where the Ruta de los Molinos begins, at the end of Calle Cabrerizas.

5 mins, 36.8644, -5.1809

13 ZAHARA DE LA SIERRA

Sitting proudly on a green hill above a still blue lake, Zahara is one of the most iconic of the *pueblo blancos*, capturing the imaginations of 19th-century Romantic writers. A frontier village, it was fought over until the 14th century when it finally surrendered to Christian rule, but its castle suffered again at the hands of French troops in the Napoleonic Wars. Today the footpath to the ruined castle is steep but offers panoramic views of the village, lake and the Serranía de Ronda. There are plenty of bars, churches and passages to explore.

→ There is parking along Camino Nazar just below the castle.

5 mins, 36.8399, -5.3893

ANCIENT & SACRED

14 DOLMEN DEL GIGANTE

This ancient Copper Age burial site is known as the giant's tomb as it is nearly 9m in length and would have been covered with a huge earth mound. From the hillside below Cima de las Granjas and Tajo Algarín, it looks out to incredible views of the Sierra Grazalema, Cerro Malaver and the beautiful Olvera below. You can follow the footpath up to these peaks.

→ From El Gastor take Calle Tajillo for 100m

17

18

18

until it joins the CA-0419; the footpath is signed from here. It is located in farmland so close gates behind you.

30 mins, 36.8441, -5.3231

15 DÓLMENES DE LOS TOMILLOS

Two ancient dolmens dating to around 2,000 BC are surrounded by oaks and olive trees in a peaceful grassy enclosure. They look out from this hilltop over the Sierra de Cádiz, and there are several stone picnic tables under the shade nearby which themselves look suspiciously megalithic.

→ From Alcalá del Valle head N towards Algámitas. At km4 on the CA-9107 turn R at the sign for Dólmenes de los Tomillos. Follow the road uphill, which briefly becomes untarmacked for 650m. The dolmens are in the enclosure but it is unlocked. Close the gate.

1 min, 36.9465, -5.1330

16 DOLMEN EL CHOPO

The remains of an ancient megalithic burial site with a beautifully preserved capstone stands on a small plateau looking out over the nearby valley. It is on private farmland and behind a fence, but you can stand 2m away. It was the ranger

of this farm who denounced Pasos Largos as a poacher. In 1916 the bandolero took his bloody revenge nearby.

→ From Grazalema take the A-372 for 13km towards Ronda. At the junction turn R and after the bend there is a dirt track on the R. Park and follow this for 1km.

15 mins, 36.7837, -5.2712

17 SENDERO CALZADA ROMANA DE UBRIQUE

A deserted stretch of Roman road winds for 3km through the Grazalema hills between Ubrique and Benaocaz. Ancient flagstones pave the way and olive and carob trees provide the occasional patch of shade. Overlooked by the Roman fortification of Ocuri on its north side and a colony of vultures on its south, the path feels timeless. Start in Ubrique, filling your bottles at the freshwater spring, and finish in the beautiful village of Benaocaz with its enigmatic medieval Nasrid quarter.

→ The way is signed from the drinking fountain, Fuente de los Nueve Caños, on Av. de Miguel Reguera, 3km to Benaocaz.

45 mins, 36.6931, -5.4334

18 YACIMIENTO ARQUEOLÓGICO DE OCURI

These enchanting ruins of a once crucial Roman fortification survey the valley pass below from its hilltop. In 1792 the entire hill was bought by a farmer and eccentric pioneer of archaeology, Juan Vegazo from Ubrique. Hoping to discover another Pompeii, he excavated the site, slowly revealing the slightly more humble yet evocative remains of a pre-Roman oppodium, Roman baths, temple, mausoleum and cisterns. From a 1000-year-old olive tree there are stunning views of Benaocaz, the nearby white village deep in the Sierra de Grazalema. There is a relaxed restaurant opposite with equally fabulous views and sofas under the trees.

→ Daily tours can be booked ahead online. Closed Mon, €2, Yacimientodeocuri.es.
1 min, 36.6873, -5.447 ⛯✝♿🍴€🎎

SUNSET HILLTOPS

19 LOS ÁLAMOS, LLANOS DEL APEO

In the foothills of the Sierra de Líbar the Cerro Tinajo hill is a perfect mini peak for scrambling up to enjoy sunset views. It is surrounded by an ancient farmland with dolmens, streams, caves, poljes, gorges, drystone walls and acres of cork oak woodland. An unsigned 10km circular footpath loops partly round the base and up Cerro Tinajo with views across the Sierras de Grazalema and Líbar.

→ From Grazalema take the A-372 towards Ronda for 3km. Turn L at signs for Ronda and R into restaurant Mesón los Alamillos parking. Continue on the track 4km to the rocky hill.
5 mins, 36.7247, -5.3272 🏞🚵🏊🏃🏇🚏

20 LLANOS DEL ENDRINAL

A short, steep hike up from the *pueblo blanco* of Grazalema leads to these rugged peaks and views out across the karstic depression named after the blackthorn which covers much of the mossy woodland here. It's a great place to watch the sunset. Keep an eye out for the *cabra payoyo* that graze this hill; their milk is used to make the cheese for which Grazalema is famed. Follow the footpath 1.5km on to Cueva de las Dos Puertas. The Sendero del Pinsapar which passes through Spanish fir forest starts nearby.

→ Take the A-372 out of Grazalema in the direction of El Bosque. At 1km after the first bend stop at the parking after Camping Tajo Rodillo. Follow Sendero Llanos del Endrinal for about 2.5km uphill and through the woodland.
30 mins, 36.7523, -5.3736 🏞🏞🏃

21 CUEVA DE LAS DOS PUERTAS

This cave is, in fact, a weathered arch formed in the rugged peaks above Grazalema. A striking natural viewpoint, it looks out to the Sierra del Endrinal and Grazalema's white rooftops huddled at your feet. The path passes a short detour to Ermita del Calvario, an 18th-century chapel burned and ruined in the Second Republic, whose picturesque arches frame further mountain views. You can follow the footpath on to Llanos del Endrinal.

→ From Grazalema take the A-372 uphill to parking at the first curve. After 450m the Sendero Ermita del Calvario is signed on the L. It's 500m to the Ermita and another 2km on the circular footpath up to the cave.
40 mins, 36.7505, -5.3653 ⬛🚶⬛

WINE & DINE

22 RESTAURANTE VENTA SALAS

Located along the road into the pretty town of Algonodales, this great traditional restaurant serves home-cooked dishes. Try the local stews, such as *potaje de tagarninas*, a local dish made from *tagarninas* (a roadside thistle once eaten out of neccessity), blood sausage and chickpeas. There is seating outside on the grass with views of the Sierra de Grazalema as well as warm places by the chimneys inside.

→ Ctra. Jerez-Cartagena, Km 72, 11680 Algodonales, 956 137 010
36.8801, -5.4038 ⬛⬛⬛

23 EL ALGARROBO

A family-run restaurant with tables spilling out onto the main square with its fountain in El Bosque. A small bodega at the back produces excellent wine and the bread is also made here. It offers a huge array of local tapas, and the landlord has a festive codeword for returning customers.

→ Calle la Fuente, 9, 11670 El Bosque, 644 926 757
36.7591, -5.5052 ⬛⬛⬛

24 BAR PEÑA ALBARRACÍN

An unpretentious, traditional bar in El Bosque that doubles as the village hunters' club. The award-winning chef, Ellie, follows recipes handed down from her grandmother, who cooked in this same kitchen. Try the *lengua mechá en manteca* (slow-cooked marinated pig's tongue), *cola de toro* (bull's tail) which melts in the mouth or *caldereta de jabalí* (wild boar stew).

→ Av. de Malaga, 14, 11670 El Bosque, 647 597 450
36.7575, -5.5040 ⬛⬛⬛

25 VENTA EL CASTILLEJO

Surrounded by views of the sierra and the countryside, this restaurant with its sunny terrace is built next to the remains of an ancient Ibero–Roman settlement. It is also a great stop for simple hearty *raciones*, plates of fried fish or cuttlefish and excellent *croquetas*.

→ Carr. de Antequera, Km 51,50, 11680 Algodonales, 625 230 288
36.9075, -5.3586 ⬛⬛⬛

26 BAR GONZALEZ

A rustic, no-nonsense restaurant, popular with locals, serving some of the best cooked local dishes in the sierra. They serve local grilled trout, shrimp in garlic, traditional stews and hearty roast wild boar.

→ C. Marques de Estella, 5, 11679 Benamahoma, 607 390 616
36.7645, -5.4662 ⬛⬛⬛

27 BODEGA AMBROSIO

A small winery and bar in Olvera that produces an organic white wine made from the native perruno grape, practically in extinction since the Great Wine Blight of the 19th century. This is a downbeat local *tabanco* where the wine is accompanied with a tapa.

→ Pl. del Matadero, 6-4, 11690 Olvera, 956 599 708
36.9370, -5.2674 ⬛⬛⬛

RUSTIC HAVENS

28 TAMBOR DEL LLANO

A beautiful, old farm converted into a guesthouse surrounded by footpaths leading into the mountains and woodland. Its 32 hectares hide allotments, stables, a luxurious eco-friendly pool and ruins said to once have been the home of the infamous gentleman bandit, El Tempranillo. They run horse trails through the mountains as well as short-stay riding courses.

→ Cañada Grande, Los Alamillos, 11610 Grazalema, 674 484 885, Tambordelllano.es
36.7486, -5.3319 ⬛⬛⬛⬛⬛⬛⬛

29 LA MOLINA

An idyllic retreat hidden just outside Setenil along the Río Trejo canyon with water running all year. There are two studios, a yurt

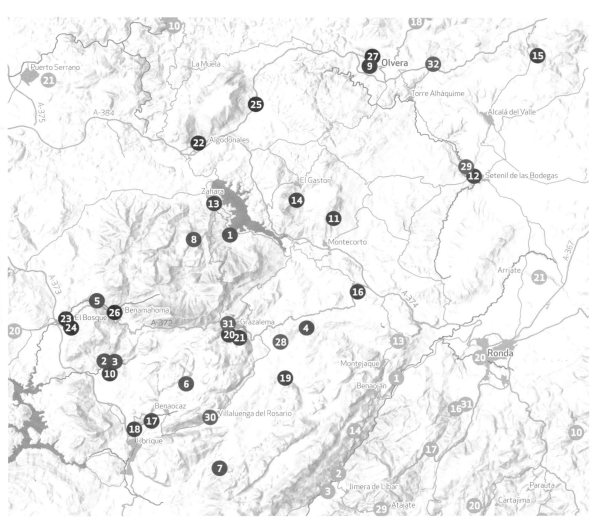

and restored campervans, as well as space for vans under the trees. Carola and Karin have created a space where guests leave as little carbon as possible. A peaceful spot surrounded by nature.

→ 11692 Setenil de las Bodegas, 660 167 981, Molinas.weebly.com
36.8704, -5.1876 🅿🚶🏕📶🔌

30 CASA DEL MUNICIPAL

Three cosy cottages with oak beams and chimneys in the tiny village of Villaluega del Rosario. It is the highest village in the Cádiz province and on either side the rugged peaks of the Sierra de Líbar and Sierra de Caíllo rise up with many caves and footpaths, the legendary haunt of El Tempranillo and Pasos Largos.

→ Calle Poeta Pérez Clotet, 8, 11611 Villaluenga del Rosario, 636 777 736, Casadelmunicipal.es
36.6968, -5.3864 🏕🚶🏕📶🔌

WILDER CAMPING

31 CAMPING TAJO RODILLO

A simple campsite under pine trees with several wooden bungalows and a pool. A short walk from the *pueblo blanco* of Grazalema, the spot overlooks immense views of the Llanos del Endrinal and many footpaths pass nearby.

→ 11610 El Bosque, 670 407 940, Campingtajorodillo.es

36.7585, -5.3740 🏕🚶🏕🔌

32 CAMPING PUEBLO BLANCO

A camping village on a low hill just outside Olvera with views across to its castle, Pruna and the distant Sierras de Cádiz. There are plenty of camping plots and bungalows as well as a pool, restaurant and climbing wall with rope bridges available for guests. It is popular with family caravans and mobile homes.

→ Ctra. Nacional 384, Km 69, 11690 Olvera, 956 130 033, Campingpuebloblanco.com
36.9385, -5.2169 🔌🏕🏕🏕🏕

SERRANÍA DE RONDA

Our perfect weekend

→ **Stargaze** under the dark silhouette of the Sierra de Líbar and wake up to dawn swims in the River Guadiaro

→ **Climb** up at sunset to the *mirador* above El Burgo and watch the hills turn purple over the Serranía de Ronda, the legendary refuge of outlaws

→ **Shudder** at the dizzying peak of the gorge of Tajo de la Caína, named after a woman accused of witchcraft

→ **Plunge** under the dark, cool waters of the waterfall and mountain pool at Charco de la Virgen

→ **Feel** the ancient cobbles under your feet following a Roman road to a hidden cave at Tajo del Abanico

→ **Hike** along a gorge at Arriate, splashing across its river, its rich woodland alive with woodpeckers, warblers and wrens

→ **Leap** from the dam at Dique El Burgo and dive into the clear, blue water

→ **Marvel** at hundreds of ancient cave paintings as you venture deep underground at Cueva de la Pileta

→ **Sink** into a natural rhythm of life at Algaba de Ronda and sleep in cabins by a prehistoric village

The Serranía de Ronda is spread between the Cádiz and Málaga provinces, running south as far as the mountains behind the Costa del Sol. Its bare peaks and rocky limestone crags jut out from wild woodland and valleys with their long, snaking green rivers. Perilous ravines, pockmarked with caves, open up at every turn. This is classic bandit country, the haunt of Pasos Largos and El Tempranillo and his gang. This is where peaceful farmhouses became the backdrop to bloody betrayals and where the roads between its pretty villages of Montejaque, Benaoján or Jimera de Líbar are full of stories and legends of bandits and stagecoaches.

A beautiful footpath follows the Guadiaro river from the train station at Benaoján, running from Ronda to the deep green swims at Jimera de Líbar. The path runs along the valley passing ruined inns, old mills, holm oaks and gall oaks. It follows a section of the Gran Senda de Málaga, an 850km circular footpath looping around the entire Málaga province and passing many of its wilder sites.

Rising above the green Guadiaro valley is the immense limestone massif of the Sierra de Líbar, the western edge of the Serranía de Ronda. In the early morning its sun-capped peaks are reflected gold in the green river. It is a karstic landscape, riddled with caves, and just outside Montejaque the Guadares river disappears into the mouth of Cueva del Hundidero. This great echoing cave is the portal to 8km of subterranean chasms, siphons and canyons. Later the river emerges into daylight at Cueva del Gato, tumbling from the cave mouth into a crystalline pool.

Málaga's beautiful long-distance path also links the Serranía de Ronda to the Parque Nacional Sierra de Las Nieves, to the east of Ronda city and its dramatic gorge. A place of sharp contrasts, it is named after its icy peaks which reach up almost 2,000m at La Torrecilla, but it could equally refer to its icy depths. At Sima GESM the chasms are some of the deepest in Europe, with drops of 1,100m, best left to professional cavers. You can hike up to the clear pools and waterfalls nearby at Poza Macías and swim in the water that gushes from this great chasm.

Further swims can be found at Charco de la Virgen with its bright, white waterfall and dark pool; the waters are said to be curative. Follow the footpath on through woodland to views of the peak at La Torrecilla and other waterfalls surrounded by a deep thicket of gorse, hawthorn and rockrose. Or you can follow the cattle track out of Tolox, passing sulphurous springs and streams winding through farmland to reach Cueva la Tinaja, caves set deep in pine woodland.

After a day exploring this precipitous landscape, you'll see that the vertiginous gorge and bridge at Ronda are only a glimpse of the breathtaking ravines and dizzying chasms the nearby sierras have to offer. It's hard not to imagine the bandoleros and their exploits across these mountains, hiding out in the caves, or Pasos Largos jumping a ravine to escape the civil guard; their spirits live on. In El Burgo, birth town of Pasos Largos and home to his family, look out for Manué. He chats in the street with other kids and deliberates whether to jump from high rocks by the cascades at El Dique in the River Turón.

Refuel on local fare under the vaulted ceiling and thick old walls of Bodega El Porfín in Yunquera, where you can try the young Yunquerano wine, and feast on hearty plates of chivo en caldereta (goat stew) or cazuela de bacalao (cod casserole). Bed down like a true bandolero under old holm oak at Zona de Acampada Libre Los Sauces, perfect for a starlit wild camp.

WILD SWIMS

1 CUEVA DEL GATO

They say this cave was the lair of a basilisk, a beast, a bandolero or a smuggler. Be that as it may, what really tumbles out of this dark cave is a waterfall, filling a wide blue pool. The River Guadares has worked its way through 8km of underground chasms, lakes, siphons and canyons to fill a breathtakingly icy pool. Hundreds of prehistoric artefacts and cave paintings have been discovered here. To explore the cave further see Cueva del Hundidero entry. This is a very popular spot in summer and you will have to pay a small entry fee, but it is an amazing geological phenomenon.

→ From Ronda follow the signs to Seville. After 4km turn L at a sign for Benaoján and follow the MA-7401 for 11.5 km. There is a parking area on the R close to the hotel.
10 mins, 36.7271, -5.2379

2 PISCINA NATURAL DE LA ESTACIÓN DE JIMERA DE LÍBAR

The deep green Guadiaro river runs slowly by this built-up grassy bank where there are a couple of small stone dams. It's popular with families picnicking and dogs. On the opposite side the Sierra de Líbar rises steeply, its woodland running along the bank. Follow the path upstream for quieter dips. The 8km footpath along the Guadiaro river starts at Benaoján train station and passes by.

→ Park in town and follow the foot tunnel under the railway. Turn R at the drinking fountain and continue to the pool.
10 mins, 36.6625, -5.2819

3 PISCINA NATURAL JIMERA DE LÍBAR

A rope swing dangles over the green pool before a small dam in the bend of the Guadiaro. Oleanders lean over the water and there are always a couple of vans by the picnic tables in summer. A little way upriver is perfect for longer swims, the limestone peaks of the Sierra de Líbar towering above the woodland and river. A 9km footpath along the Guadiaro river, part of the GR249, starts at Benaoján train station and leads here.

→ From the train station in Jimera de Líbar, cross to the side closest the river and head S on Av La Barca for 1.5km to the picnic area.
30 mins, 36.6507, -5.2900

4 POZA MACÍAS AT SURGENCIA DE ZARZALONES

A little way upstream from this pool is El Nacimiento del Río Grande, where water

gushes from the depths of the Sierra de las Nieves. It is also known as the Surgencia de Zarzalones and is the largest natural siphon in Andalucía, with more than 2,000m of flooded cave galleries linked to the Sia GESM caves yet to be fully explored. This turquoise pool is fed by a spectacular waterfall that marks the end of the sporty canyoning descent. The GR243 footpath passes by. For canyoning call Montaña Viva – 626 720 720.

→ From Yunquera take the Calle Agua S for 1km and park at the ford (36.7247, -4.9203). Follow the GR243 signed footpath for 2km.

40 mins, 36.7165, -4.9282 🏊👜🅿🚶

5 DIQUE DE EL BURGO

Deep in the Sierra de las Nieves the Río Turón forms a large, deep blue pool under a 5m-high stone-wall dam. Several cascades spout out of its side and you can swim up under their waterfalls. It is a peaceful spot with smooth rock banks for drying off, and local kids like to jump from the top of the dam over the cascades. Behind this dam are further deep swims.

→ From the centre of El Burgo take the A-366 towards Yunquera and there is a nice 2km walk

along the river signed (at 36.7881, -4.9492) on the R just after the bridge.

30 mins, 36.7853, -4.9688 🌲👜🏊🏕

RIVERS & WATERFALLS

6 CHARCO LA SILLERA

A very tiny, clear pool near the old mills and sulphurous springs of Agua Amargosa in the Arroyo de los Horcajos. It lies along the 3.6km footpath to the Virgen de las Nieves chapel from Tolox.

→ See directions to Cueva de la Tinaja. The pool is about 1.5km from the *ayuntamiento* in Tolox.

20 mins, 36.6931, -4.9164 🚶👜🏕🎋

7 CHARCO DEL PONTÓN ALTO

Limestone rocks slope gently down on either side of the Río Grande, where small bright pools form under small dams and waterfalls. The banks are overgrown with oleander and willow and there are large sun-warmed boulders for drying off. Wander upstream beyond the derelict Hidroeléctrica San Augusto to a large, river-smoothed pool. Look out for otters on the riverbanks.

→ From Alozaina follow the A-366 towards Coín. At km46 turn R at the recycle bins. The

pools begin after 500m along this road, so continue and park where you can.
10 mins, 36.7021, -4.8818 🐾🍴📶📷

8 CHARCO DE LA VIRGEN

A dark pool under a bright white waterfall which forms as the Arroyo de los Caballos plummets from a high ridge. Ferns and moss hang down from the semi-circle of rock and wild olives reach over the pool. A small ledge under the surface of the water by the waterfall makes a good seat. The footpath from Tolox passes several other pools and the water is said to be curative. Further on there are other waterfalls: Cascada la Rejía and Cascada Horcajuelo.

➜ Follow the main road straight through Tolox for about .2km and park at the Balneario de Tolox (36.6793, -4.9089). There is an easy 2.5km footpath signed 'Charco de la Virgen'. Follow this path to the waterfall. To discover further waterfalls follow the 10km circular walk signed 'Sendero Las Cascadas'.
30 mins, 36.6686, -4.9251 🏊🚶🥾⛰️

9 CHARCO DE LA CALDERA

A 25m-high waterfall splashes into a small but deep pool by the orchards at Jorox. Millennia of mineral deposits have created a mossy petrified waterfall with a small cave behind.

➜ From Yunquera take the A-366 towards Jorox. Turn R at signs for Jorox and park at the first bend. Follow the track down to the water.
10 mins, 36.7332, -4.8865 🏊🚶🐾

10 CASCADA MALILLO

Opposite the mossy spring of Fuente de Huerto Malillo, and just next to the cattle path, lies this waterfall and small, shallow pool. The way is the old livestock route, Vía Pecuaria Cordel de Ronda, and it is best to hike or cycle. A little way upstream is another spring, and at this point in its journey it becomes the Río Grande, or Guadalevín, which carries on to pass under the Puente Nuevo in Ronda.

➜ The way is signed from Área Recreativa Las Conejeras. Park here and follow signs for Cordel de Ronda. Stay on the path for 4.5km.
1 hr, 36.6946, -5.0920 🏊🚶🚶🚴⛩️

11 CASCADA Y TORRE DE LIFA

A beautiful waterfall with a shallow pool that forms as the Arroyo de la Higuera courses through a narrow limestone gorge in the Valle de Lifa. At the top of the limestone outcrop is an enigmatic, medieval watchtower, Torre de Lifa, with scenic views

over the valley to the Sierra Blanquilla. The footpath here is the GR243, which follows the ancient way linking El Burgo to Ronda. Come in autumn to see the leaves of the *cornicabra*, or turpentine tree, turn a dark burnt orange.

➜ From El Burgo take the Caril del Dique for about 8km to reach the beginning of the walk, signed in red and white on the R. Park here (36.7616, -5.0040) and the walk is about 3km, following the GR243 signs, to the waterfall.
1 hr, 36.7537, -5.0283 ⛩️🚶🚶⛰️

HIDDEN CAVES

12 FUENTE DE LA CUEVA DEL AGUA

This beautiful cave is hidden deep in protected *pinsapo* forest, home to foxes, wild boars and mountain goats. The walk here and views from the cave mouth are some of the most spectacular in the Sierra de las Nieves. Look out for the pygmy marbled newt, a mottled green creature, and the common salamander, black with yellow spots. To further explore the rich cultural and natural heritage of this sierra contact Abeto del Sur Ecoturismo - Call 616 158 546, Abetodelsur.es.

→ From the campsite and sports grounds at Yunquera take the Camino de la Sierra for 5km to the parking area near the Puerto Saucillo viewpoint. The footpath is signed from here and it's about 2km to the cave.

30 mins, 36.7322, -4.9683 🗺🏔🔆🏃📷🐦📹🚗

13 CUEVA DEL HUNDIDERO

This immense 50m-high cathedral of a cave is the other entry into the 8km-long Hundidero-Gato system and home to a large bat colony. Its impressive entrance stands at the bottom of a rocky gorge carved by the Guadares or Campobuche river, which flows through the Sierra de Grazalema. It is in the northernmost foothills of the Sierra de Líbar, with its *poljes* and sinkholes. They once tried to build a reservoir, but the river escapes through the karstic terrain to emerge later at Cueva del Gato. To explore the Hundidero and other local cave systems further with expert guides contact Pangea Activ Nature – Call 630 562 705, Pangeacentral.com.

→ From Ronda take the A-374 for 13km towards Grazalema. Turn L onto the MA-8403 and continue for 3.3km to reach parking on the R. Follow the footpath for 1km to the cave.

20 mins, 36.7519, -5.2375 🗺🚴🏃🏞

14 CUEVA DE LA PILETA

This deep and echoing cave system was discovered in 1905 by a farmer, José Bullón Lobato, on the hunt for bat guano to fertilise his fields. What he found were bones, ceramic pots and hundreds of ochre paintings dating back 20,000 years. Further paintings, equally as ancient, are thought to be covered by a millennia's worth of flowstone. You can visit by daily guided entry; the excellent conservation project is still run by the Bullón family. Call 677 610 500, Cuevadelapileta.es.

→ From Ronda take the MA-7401 to Benaoján, continue through town and at the T-junction with the MA-8401 turn L and follow for 4.5km, the cave is signed on the R. Parking.

15 mins, 36.6912, -5.2699 🌊🚴🚻🅿️🚂

15 CUEVA DE LA TINAJA

Ceramic fragments from the Bronze Age and earlier Neolithic Age have been found in this ancient wild cave deep in the Sierra de la Nieves. A footpath following the course of the pools in the Arroyo de los Horcajos takes you to the dark cave with its long stalactites. Rosemary, thyme, rockrose, gorse and juniper grow in the pine woodland surrounding it; it's a peaceful place.

→ From the *ayuntamiento* in Tolox follow signs for the Ermita Virgen de las Nieves and follow the SL-A238 footpath along the Horcajos stream for 3.6km, passing fountains and a small river pool, to reach the chapel. Continue on the footpath along the same stream for 2.6km to the cave.

105 mins, 36.6955, -4.9580 🌊🚴🚻🏔️🅿️🚂📷♿

16 TAJO DEL ABANICO

A beautifully eroded cave by a small river which was used as the location for Franceso Rosi's 1984 film *Carmen*. The path here follows the old Roman road, with its ancient cobbles, linking Ronda to Algeciras.

→ The way is signed from Ronda new town at Calle Pila Doña Gaspara, 18. Follow green and white signs for 4km.

1 hr, 36.7079, -5.1895 🚶🅿️🚴

ANCIENT & SACRED

17 DOLMEN DE ENCINAS BORRACHAS

This Copper Age burial site is named after the *encinas* (holm oaks) that appear to be drunkenly growing in all directions on this plateau in the Genal valley. Several granite boulders sunk into the ground were said to have been the graves of giants. Cattle graze lazily around this sacred

139

site dating back to around 3,000 BC. Continue along the valley footpath for 1km for stunning views of Ronda. The GR141 footpath, or Gran Senda de la Serranía de Ronda, passes by.

→ From Atajate take the A-369 N towards Ronda. After 6km there is a sign for the dolmen on the L. Park here in the layby and walk 50m along the track to the dolmen on your L. Close gate for livestock.

5 mins, 36.6805, -5.2082 🐾🚶🌲💫

RAVINES & GORGES

18 TAJO DE LA CAÍNA

Overlooking the Cañada de Carnicerías ravine, this imposing, natural viewpoint has a vertical drop of more than 100m. They say the ravine is named after a woman nicknamed 'La Caína', whom the Inquisition ordered to fall from the top after she was accused of practising witchcraft. You'll pass through *pinsapo* forest, where very little light penetrates, creating a drop in temperature and lending atmosphere to the legend. It also passes the old threshing ground, Era de los Gamones, with views to Yunquera and the Sierra Prieta behind. On clear days you can see the Málaga coast and the sea.

→ See directions to Fuente de la Cueva del Agua but before reaching the Puerto Saucillo

viewpoint follow signs L for Mirador de Luis Ceballos. The 4.2 circular trail is signed in white and green from here.

45 mins, 36.7026, -4.9654 🚶🏕️💧❄️

19 MIRADOR DEL GUARDA FORESTAL

A stunning place to watch the dawn break, on the rocky outcrop overlooking El Burgo with views of the Turón valley and Sierra Blanquilla beyond. These wild hills still evoke the spirit of the folk hero and last bandit of the Serranía de Ronda, Pasos Largos. Shot by the Civil Guard in the Sierra Blanquilla in 1934, he is remembered in a monument in El Burgo, and if you are lucky you might meet his great-grandchildren who live in the village and swim in the river at El Dique.

→ From El Burgo take the A-366 towards Ronda for 8km. Turn R on to an unpaved road, Carril de las Víboras, for 2km. Turn R at the crossroads and continue 1km to reach the forest guardhouse. Watch out for the steep drops by the guardhouse.

5 mins, 36.7948, -4.9854 🏞️🏔️💫

20 LOS MOLINOS DEL TAJO TRAIL

This 5km walk curls down the steep hillside from Ronda's bridge and dramatic gorge to

the Guadalevín river beneath. The famous 18th-century bridge with its towering arches is best viewed from along this dusty track. And if you follow it all the way down, you can cross the river and stop for a paddle. There is no swimming but it's a good way to escape the crowds and enjoy incredible views.

→ Follow the paved path downhill from Mirador María Auxiliadora (36.7383, -5.1669); there are information boards along the way. The path finishes in Calle Jerez.

1 hr, 36.7427, -5.1712 🏛️🚶

21 ARROYO DE LA VENTILLA

Just 10 mins north of Ronda, near the village of Arriate, is this signposted footpath which heads up a shady and leafy gorge. There are some small river pools, rope swings and a picnic area.

→ Take Calle Málaga out of Arriate and continue straight for 700m. The 3km circular path is signed on the L and passes dips along the way.

30 mins, 36.7976, -5.1257 🚶🚲📷🛍️📹

LOCAL FOOD

22 MIRADOR DE LA SIERRA DE LAS NIEVES

Great local dishes with views from its terrace to the pretty mountain village of Alozaina with its medieval Islamic fortress.

→ Lugar Curva Colorada, 3, 29567 Alozaina, 607 880 801

36.7293, -4.8679 🏛️🍴🍷

23 LAS MILLANAS

A typical *venta*, or roadside restaurant, serving excellent tostadas for breakfast as well as good local *raciones* (sharing plates). Very close to the Río Grande and its pools.

→ Carril de Tolox a Golondrina, 29109 Tolox

36.6989, -4.8754 🏛️🍴🍷🏊🚶

24 EL RINCÓN DE RAFAEL

A cosy tapas bar with barrels outside and a traditional flamenco feel inside. They offer a wealth of local tapas to enjoy after a nearby hike and specialise in *marisco* (fresh seafood) and *las tablas de chacina* (ham and cheese boards).

→ C. Polito, 78, 29109 Tolox, 615 248 454

36.6850, -4.9054 🏛️🍴🍷🚶

25 BAR EL CASINO

A great bar in the heart of the mountain village of El Burgo, home to the infamous Pasos Largos, last bandolero of the sierra

who died in 1934. There are a few good places to eat but here El Nene and Inma offer moutherwatering, home-made tapas in a relaxed atmosphere.

→ Calle Real Comandante Benítez, 17, 29420 El Burgo, 952 160 006

36.7891, -4.9475 🏛️🍴🍷

WINE & DINE

26 BODEGA EL POR FÍN

Located in the middle of Yunquera, this surprising tavern gives little away from the outside. Head inside to discover the 18th-century vaulted cellar and winery, where the young musts fill the establishment with a heady aroma. They serve typical stews and meaty dishes. Try the aloreña olives, a local variety from Málaga.

→ Calle Agua, 26, 29410 Yunquera, 952 482 825

36.7316, -4.9216 🏛️🍴🍷

WILDER CAMPING

27 ZONA DE ACAMPADA LIBRE LOS SAUCES

A grassy picnic park under the shade of an enormous holm oak with fountains, tables and BBQs. Paths lead to ruins of a 17th-century

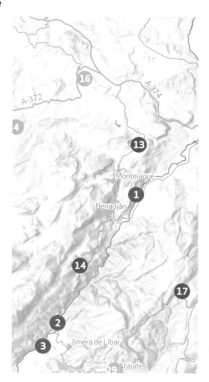

convent that gives the Sierra de las Nieves its name and an 8km footpath signed to Yunquera.

→ Permission to camp here is dependant on seasonal conditions and granted by the Junta de Andalucía online or by calling 670 948 894 with 2 weeks' notice.
36.7475, -4.9799

28 CAMPING SIERRA DE LAS NIEVES

A great campsite with bungalows, cabins and hostal rooms as well as a restaurant. It is a short stroll into the pretty white village of Yunquera, and nearby several footpaths lead to forests, caves and rivers.

→ Camino Forestal, 29410 Yunquera, 607 640 485, Campingsierradelasnieves.com
36.7356, -4.9273

RURAL HAVENS

29 CASA RURAL MOLINO LA TEJA

A cosy cottage built in the remains of the old village flour mill in Yunquera. The crystal-clear water of the river Plano rushes by the terrace, where there is a hammock, table and BBQ. There is an old millstone in the porch and rustic decor throughout, including wooden ceilings and terracotta floors. Several footpaths lead into the sierra. Sleeps 7.

→ C. Zauquillo, 29410 Yunquera, 952 482 775
36.7318, -4.9239

30 FINCA MARTINA

A romantic retreat with ecological sensibilities at its heart. It is surrounded by lemon, orange and olive groves, and they encourage you to pick and enjoy a host of other wild goodies and seasonal produce from its gardens. A 2.5km walk through the valley takes you to the mountain village of Casarabonela. A garden studio sleeps 2 and a traditional cottage sleeps 4.

→ Lugar, 29566 Partido Martina, 644 674 620, Fincamartina.es
36.7993, -4.8213

31 ALGABA DE RONDA

An award-winning, restored farmhouse, elegant cottages and a bioconstruction cabin surrounded by acres of farmland and woodland. There are beehives, and black pigs graze under the holm oaks. They run various ecological and archaeological projects and have built a perfectly reconstructed prehistoric walled village.

→ Carretera Ronda-Algeciras Km 4.5, 29400 Ronda, 952 114 048, Algabaderonda.com
36.7112, -5.1815

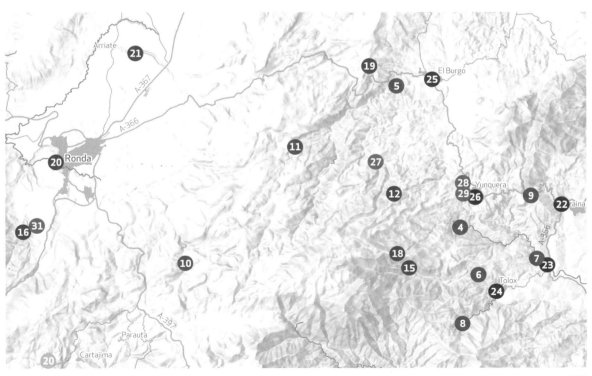

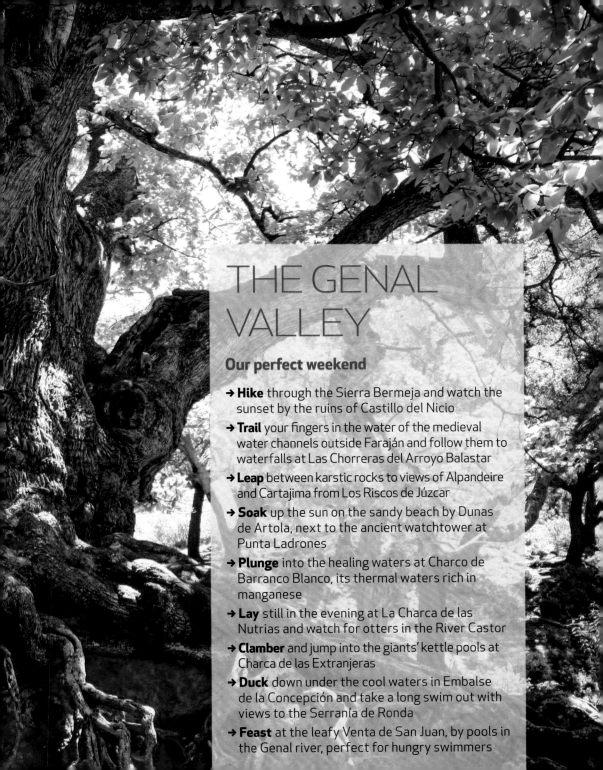

THE GENAL VALLEY

Our perfect weekend

→ **Hike** through the Sierra Bermeja and watch the sunset by the ruins of Castillo del Nicio

→ **Trail** your fingers in the water of the medieval water channels outside Faraján and follow them to waterfalls at Las Chorreras del Arroyo Balastar

→ **Leap** between karstic rocks to views of Alpandeire and Cartajima from Los Riscos de Júzcar

→ **Soak** up the sun on the sandy beach by Dunas de Artola, next to the ancient watchtower at Punta Ladrones

→ **Plunge** into the healing waters at Charco de Barranco Blanco, its thermal waters rich in manganese

→ **Lay** still in the evening at La Charca de las Nutrias and watch for otters in the River Castor

→ **Clamber** and jump into the giants' kettle pools at Charca de las Extranjeras

→ **Duck** down under the cool waters in Embalse de la Concepción and take a long swim out with views to the Serranía de Ronda

→ **Feast** at the leafy Venta de San Juan, by pools in the Genal river, perfect for hungry swimmers

The wild hills of the Serranía de Ronda continue well into the Genal valley, its dense Spanish fir woodland, hairpin bends and tight switchbacks climb up to mountain villages – Atajate, Benarrabá, Algatocín – perched like eagles' nests on its dramatic peaks. As you sail along its high roads at sunset, with the hills falling away either side, it feels as though you're flying over dusky blue and purple hues. At the twilight hour, the old road from Gibraltar to Ronda running along this mountain spine is at its most evocative. It has seen the footfall of bandits and smugglers – Tragabuches, Diego Corrientes or Juan Caballero 'El Lero' – as they hid out in the hills, putting distance between themselves and the frontier. But it is also known as the Camino Ingles, a route taken by soldiers on excursions from Gibraltar and by Romantic writers, such as Richard Ford or Mérimée, who passed through en route to Ronda.

Many of the high places and villages of the Genal valley look out to the distinctive crests of the Sierra Bermeja and Sierra de Crestellina, which reach up 1,449m. While only 10km inland from the busy Costa del Sol resorts, these mountains are a world away and demand time to navigate them; and quite literally in the case of some of the tortuous roads whose tight bends echo the wily ways of its notorious bandits, leading you to villages largely unchanged since their day. It is best to hike, and you can follow numerous footpaths as well as the long-distance GR249, the Gran Senda de Málaga, down to hidden waterfalls and up to ancient castles. The Pasarelas del Río Genal footpath follows the Genal river valley to hidden pools.

The Sierra Bermeja and the Genal valley are home to some of the most picturesque *pueblos blancos*, and each has its own distinct character. The flowering squares and white streets of Genalguacil are filled with contemporary artworks from its biennale; Gaucín is home to a dramatic castle named after eagles; Faraján was the "white swan on a pond of green hope" for Hemingway and at Igualeja, the caves and source of the river Genal were home to outlaws such as Flores Arrocha, Juan el Nene and Zamarrita.

The orchards and woods around these villages are bursting with fruit trees, holm oaks, chestnuts, cork and *pinsapo*, whereas the Sierra Bermeja contains one of the largest outcrops of volcanic peridotite. Rich in platinum, it gives these mountains their characteristic crimson colour and their name, Bermeja, means 'reddish'. Great swathes of this rich wilderness have survived the golf courses along the coast. You can hike up to Castaño Santo, an 800-year-old chestnut tree deeply rooted in the Costa del Sol's history and reddish rock, whose gnarly girth saw the 16th-century Morisco Rebellion under the Catholic Monarchs' rule.

Head further east into the Serranía de Ronda to hike to Charco Azul, where waterfalls gush into a clear plunge pool. Baños de la Hedionda is a magical swim in the overgrown ruins of Roman baths, and Lago de las Tortugas is an unexpected oasis among Marbella's built-up resorts.

After the first rains of autumn, these hills are a great place for mushrooms, boletus and amanitas mainly, although there are also chanterelles, mountain elvers as well as chestnuts. Hotel Bandolero in Júzcar, a *pueblo blanco* painted blue, is a great place to try dishes made with this seasonal produce. Follow mountain paths in the foothills of the Sierra Bermeja back to thatched cottages, such as Casa Rural El Balatín, for a woodland rest.

RIVERS & POOLS

1 CHARCA DE LAS EXTRANJERAS

As the River Padrón courses through the southern slopes of the Sierra Bermeja, it fills these startling green giants' kettles known as the Foreign Ladies' Pool. It is a great place to see the reddish peridotite rock, which gives the Sierra Bermeja its name, as well as the monumental striped marble reshaped by water over millennia. The walk here through pine forest and rockroses has beautiful views across the sierra.

→ From Estepona take the coastal road E for 3km. Take exit 160 off the A7, at the roundabout take the third exit, L, under the bridge and continue straight over the second roundabout and turn L at the third. Follow the Camino de Montesol for 6.5km, passing under the flyover, to a fork in the dirt track. Park here and take the R fork uphill for 1km. Keep L at the fork to drop down to the river.

30 mins, 36.4798, -5.1471

2 RÍO GENAL POOLS

Several large pools in the Genal valley beneath the bridge next to Venta San Juan. It is a popular spot with picnicking families on a Sunday but trek upstream for 2km to find quieter and wilder spots.

→ From Algatocín, follow the MA-8305 towards Genalguacil for 7km. Stop when you reach the bridge and park by the restaurant, Venta San Juan. Follow the river upstream for 500m.

5 mins, 36.5705, -5.2449

3 RÍO GENAL, GAUCÍN

Several small pools and a dam in the Genal river hidden behind bamboo canes. Small barbel fish nibble your toes if you stay still a moment and on clear nights there is great stargazing.

→ From Manilva, travel N for 20km on the A-377, and 6km S of Gaucín you'll cross a river. Turn immediately R after the bridge down a small stone track and after about 100m you can park and swim.

1 min, 36.4931, -5.3053

4 FINCA LA ESCRIBANA

The Genal river collects behind a small stone dam in the valley below Benarrabá. Wild olive trees provide shade and at night the valley is canopied with stars. There is a kids' play park on grass next to the river and sheep often pass through. The footpath here follows the river upstream to Venta San Juan; this walkway, the Pasarelas del Río Genal, is well maintained and forms part of La Gran Senda de Málaga (GR249).

→ From Venta San Juan, opposite Camping El Genal on the MA-8305, follow the signed footpath downstream for 3.8km.

1 hr, 36.5489, -5.2584

5 SAN PABLO DE BUCEITE

This grassy clearing alongside the bend in the Río Guadiaro offers a small haven just outside the village. It is popular with dog walkers in the mornings, and kids have made a shallow dam and pool with the colourful river stones. Great stargazing.

→ From the village take the A-405 in the direction of Gaucín. Just before the bridge over the river there is a roundabout with an olive tree. Park here and look carefully in the hedgerows for a gravel track which leads down to the river.

5 mins, 36.4690, -5.4064

6 CHARCO DE LAS VIÑAS

A tiny pool and waterfall in the Arroyo del Tejar, on the outskirts of the *pueblo blanco* of Ojén.

→ Park in Ojén and follow the road signed for the cemetery. After 1km, just before the cemetery, there are some steps down to the R.

20 mins, 36.5603, -4.8476

WILD WATERFALLS

7 CHARCO AZUL

A beautiful plunge pool in the Sierra Bermeja formed as the Arroyo del Quejigo, stream of the gall oaks, divides into two cascades over smooth stone. Follow upstream to discover larger plunge pools.

→ From Genalguacil take the MA-8304 S for 9km to the dirt track on the L next to the 'Incendios' sign. Park here and walk 1km down the track. The pool is on the R over the rocks.

20 mins, 36.5339, -5.1955

8 LA CHARCA DE LAS NUTRIAS

Striking marble walls flank the River Castor as a small waterfall tumbles into this clear pool. Pineforest continues above the river and roots hang over the high stone lip. This is one of many rivers in the Sierra Bermeja that have been declared a Special Conservation Area thanks to the habitat they provide for wildlife, in this case otters. Follow the river upstream to find further crystal-clear pools.

→ From Estepona take the coastal road E for 3km. At the roundabout take the third exit under the bridge and continue straight over the next two roundabouts. At the junction turn R and continue on this road for 4km. Cross under the flyover and continue for another 2.2km to reach a closed white gate. Park where you can and follow the footpath to the R of the gate to the river. Cross the river and follow the footpath and then the river 600m upstream.

20 mins, 36.4849, -5.1334

9 CHARCO DEL CANALÓN, ISTÁN

Several sparkling pools in the Río Verde before it meets the Arroyo Balatín make up this hidden paradise. Climb up the rocks behind the waterfall to find more secluded pools.

→ From Istán townhall take Calle Calvario out of town for 400m. Keep L and follow the road down over the bridge at Nacimiento de Río Molinos. Continue on this road, great for cycling, for 5.2km. If you drive, the last 2km must be done on foot. The path is signed and passes dips along the way.

40 mins, 36.6149, -4.9376

10 CHARCA DE LAS MOZAS

Escape the Costa del Sol crowds and head to this sparkling river hidden in the woodland on the southern slopes of the Serranía de Ronda. The River Guadalmina has carved several pools and waterfalls in the limestone gorge. Bring water shoes as there is about 1km of river to explore between the pools.

→ From Benahavís, head S on the A-7175 to the roundabout and take the second exit. Continue and you'll see the river on your L and parking on your R. If it's full, there's another car park 100m on your L or, alternatively, a larger car park 1km further on at the second swimming spot. Steps down to Charca de las Mozas are 100m N of the first parking spot. Head S down the river to the second, larger pool (36.5132, -5.0344).
5 mins, 36.5172, -5.0400 🏊📶

11 CHARCO DE LA CAL

A beautiful waterfall and pool where farmers from nearby Igualeja used to wash their sheep after shearing them. The path here leads through chestnut woodland and can be followed from the village; you'll need to walk the first part along the road.

→ Take the MA-7300 S out of Igaleja, passing the medicinal herb fountain on the R, and continue along this road for 1km to a hairpin bend. The footpath is signed on the L. Follow for 3km to reach the pool.
45 mins, 36.6174, -5.1005 🏊📶🚶🚴🚵

12 LAS CHORRERAS DEL ARROYO DE BALASTAR

A couple of beautiful waterfalls that jump and splash down travertine rock, a short walk from Faraján. The path passes green orchards with fruit trees, old Arabic mills and water channels to reach the signed 'chorreras' (waterfalls) and a large walnut tree.

→ The 2.4km circular footpath is well signed from the town hall at Faraján.
20 mins, 36.6199, -5.1934 🏊📶

13 CHARCO DEL MOCLÓN

A short and wooded footpath from Júzcar leads to several pools in the river Genal formed in summer by small dams. Head upstream towards the 18th-century tin factory, now a bodega, for further pools. Nearby is the Sima del Diablo gorge, if you are feeling more adventurous you can try canyoning here. Contact Montañaviva.es for canyoning and access – 626 720 720.

→ From Júzcar, take the road towards Faraján, after 1.5km the track that goes to the river is signed on the L. Follow this for about 3km to the bridge over the river and pools.
45 mins, 36.6076, -5.1742 🏊📶📷⛺🍴📶📶

COASTAL HAVEN

14 DUNAS DE ARTOLA O CABOPINO

The protected dunes along Playa Artola provide a welcome break from the Marbella resorts and urbanisation. They lie along

the Punta Ladrones, or Robbers' Point, and to the east is the square-built watchtower known as Torre de Ladrones. The square watchtowers are the oldest, possibly of Muslim origin, while the circular ones were built in the 19th century. Nudist friendly.

→ From Marbella take the A-7 for 13km. Take the exit to Cabopino and at the roundabout take the first exit to the parking. Follow the dusty track that runs parallel with the coast for 150m to the wooden walkway through the dunes.
10 mins, 36.4859, -4.7496 🏖📶🏄

HIDDEN LAKES

15 EMBALSE DE LA CONCEPCIÓN

A short drive from Marbella, grassy banks slope down to this peaceful and secluded lake, and a wooden pontoon looks out over a green valley. Good for longer wild swims, fishing, kayaking and paddleboarding. The track down to the lake is not signposted and is in bad condition. Best to park at the top of the road and walk down.

→ From Istán take the A-7176 S. After 3.2km you will see the entrance to Ermitá de San Miguel on your L. Park here and walk 100m along the A-176, taking the first unmarked road on your R to reach the reservoir.
20 mins, 36.5697, -4.9590 🏊🍴

16 LAGO DE LAS TORTUGAS

A very unexpected haven for wild swimmers and wildlife after the seemingly endless rows of Marbella holiday villas. The deep, green lake provides a great spot for longer swims with a gentle entry. There is a children's play area and at night surprisingly little light pollution.

→ From Marbella take the A-7 towards Algeciras for 5km. Take exit 176 and at the roundabout take the third exit and continue for 2km straight on over all the roundabouts. Turn L on to Av. Del Prado, then L onto Calle Aries. At the end turn R, pass the building sites on the L and after 500m park where you can and walk down to the lake.
1 min, 36.5221, -4.9659 🏊🏻

HEALING WATERS

17 BAÑOS DE LA HEDIONDA

You will smell these hot springs in the River Manilva before you see them. The sulphur-rich water gives off a pungent eggy odour and *hedionada* literally means 'stinking'. But this milky turquoise river has been visited for its healing properties since Roman times. Legends say the sulphur stink is the lingering breath of a demon expelled by Santiago. In the 1st century BC Julius Caesar's troops stopped here to heal a blight of scabies. Pleased with the results, he ordered a bathhouse to be built. You can swim in the wild ruins of these ancient vaulted baths today. Wander downstream to muddy hollows in the banks to take a green clay body mask. A beautiful walk through the nearby weathered limestone ravine of Canuto de la Utrera is signed from here. Access to the natural pools in the river is free but to swim at the baths, call Ayuntamiento de Casares – 952 895 521.

→ From Casares take the A-7150 to Gaucín for 1km. At the junction turn L on to the A-377 in the direction of Manilva and follow for 9km. At the roundabout, take the third exit, which runs alongside the motorway, and follow for 1km. Before the flyover turn L and follow the dirt track along the river for 200m to parking on the L.
15 mins, 36.3964, -5.2614 🏊🏻🚲📷

18 CHARCO DE BARRANCO BLANCO

Known unceremoniously as Poza de los Huevos, Well of the Eggs, or Stinking Baths, its thermal waters spring from an upwelling on the left bank of the river, which has a large amount of manganese, a mineral with medicinal benefits for asthma and healing skin. Nearby are other pools and waterfalls. It can get busy in summer.

→ From Coín take the MA-3303 S for 5km. The casacadas are signed on the L. Park here and follow the footpath for 2.5km.
40 mins, 36.6093, -4.7418 🏊🏻🚶

20

CAVES & CLIFFS

19 CUEVA EXCÉNTRICA IGUALEJA

A hidden cave with stalactites just outside Igualeja. For caving call Pangeacentral.com, 630 562 705.

→ From the Nacimiento del Río Genal follow the road out of Igualeja for 200m and the cave is signed on the R.

5 mins, 36.6358, -5.1174

20 LOS RISCOS DE JÚZCAR

A 3km, signed, circular footpath leads to these wonderfully shaped karstic rocks with beautiful views of the *pueblos blancos* of Cartajima and Alpandeire. The limestone plateau has been carved by millennia of water erosion into a maze of gullies and corridors, some of which were once used as natural threshing grounds. It's a great place for some scramble climbing or to view the sunset.

→ From Júzcar take Calle de los Riscos out of town. Turn L at a brown sign for Los Riscos and follow the dirt track, not the road, uphill for 1.7km. The Sendero de las Eras is signed on the R.

45 mins, 36.6443, -5.1720

SUNSET HILLTOPS

21 GENALGUACIL

This *pueblo blanco*, sitting brightly on the northern slopes of the Sierra Bermeja, is known as the *pueblo museo*, as it sees art and nature as the engines for growth in its community. Its cobbled streets are alive with quirky, ever-changing artworks from its biennale festival in early August. Several circular footpaths begin here and lead through the *pinsapo*, or Spanish fir, woodland.

→ Parking is signed off the MA-8304 as you come into town.

5 mins, 36.5457, -5.2348

22 CASTILLO DEL ÁGUILA

This dramatic castle is perched like an eagle's nest on the craggy peaks above Gaucín. It has seen successive waves of history, including Roman campaigns, the burning of Arab ships in Algeciras, medieval reconquests and Napoleon's siege. It's a short and very steep climb up but worth it for the immense views across the Serranía de Ronda.

→ From Gaucín follow Camino al Castillo up to the castle.

20 mins, 36.5176, -5.3131

23 CASTILLO DEL NICIO

A 9th-century Islamic castle in the foothills of the Sierra Bermeja. It has Bastulo, pre-Roman, origins and was one of the last stongholds before yielding to Christian forces. It is overgrown now and makes a wonderful spot for sunset.

→ See directions to Charca de las Extranjeras but at the very last fork, keep on going R uphill for another 1.5km rather than dropping down to the river.

30 mins, 36.4862, -5.1374

ANCIENT & SACRED

24 CASTAÑO SANTO

This ancient and sacred chestnut tree, the trunk of which measures 14m in circumference and the crown 27m in diameter, is thought to be over 800 years old. According to the tales of the 16th-century chronicler Mármol Carvajal, it saw the rebellion of the Mudejar Muslims who fled for their safety and secured themselves here, in the 'wildest part of the Sierra Bermeja' near Istán. In about 1501 King Ferdinand held a Catholic mass under its heavy branches to commemorate the bloodshed.

→ The hike starts from La Quinta Golf and Country Club in Marbella. Go around the back

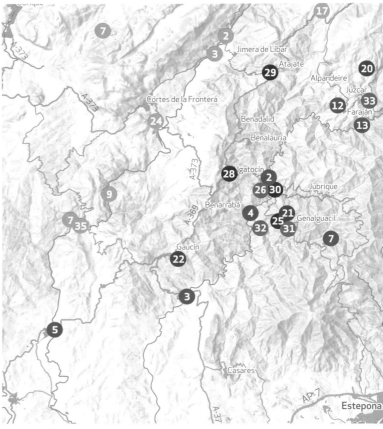

of the golf course towards the River Guadaiza. Don't cross it but take the road N with the river on your R for 1.5km, then cross the river. Park here and follow the road around to the R before it curves back N. Follow this track for 13km.

2.5 hrs, 36.6136, -5.0145 🅿🚻🚶

LOCAL FOOD

25 BAR EL REFÚGIO

Hidden away down a side street in the pretty white village of Genalgaucil is this bar with great views across the wooded Genal valley. Generous and well-priced, the *croquetas* are great.

→ Calle Duende, 8, 29492 Genalguacil
36.5443, -5.2364 🅿🚻🍴♿

26 LA VENTA SAN JUAN

A rustic restaurant deep in the woodland on the Genal river. Dappled sunlight and rustling leaves brush the brick porticos that shade the terrace. A good stop for hearty dishes and freshly grilled meats; the chorizo and *morcilla* (Andalucían-style black pudding) are homemade.

→ Calle Algatocín, Km 7, 29492 Jubrique, 952 152 055
36.5670, -5.2454 🏕🚻🍴

27 RESTAURANTE EL NACIMIENTO

A good stop for simple, traditional dishes and a sunny terrace a stroll away from Igualeja. It is right by the spring of the River Genal and is a great place for a cool paddle.

→ Travesia Pio XII, 70, 29440 Igualeja, 951 452 780
36.6328, -5.1181 🍴🚶♿

28 MESÓN LA ERMITA

A great stop in Algatocín for home cooking: stews with local vegetables and locally-reared meats. Opposite, is a hike up to Ermita del Calvario, worth it for the dramatic views.

→ Calle Ronda, 2, 29491 Algatocín, 666 722 151
36.5740, -5.2755 🍴🚻

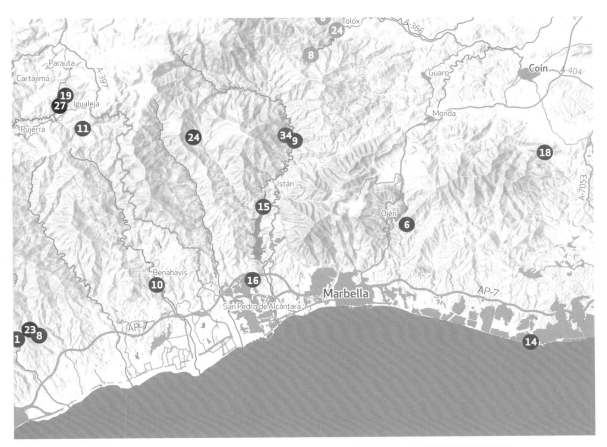

29 MESÓN LA SIERRA

In the tiny *pueblo blanco* Atajate, deep in the Serranía de Ronda on the south side of the Genal valley, all the houses are named, not numbered, after the women who live there. This restaurant and hostel is a great stop for some home cooking and traditional hearty fare.

→ C. Nueva, 47, 29494 Atajate, 952 180 165, Atajate.net/lasierra

36.6400, -5.2466 ⊞♨⊠⌖

WILDER CAMPING

30 CAMPING SAN JUAN

A peaceful and simple camping park deep in the Serranía de Ronda along the Genal riverbanks. There are plenty of pools in the Genal river within a short walk and various footpaths run into the woodland. Some cottages are also available.

→ Carretera Algatocín, Km 7, 29492 Jubrique, 620 612 323, Campingsanjuan.net

36.5665, -5.2455 ⊞♨⊠⊠⊠⊠⌖

RUSTIC RETREATS

31 JARDINES DEL VISIR

Several beautiful, rustic cottages in the *pueblo museo* of Genagaucil, with terraces and views across the wooded Genal valley. Rooms are also available in the *posada* above the Refúgio bar.

→ Calle Estación, Calle la Lomilla, 4, 29492 Genalguacil, 669 808 270, Jardinesdelvisir.com

36.5450, -5.2347 ⊠⊞⊞♨⊠⌖

32 CLOUD HOUSE FARM

A wild hideaway in the Genal valley with family lodging among several acres of woodland. The farm is off-grid, making use of a natural spring in its grounds and solar energy. Two large yurts are hidden in the trees; each has a rustic kitchen and showers on the wooden decking outside. Located near footpaths and river pools.

→ Finca Casa Nube, Genalguacil, 29492, 645 238 742, Cloudhouse.es

36.5394, -5.2502 ⊠⌖⊠⊠⊠

33 HOTEL BANDOLERO

A great rural hotel with an excellent restaurant deep in the Serranía de Ronda. Many walking routes start from the village, which is Andalucía's only *pueblo azul*. Historically, a *pueblo blanco*, Júzcar was painted blue to launch the *Smurfs* movie in 2011 and the village voted to keep it that way. This blue hotel has elegant rustic rooms, a leafy terrace and an outdoor pool.

→ Av. Havaral, 43, 29462, 640 103 494, Hotelbandolero.es

36.6236, -5.1693 ⊠⊞♨⌖

34 CASA RURAL EL BALATÍN

Three cosy, thatched cottages in the hills just outside the Sierra de la Nieves and near footpaths to bright pools along the Río Verde. Each cottage runs on solar energy and is built with local stone and wood.

→ El Balatín, 2961 Istán, 951 193 117, 951 193 117 Elmundoenmicamara.com

36.6165, -4.9430 ⊠⊠⊠⊠⌖

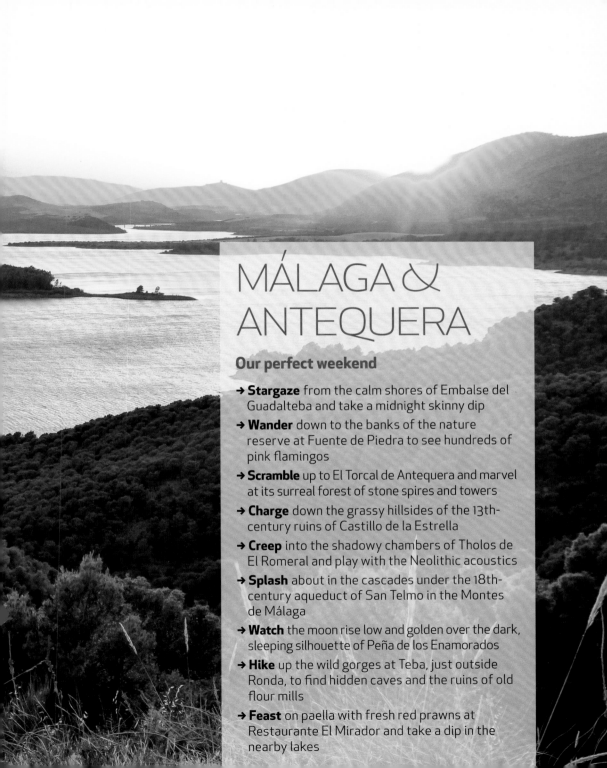

MÁLAGA & ANTEQUERA

Our perfect weekend

→ **Stargaze** from the calm shores of Embalse del Guadalteba and take a midnight skinny dip

→ **Wander** down to the banks of the nature reserve at Fuente de Piedra to see hundreds of pink flamingos

→ **Scramble** up to El Torcal de Antequera and marvel at its surreal forest of stone spires and towers

→ **Charge** down the grassy hillsides of the 13th-century ruins of Castillo de la Estrella

→ **Creep** into the shadowy chambers of Tholos de El Romeral and play with the Neolithic acoustics

→ **Splash** about in the cascades under the 18th-century aqueduct of San Telmo in the Montes de Málaga

→ **Watch** the moon rise low and golden over the dark, sleeping silhouette of Peña de los Enamorados

→ **Hike** up the wild gorges at Teba, just outside Ronda, to find hidden caves and the ruins of old flour mills

→ **Feast** on paella with fresh red prawns at Restaurante El Mirador and take a dip in the nearby lakes

The terrain of the Málaga province changes considerably from west to east. Stunning blue lakes near Ardales, the vertiginous gorge and its hanging bridges at Caminito del Rey give way to the surreal, twisted rock formations, carved by water, ice and wind, at El Torcal de Antequera. The origins of this sculptural plateau date back several hundred million years, to when much of Europe was under the ancient Tethys Sea. Deposits of this salty ocean emerge at Fuente de Piedra in its salty springs and lagoon, home to hundreds of pink flamingos.

At the heart of Andalucía lies Antequera, a natural crossroads and meeting place of ancient roads leading to Seville and the coastal ports of Cádiz and Lisbon. Cave art, crusader castles and rupestrian chapels are scattered throughout its hills. Dolmen de Menga, perhaps the most emblematic of these ancient sites, is one of Europe's largest Bronze Age passage tombs. Its upright monoliths and dark chamber face the summer solstice sun rising behind the striking Peña de los Enamorados. Rising out of the plains, and dramatically visible from the surrounding roads, this limestone mountain unmistakably resembles a sleeping woman's profile. A theatrical landmark, registered by the ancient cultures who built the tomb, it also figures in medieval legends, the backdrop to star-crossed lovers who leapt from its rock.

To the east of Antequera, golden eagles soar over the breath-taking ravine of Desfiladero de los Gaitanes. Its limestone and dolomite sides plunge 300m down to the Guadalhorce river. The vertiginous Caminito del Rey pathway was built into its sides for workers at the hydroelectricity station. It became treacherously derelict but was recently renovated and is now a popular tourist route, its caves and *vía ferrata* attracting climbers worldwide. It's a staggering experience, but you can find wilder ways to explore these hills. At Embalse de Gaitanejo, take the path along a tunnel to wild swims under *tafoni*: sandstone weathered like honeycomb, used for ancient cave houses.

Nearby Roman ruins at Bobastro are a reminder that these dramatic rivers and ravines were the dwelling place of fascinating and almost forgotten characters, such as the outlaw and rebel leader Umar ibn Hafsun and his daughter, the saint and martyr, Argéntea. Hafsun settled in the riverside ruins of this Roman castle in AD 880 and led a devastating rebellion against the Caliphate of Córdoba. Bobastro and its river witnessed bloody scenes, a murdered Emir and the crucifixion of Hafsun's unearthed corpse, but it was also the site of Argéntea's hermitage and a rare Mozarabic chapel dug into rock, which you can visit today.

The chapel was already in ruins when Castilian forces arrived in the 13th century, among them Black Douglas carrying the heart of Robert the Bruce to battle. You can hike up to Castillo de la Estrella, overlooking this battle site. But perhaps one of the most moving places you can visit is the Necrópolis de las Aguilillas: sandstone caves strategically overlooking three valleys and lakes of Guadalteba, Guadalhorce and Turón. Hollowed out as burial chambers over 4,000 years ago, items belonging to Republicans hiding out during the civil war were found among older grave goods. It's an unearthly site with sweeping views, perfect to visit at sunset and dwell on the lives lived out here.

In summer, try *ajo blanco*, considered to be the original gazpacho. It has its origins in Al-Andalus, before tomatoes were introduced, and is made with almonds, garlic, and olive oil, served with fresh white grapes. Enjoy with a glass of Montes de Málaga wine before hitting the hay in your tent in the olive groves outside Álora.

LAKES & LAGOONS

1 EMBALSE DE GAITANEJO

A beautiful spot for a long swim near the Caminito del Rey. It is next to the Tunel de los Tafonis, which was built for the workers of the hydroelectric station out of weathered stone known as tafoni. On the nearby banks you can spot more strange geology known as the Gothic Arches. Black redstarts, peregrine falcons, Bonelli's eagles and many vulture colonies live in the rocks, as well as water birds such as cormorants, grey herons and common egrets

➜ From the bus stop at Restaurante El Quiosco on the MA-9006 walk through the small, low tunnel to the R of El Quiosco; this will join the Camintio del Rey. Follow signs to the R for 1.8km to the picnic area.
35 mins, 36.9303, -4.7932 🏊🚶📷🏔️

2 EMBALSE DEL CONDE DE GUADALHORCE

A sparkling swim in the wilder part of the reservoir away from the busier area near Restaurante El Quiosco. These three artificial lakes, created by a dam across the 200m-high sheer cliffs of the Guadalhorce river gorge, are bordered by pine forests and known as Málaga's 'Lake District'. This is a lovely spot for a swim across the lake and back.

➜ Park near the bus stop on the MA-9006, opposite Restaurante El Quiosco, and follow the steps down to the lake.
5 mins, 36.9312, -4.8017 🏊🏞️

3 LA ISLA EL CHORRO

Just 1km south of the beach area opposite Restaurante El Quiosco are more spots for a swim by shady pine trees. It can get a bit busy around the parking area but wander on through the trees to find quieter spots.

➜ Head S from Restaurante El Quiosco for 1km to a parking area on your R. Park here and wander down.
5 mins, 36.9258, -4.8028 🏊🏕️

4 EMBALSE DE TAJO DE LA ENCANTADA

This spot offers easy entry for a long swim with views up to the end of the sheer limestone gorge, Desfildero de los Gaitanes, and the exit of the Caminito del Rey path. The popular and challenging climbing route of Via Ferrata El Chorro starts nearby.

➜ From the train station in El Chorro follow the path keeping the reservoir on your L for 650m to the free parking area. Scramble down to the water.
15 mins, 36.9108, -4.7618 🚆🏊

springs, known as 'the stone spring' and to which the town owes its name, was known to the Romans as *Fons Divinus* for its power to cure kidney stones; even Emperor Trajan took some water to Italy for this purpose. The spring was stemmed in 1959, but you can still enjoy views out over the lagoon to the distant hills of the Sierra de las Nieves and Sierra Blanquilla on the horizon.

→ Take the MA-454 out of Fuente de Piedra town towards Sierra de Yeguas. Cross the train track and take the first L. Follow for 500m to reach the parking. Walk down behind the centre to wooden walkways leading to the bird hides.

1 min, 37.1315, -4.7422 🌳📷🏨

WATERFALLS & POOLS

7 CHARCO DEL INFIERNO

A long, deep pool in the smooth limestone and marl riverbed of the Campanillas before it becomes the Casasola reservoir. While the river dries up over summer, this pool remains all year long.

→ From Málaga take the A-7075 towards Antequera. At Km18, turn L on to a dirt track leading to a wide esplanade and a section of the old road. From here, you will be able to see the now abandoned bridge a short distance away. There is plenty of space to park here. Walk up the riverbed a short distance, and in a few minutes you will reach a narrow stretch where this beautiful, elongated pool lies.

10 mins, 36.8259, -4.5091 🏞️⛰️

8 ACUEDUCTO DE SAN TELMO

This 18th-century aqueduct, which winds for 11km into the Montes de Málaga Natural Park, once carried water from the Guadalmedina to Málaga city. At this point you can see some of its most picturesque remains. Under its elegant arches there is a small cascade, only large enough for a shower, in the stream below. The Salto de Picapedreros footpath passes by.

→ From Málaga take the Camino de Casabermeja, which runs parallel with the A-45, out of town for 500m. Turn R at signs for 'sendero' and park where you can before the entrance gates to the park. Walk through the gates and follow the path down to the R and cross the river. Walk downstream 280m.

5 mins, 36.7627, -4.4203 🏞️⛰️🚶

9 CASCADA DE PICAPEDREROS

On the outskirts of Málaga this footpath follows the San Telmo Aqueduct to a

5 EMBALSE DEL GUADALTEBA

One of three giant reservoirs that fill the valleys of the Guadalhorce, Guadalteba and Turón where they meet. Here you can push out for long swims in the calm water under the massive Peñarrubia rock formation whose ledges and crevices provide a roost for griffon vultures. Tenants of the village of Peñarrubia were evacuated to Málaga city before the flooding in 1971; a short film called *Borrados del Mapa* (2007) documents this event. There is wonderful stargazing under open skies and there are usually a couple of campervans.

→ From Campillos head S on the A-357 towards Ardales for 15km then turn sharp L on to a gravel track. Follow for 1.5km and at the sharp bend R, which turns downhill, keep on the dirt track for 500m to a turn-off on the L. It's a short walk down to the water.

15 mins, 36.9456, -4.8439 🏞️➕🌳🚗

6 RESERVA NATURAL DE LA LAGUNA DE FUENTE DE PIEDRA

This enormous inland salt-water lagoon is home to thousands of flamingos and other migratory birds during winter. It is fed by underwater springs which pass through ancient mineral salt deposits. One of these

spectacular waterfall. It is often dry so make sure to visit after rain.

→ See directions to Acueducto de San Telmo and follow the footpath upriver for 1km.
20 mins, 36.7680, -4.4121 🏕🏔🎫🏊

ROCKS & CAVES

10 TORCAL DE ANTEQUERA

About 1,171 hectares of the most spectacular karstic landscape in Europe forms this nature reserve, which is popular with climbers and boulderers. The Jurassic limestone is about 150 million years old, and three colour-coded footpaths lead through deep canyons and rock passages. Look out for griffon vultures, Bonelli's eagles and, of course, ibex, or mountain goats. The green route passes the Hoyo de la Burra, a known energy point, visited by meditation lovers. You can visit the prehistoric Cueva del Toro by appointment; see – Torcaldeantequera.com

→ From Antequera head S on the A-7075 for 15km to the parking area. The walks are all signed from here. For stargazing nights call Astrotorcal.es, 600 703 700.
15 mins, 36.9512, -4.5457 🅿🚻🏔🎫

11 CUEVA DE ARDALES

This labyrinthine cave system with its dark lakes and beautiful stalagmite formations was rediscovered in 1821 following an earthquake. It houses around 50 engravings, mostly of animal figures, dating from about 20,000 BC, as well as later burials from about 4,000 BC.

→ Visits can be made in small groups and booked ahead either at the Guadalteba Prehistory Museum in Ardales or by calling 952 458 046. Av. de Málaga, 1, 29550 Ardales
5 mins, 36.8727, -4.8289 🚲🎫🐕🏕♿

12 CIMA DEL MONTE HACHO

A long-time refuge for shepherds and bandits, the hills and caves here are surrounded by pines, mastic, rosemary and rockroses with views of Álora. The karstic curtains of stalactites covering the rocks near its peak give the appearance of a suspended wax waterfall.

→ The 14km circular route is signed from Álora, where Calle Puerto meets Calle la Viñuela, and also from its train station. It is about 3km to the peak.
50 mins, 36.8244, -4.7278 🧗🏔📷🚶🚴

15 VÍA FERRATA EL CHORRO

The vertiginous Vía Ferrata El Chorro is open to all properly equipped climbers. For expert guides to this vía ferrata, rock climbing, canyoning and a host of wild local adventures contact Local Experiences - 675 647 355, Localexperiences.es.

→ From El Chorro train station walk 600m towards the Caminito del Rey until the parking area on your L by the lake. The Vía Ferrata is signed on the R.

5 mins 36.9125, -4.7612 🚶🧗‍♀️🏊‍♂️🚵‍♂️

ANCIENT & SACRED

16 DOLMEN DE MENGA

This is one of the largest known megalithic structures in Europe. Enormous slabs and mighty pillars support the weight of its stone ceiling. The heaviest stone weighs around 180 tons. To put that in context, the heaviest stone at Stonehenge weighs only 40 tons. It dates to around 3500 BC. Standing on a small hill, it faces the summer solstice sunrise and the enigmatic skyline of the mountain of Peña de los Enamorados, which uncannily resembles the profile of a giant sleeping woman. Open 9am – 6pm, closed Mon; entrance is free or a small donation. Normally very empty.

→ Carr. de Málaga, Km 5, 29200 Antequera

15 mins, 37.0240, -4.5483 🚵‍♂️🚶🚗➕✝️

17 THOLOS DE EL ROMERAL

This ancient passage grave was constructed in around 1800 BC. A long, narrow passage made with an ancient drystone walling technique leads into the earth mound. If you stand and speak in the middle of its dark, domed chamber, it feels as if your ears are muffled and your voice can only be heard in your head. In fact, to your audience standing at the edge of the circular chamber your voice is amplified. Its Neolithic acoustics are still tuned. Along with the nearby Dolmen de Menga (see entry) this is a little known UNESCO World Heritage Site. Closed Mon. Entrance is free and guided 9am – 6pm.

→ Cerro Romeral, 29200 Antequera

1 min, 37.0342, -4.5350 🚵‍♂️🚶🅿️

18 PINTURAS RUPESTRES DE PIEDRAS DE CABRERA

On this small hill, Cerro Mojea, outside Casabermeja are some forgotten cave paintings hidden in the olive and cork oak woodland. This is farmland and goats trot by the hard sandstone outcrops. Weathered and eroded, their cavities hide numerous red

13 TAJO DEL MOLINO

A beautiful, curved gorge, wilder and less visited than those nearby. Carved by the Venta river, these caves and cavities abound, the largest being the Cueva de las Palomas.

→ From Teba take the road towards Mayorazgo for 3km and turn R at signs for Tajo del Molino parking. Parking is after 100m. The way is indicated from here. Walk under the bridge and along the river for 1km.

15 mins, 36.9826, -4.8804 🚶🚵‍♂️🏕️

14 MONTE SAN ANTÓN

Rambling footpaths wind up through gorse and rosemary to this streaked limestone crag with caves and popular with rock climbers. It is just 3km inland from the busy coast, climb up in the morning to see the sea mists moving over the sleepy hills.

→ From Málaga take the A7 east towards Torre del Mar, take exit 246 and follow signs inland for 'Pinares de San Anton', after 500m turn L onto Calle Almendros. Follow signs for Parque Lagrillo Blanco for about 1km until a parking area. Follow track for 600m where tracks lead up to the peak.

15 mins 36.7423, -4.3656 🚶🚗📷🚵‍♂️🏕️

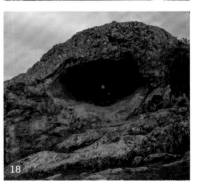

ochre paintings dating to around 6,000 BC. In the evening the only sounds are goat bells and the swallows that dip and soar out of their nests in these caves. Climb the stone steps roughly hewn into the rock – possibly steps to an ancient stone altar – for views out across the Sierra del Torcal.

→ From Casabermeja take the A-356 towards Colmenar for 4km then turn R, cross the bridge and follow the first L along the river. Park at signs for the hunting ground and follow the path up, curving to the R and then veering off up over the hill to your L. Close any farm gates behind you.

20 mins, 36.8952, -4.3880 🌲🐾✦◈

19 NECRÓPOLIS DE AGUILILLAS

These ancient caves with their corridors and chambers were dug into the sandstone around 4,000 years ago. They were used as burial chambers by the people living in the two fortified towns at the meeting of the three valleys carved by the rivers Guadalteba, Guadalhorce and Turón. It became a village of the dead, close to the living. All of the caves look out over valleys, woodland and rivers. In the winter of 1936, when Spanish Nationalist forces seized the province of Málaga and settled in the now flooded village of Peñarrubia, it was used as a hideout by Republican forces. Excavations in 1994 found Republican artefacts mixed in with ancient bowls, necklaces, arrows and amulets and a curious egg-shaped bethel, or large polished stone, its burial suggesting a belief in an afterlife or death as part of a cycle.

→ From Ardales take the MA-5403 N towards Campillos for 10km. Just before the bridge crossing the dam of Embalse de Guadalteba, take a L on to a dirt track. Follow for 2.5km to a small parking area at 36.9465, -4.8204 and signs for the necropolis on the L. There are lots of information panels, and the walk itself is a signed circular route of 2.5km which passes the tombs and caves in shady pine woodland.

20 mins, 36.9429, -4.8186 🌲✝🏞🐾

20 RUÍNAS DE BOBASTRO

The dusty ruins of a Roman fortress and cave church hide in the woodland south of the Desfiladero de los Gaitanes. They were once the stronghold of the 9th-century outlaw and rebel leader Umar ibn Hafsun, who led the resistance against the Córdoban Caliphate. The cave church was built by Hafsun after he strategically converted to Christianity. He was buried here in 918 only to be unearthed 10 years later and crucified at the gates of Córdoba for his betrayal. Visting hours apply; see Malaga.es or call 952 458 046.

→ From Ardales take the MA-5403 towards Caminito del Rey for 5.3km. At the visitor centre roundabout take the first exit and continue for 3km to a sharp R at a sign for Bobastro. Continue for 3km to the parking on the R.

15 mins, 36.9023, -4.7813 🌲✦🖼✝€

WOODLAND PICNICS

21 LAGAR DE TORRIJOS

A picnic park with BBQs for communal use and a free camping space in the middle of the Montes de Málaga Natural Park. There are toilets and showers, and the small stream and its undergrowth are popular with kids. A great place for lazy Sunday picnics.

→ Park the car at the olive press museum and follow the path down to the river.

10 mins, 36.8271, -4.3640 🛶🎒✦🏕

CRUSADER CASTLES

22 CASTILLO DE TURÓN

The ruins of this medieval fortress crown the limestone cliffs above the River Turón, with spectacular views over the green Serranía de Ronda. It was built by the Nasrids to defend the Kingdom of Granada from Castilian attack based at Castillo de la Estrella in Teba.

➜ Park at the Roman bridge at Ardales and follow the road along the riverside for 1km. At the fork keep R and continue for another 2km to a bend and a sign on the L for PRA-90. Follow the track uphill to the castle. Scramble climb.

1 hr, 36.8701, -4.8790 🏔🏞🚴🚶🧗♻

23 CASTILLO DE LA ESTRELLA

This 13th-century castle built on a high rock overlooking the Guadalteba valley was once Málaga's biggest medieval fortress. A Scottish lord, Sir John Douglas, or Black Douglas, fought here in the Battle of Teba. He carried Robert the Bruce's heart in a silver casket around his neck to the crusade, and his rash dying act, flinging the heart under the feet of Uthman's soldiers, was immortalised by Sir Walter Scott. The heart and his body were found and later buried at Melrose Abbey.

➜ A short walk uphill from Calle la Estrella in Teba.

10 mins, 36.9798, -4.9181 🚵🚗♿

RURAL RESTAURANTS

24 CASA PEPA

If you want home-cooked *croquetas* and traditional Andaluz grandma-cooking, then this is the place to come. The tiny kitchen and restaurant, with its dresser and plates, looks like home. You will be served whatever Pepa has made that day: *puchero* (chicken broth soup), *potaje de callos* (tripe stew), *gazpachuelo malagueño* (a hot fish-stock broth with mayonnaise, garlic, egg yolk and oil); they are all excellent.

➜ Calle Baños, 18, 29551 Carratraca, 952 458 049, Labocacha.com/lafonda.html
36.8520, -4.8189 📶🍴♿

25 RESTAURANTE EL MIRADOR

Heaps of pumpkins and gourds hold down the tin roof of this rustic restaurant which has views across the sparkling Conde de Guadahorce reservoir. Come here for hearty roast meats, hunters' stews and local specialities such as stuffed cabbage with a sweet Málaga wine sauce. There is a children's play park in the garden. It can be very busy on Sundays and public holidays, so book ahead.

➜ Parque de Ardales Zona Cuarta, 29552 Ardales, 952 119 809
36.9282, -4.8012 📶🍴♿

26 PANADERÍA CONFITERÍA JUSTA

A dark den with a bar and the grumpiest owner in all of Andalucía on first

appearances, but he's kind really. It's a great stop-off for bread, local products, meats, honey and a great source of local olive oil.

➜ Lugar Urbanización La Almazara, 0, 29160 Casabermeja, 952 758 843
36.8956, -4.4309 📶🍴♿

27 BAR CAFETERÍA TEJADA, 'MANOLITO REY'

A great bar and restaurant in the main square of sleepy Fuente de Piedra. It is right next to one of the town's beautiful, old salty water fountains.

➜ Pl. de la Constitución, 10, 29520 Fuente de Piedra, 952 735 332
37.1362, -4.7297

28 RESTAURANTE CHAQUETAS II

Also in Fuente de Piedra, but not in a beautiful spot, this restaurant is the place to try an excellent *ajo blanco* (cold almond soup) and true Malagueña cooking.

➜ Polígono industrial Fuente Piedra, s/n, 29520 Fuente de Piedra, 952 736 291
37.1346, -4.7231 📶🍴♿

29 BAR FUENTE DE LA REINA

A great stop by an old stone drinking fountain in the Montes de Málaga serving seasonal tapas, great *migas* and homemade sweet wine. Good place to refuel for hikers and bikers.

➜ Camino del Colmenar, s/n, 29013 Málaga, 952 110 123
36.8130, -4.3720 🍴♿🚶🚴

CAMPING & STARGAZING

30 CAMPING ARDALES

A beautiful campsite in pine woodland on the banks of the Conde de Guadalhorce reservoir. The cool blue water of the lake is easily accessible, and there are plenty of pitches for tents where you can wake up to spectacular, dazzling views of the lake. Caravans are also welcome in an alotted area and dogs are permitted. Restaurant open in summer. For kayak rental call Indian Sport – 686 479 288.

➜ Carretera de los Embalses Km 7, 29550 Ardales, 951 264 924, Parqueardales.com
36.9170, -4.8244 🍴🏕🛶🏊🐕♿

31 HIDDEN VALLEY

Stay in a glorious bell tent in the olive groves, just a 20 minute walk from Álora.

➜ 29500 Álora, 630 982 413, Hiddenvalleyandalucia.co.uk
36.8367, -4.7143 🛖♿🏕🚶

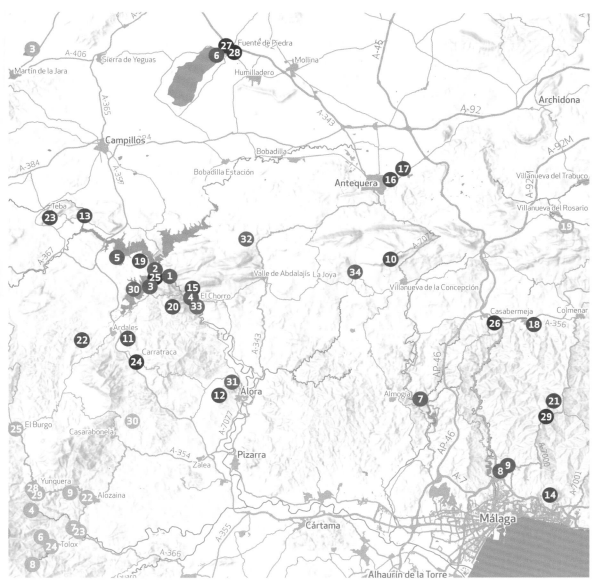

32 CORTIJO DOS SANTOS

Several vintage safari lodges with terraces, wood-burning stoves and views out to La Huma mountain. Close to footpaths and swims in lakes.

→ Partido Veja Beja Apartado 80, 29240 Valle de Abdalajis, 629 574 002, Cortijodossantos.com

36.9659, -4.7035 🔲🎿⛰️🎨🏊

33 LA GARGANTA HOTEL

A pet-friendly hotel and restaurant in the Old Flour Mill right next to El Chorro train station and the Caminito del Rey. The García family have been running the business for over 50 years and they've recently won awards for their sustainable use of energy. The hotel has great views of the gorge and the lake, and they run climbing expeditions on the Vía Ferrata El Chorro.

→ Barriada El Chorro, s/n, 29552 El Chorro, 952 495 000, Lagarganta.com

36.9062, -4.7593 🏨🎿🍴💧🐾🚆

34 VILLA CEREZA

Cosy cottage in the foothills of El Torcal near footpaths. Pool has views of the mountains; very peaceful. Sleeps 6 and dogs welcome.

→ El Robledillo La Higuera Buzon 80, 29230 Antequera, 609 203 666

36.9385, -4.5840 🎿🐾🏊🚶🏕️

LA AXARQUÍA

Our perfect weekend

→ **Unwind** on the black-sand cove at Caleta de Maro and swim in crystal-clear water

→ **Soak** in the healing water of the Guaro river at Baños de Vilo, in wild baths carved a thousand years ago

→ **Dive** down beneath the waves at Cerro Gordo to see waters teeming with sea life, fishes glinting among reefs and seagrass

→ **Kayak** out to Cascada de Maro, a waterfall tumbling from high cliffs into turquoise sea

→ **Lose** yourself in the landscape as you follow the River Higuerón along its gorge from the white mountain village of Frigiliana

→ **Tread** on ancient cobblestones as you cross the Roman bridge at Canillas de Albaida and follow the path winding up green hills

→ **Bed** down under tropical palms a short stroll from the sea at Camping Cortijo San Miguel

→ **Ramble** along muleteer paths passing cacti, prickly pears and pomegranates as you wander into pretty mountain villages

→ **Sip** on a sweet glass of Muscatel from the steeply sloped vineyards near Cómpeta, or a refreshingly dry *seco* made from the same local grape

The mountains and sea to the east of Málaga, with their flaming sunsets that turn the hills and coastline a deep golden orange, form one of the most beautiful corners of the province. The name Axarquía comes from the Arabic for 'land lying east' of Málaga, and the Arab influence can be seen in its lush valleys and orchards watered by ancient stone channels and peppered with white villages looking out to the blue Mediterranean Sea. Rising to over 2,000m behind these streams and settlements are the Sierras de Tejeda, Almijara y Alhama. Their wild beauty stands in stark contrast with the sprawling developments along the Costa Tropical.

As you climb up from Axarquía's white villages to the Sierras de Tejeda, the landscape changes dramatically. Rivers have carved the valleys and mountains into a labyrinth of fissures, caverns and caves, forming a vast arena of limestone resembling a moonscape. Entering this scene at Cerro del Espino, the road winds by perilous plunges and hills without any sign of human habitation for as far as the eye can see. Wander slowly into this landscape to find the Cascada de los Árboles Petrificados. Pine, juniper and mastic woodland opens up to reveal a waterfall with several tree trunks 'turned to stone' by mineral deposits and a glittering cave hidden behind a curtain of travertine rock.

While the dazzling display of stalactites and underground lakes at the famous Nerja caves is now very popular, other natural wonders of water and rock are scattered across the mountains. Hike up to the Fájara caves near the Bermuza springs or follow the Gran Senda de Málaga from the pretty village of Canillas de Aceituno to El Saltillo, a hanging bridge over a steep gorge. At Junta de los Ríos you can plunge into sparkling rock pools under forested peaks, home to many raptors, including booted eagles and Egyptian vultures.

Mountains meet sea at the cliffs of Maro-Cerro Gordo, where gnarly limestone plunges into the turquoise Alborán Sea. This protected natural park continues underwater with reefs, endangered orange coral and sea caves that are home to eels, octopuses and colourful fish. Much of this wild and untouched coast, with its secluded beaches and coastal caves, can only be reached by kayak. Looking up to the hills from Playa de Calaiza, you might spot the distinctive horned head of an ibex, a mountain goat, fixed on its rock on the skyline. As evening draws in, keep an eye out as they come skidding down from the mountain to the sea, their cloven feet clattering across the coastal roads.

In the 16th century, these shores saw constant attacks from Barbary pirates and from the likes of Jack Ward: an English privateer who turned pirate, converted to Islam and became a corsair himself. The old watchtower at Cerro Gordo formed part of a defensive line, their towers filled with smoke and lit up by bright flames. It is a quiet spot to reflect on its wild history and watch the sunset flash pink, gold and orange across the sea.

SECRET BEACHES

1 PLAYA DE BARRANCO DE ENMEDIO

A sheltered pebbly cove with black rocks
for jumping or fishing. It is much quieter
than the beaches closer to Almuñécar
and has a small community of campervan
families in summer. It is overlooked by an
18th-century watchtower known as Torre
del Diablo, which owes its name to a legend
about a group of thieves who dressed
as devils and robbed a party of passing
travellers.

➜ From Almuñécar take the N-340 E for 7km
and turn sharp R at sign for 'urbanización
Alfamar'. Slightly double-back on yourself and
follow the road for 900m down to the cove.
1 min, 36.7437, -3.6444 🏖🤿🐚

2 CALA DONCELLA

A secret sandy cove by the Ancantilados
de Maro cliffs and Cerro Gordo hills.
Overlooked by the 16th-century
watchtower of Torre de la Caleta, it is a
great snorkelling spot.

➜ The path starts at the Playa del Cañuelo
car park. Head straight down the dusty road
that leads to Cañuelo. In about 400m the trail
starts on your L. Follow this path past the
ruins and down to the beach. It is a scramble
and very overgrown, so take care.
25 mins, 36.7418, -3.7857 🏖❓🤿🐚🚶

3 PLAYA DE CALAIZA

This secret cove hidden behind the western
arm of La Herradura is much quieter than the
busy beaches further west. The wild wooded
hill of Cerro Gordo falls away to meet this
pure, gem-like water. Look back up the hill
to see ibex, or wild mountain goats, their
distant horned heads silhouetted against
the skyline.

➜ From La Herrdura drive 3km on the N-340
in the direction of Málaga. Turn L at signs for
Carmenes del Mar and pass under the arch
into the residential area. Park where you can
on Calle Enebro. Opposite the zebra crossing
is a paved footpath; follow it for 150m
towards the sea. At the roundabout turn R and
follow the track to a woodland clearing. Behind
the information board there is a small path
through the trees on the L down to the cove.
It's a scrabbly track; be careful with kids.
20 mins, 36.7351, -3.7619 🏖🚶🤿🐚

4 PLAYA DEL PINO

From the road high above these beaches,
the sea appears as a calm turquoise mirror.
These are quieter beaches because of the
steep climb back up, but the sandy track
is safe if challenging. Nearby, the old
watchtowers of Torre de la Miel and Torre del
Pino still guard the sea.

➜ From Nerja take the N-340 in the direction
of Almuñécar. After 6km there will be signs
for parking for Playa de las Alberquillas but
continue for 100m and take the third dirt
track. Park where you can and follow the
footpath down to the beach.
5 mins, 36.7463, -3.7998 🏖🤿🐚

5 PLAYA DE LA CALETA DE MARO

A beautiful black-sand cove with shallow,
gentle water. In summer there are normally a
couple of Shangri-La shacks and wild campers.

➜ From Nerja take the N-340 to Maro.
Continue through Maro and at the roundabout
turn R to 'Playa'. Parking after 100m. Follow
the road L to a signed footpath on the R to
the beach.
10 mins, 36.7535, -3.8448 🏖🤿🐚🚶

SEA CAVES & WATERFALLS

6 CASCADA DE MARO

This beautiful waterfall tumbles over
the cliffs and into the blue sea. It is only

167

accessible by kayak, a great way to see more of the secluded coastline with its shimmering fishes and hidden sea caves. Call Local Experiences 675 647 355 for kayak trips with pirates and mermaids; great for kids.

→ See directions to Playa de la Caleta de Maro and from signs to Caleta de Maro continue on foot for another 700m down to the beach. There are also kayaks for hire here with Kayakmaro.es. It can get busy in summer months.

30 mins, 36.7495, -3.8678 🏖🚻🏊🛶⚡🛥🏕

7 CUEVA DE LAS PALOMAS
These wild sea caves are hidden like gems along the coast and accessed only by kayak.
→ Call Localexperiences.es for a kayak trip – 675 647 355.

30 mins, 36.7311, -3.7698 🏖☀🏊🛶⚡

HIDDEN WATERFALLS

8 JUNTA DE LOS RÍOS
An idyllic spot for wild swimming where the Río Verde meets the Río Negro. Its deep ravine hides shimmering rockpools, high jumping spots for adrenaline junkies and rushing cool waterfalls. There are hanging bridges, stepping stones and numerous other secrets and places to explore along the footpath which follows the river. Be prepared to do some wading and clambering if you want to find the deepest pool and waterfall.

→ From Otívar head N on the A-4050 for 6km. Stop at a gateway on the L by a yellow hut and pay the entrance fee (key available at El Capricchio Bar, Otívar, in winter). Drive 5km (25 mins) down the rough, steep track. Stop at an abandoned pump house on your R. Park here and walk to the first pool or drive up the steep hill for 200m and park. Head NW, keeping the river on your R, and pass the dam. Clamber down the rocks to meet the river. Cross and follow NE for 20m. Climb over the rocks and follow the rocky path to first pool. It is about 1.5km from the first river crossing to the deepest waterfall pool. There is little or no phone signal here.

15 mins, 36.8343, -3.7360 🏊🚻🚶🏔🔆

9 CASCADA DE LOS ÁRBOLES PETRIFICADOS AND EMBALSE DE LA CUEVA DE FUNES
A strikingly beautiful waterfall deep in the wilderness of the Sierras de Tejeda, Almijara y Alhama. It splashes over long shards of travertine rock, striped with colourful mineral deposits, into a very shallow pool. Its name refers to the tree trunks that have

been calcifying in the waterfall since the 1920s, when the river was used to transport wood to the lumber mill. Follow steps up to the right behind the waterfall to discover a secret cave dripping with glittering stalactites. Continue downstream for several brilliant turquoise pools or follow the footpath uphill to the Embalse de la Cueva de Funes, which has beautiful clear water accessible from a narrow dirt track on the left with gaps in the reeds.

→ From Otívar follow the A4050 N for 16.5km. There is parking signed on the R (36.8605, -3.7234) opposite the information board. Follow the footpath for 5.5km. Amazing views but a steep and steady climb back!

1.5 hrs, 36.855, -3.7385 🛇🏕🏔🏃🦮🐕🌳🏊⛵

10 RÍO CHILLAR, NERJA

The Río Chillar carves a gorge through limestone rock on its way from the Sierra de Almijara to the sea. Escape the summer heat with a long, cool walk upstream along the riverbed. You'll find several pools and a series of waterfalls if you venture far enough. Take water shoes.

→ From Avenida de la Constitución in Nerja, follow the road uphill and take a sharp L onto Calle Mirto (with a field in front of you) and drop down onto a small place where you can park. To get closer to the river drive through the urbanisation following the road upwards to the R, passing under the motorway. See the river on your L. The concrete road dips back down towards the river and becomes a track. Keep following this track as far as you can near a concrete factory. Park anywhere you legally can and walk upriver.

15 mins, 36.7716, -3.8794 🛇🏊🏃🏔

11 LOS CAHORROS DEL RÍO CHILLAR

The Río Verde tumbles down the hillside at Los Chortales and plunges over a high waterfall, forming a deep pool beneath. You can take long swims here, and a small opening behind travertine rock by the waterfall leads to a secret cave. Wander upstream along the footpath for 2km to find further pools at Poza de los Patos.

→ See directions to Río Chillar above but continue walking upstream for 3.5km.

1 hr, 36.7951, -3.8735 🛇🏊🏃🏔

HEALING WATER

12 EMBALSE DE LA VIÑUELA

A glassy, blue expanse of water as warm as a bath on entry and silent but for the lapping of the water. Dry off on warm rocks, looking across to the white villages on the opposite banks and to the Axarquía mountains dominating the horizon beyond.

→ Heading E from Málaga on the Autovía del Mediterráneo (A-7), turn off at exit 272 and take the A-356 towards Viñuela/Colmenar. Drive N for 10km, then take the A-402 towards Alcaucín/Zafarraya. After 1.4km take the L turn signposted 'Villas del Lago', then turn immediately L again down a tree-lined road. You'll see the reservoir in front of you. Park where you can under the trees.

15 mins, 36.8781, -4.1664 🛇🏕🏔

13 BAÑOS DE VILO

The ancient Arabic baths in this small hamlet are filled with the milky blue water of the Guaro river, rich in sulphur and famed for its healing properties. The humble curbstone pool, carved over a thousand years ago, lets you feel as though you've travelled back in time – but it smells diabolical. Popular in the 19th century, it suffered due to heavy flooding in 1907 and never really recovered its prestige. It is possible you'll have this little nook to yourself, but don't wear silver; the water turns it black. The Ruta del Água footpath from Periana passes by.

→ From Periana take the A-7204 towards Riogordo. After about 3.5km you will cross a narrow bridge over the river Vilo. Continue up the road for 200m to a parking area on the L just before a white sign on the R. Park here, cross the road and walk through the large iron gates into the patio area. It looks like someone's home but it's not! Follow the path to the R to the footbridge and little pool.
5 mins, 36.9508, -4.2067

SUNSET HILLTOPS

14 TORRE VIGÍA DE CERRO GORDO

This strategically positioned watchtower was built during the medieval Nasrid rule and later became part of a defensive system against the endless raids from Barbary pirates. It is a beautiful spot to watch the sunset. On one side you have La Herradura cove and on the other you can see along the Acantilados de Maro-Cerro Gordo almost as far as Málaga.
→ From La Herradura head W on the N-340 for 3.5km. Turn R before the tunnel at signs for Cerro Gordo and continue on the mountain road for 1.6km to reach Restaurante Mirador de Cerro Gordo. Park here and follow the signed footpath for 100m to the watchtower.
5 mins, 36.7323, -3.7674

15 FÁBRICA DE LA LUZ

Crystal clear streams and small waterfalls splash by the remains of the old power plant in the sierra outside Canillas de Albaida. Until the early 20th century it generated electricity using the kinetic energy of the water. Now it is a great picnic space with wooden tables under the shade of walnut trees and wild camping is permitted here. Climb the track further into the hills to find Cueva del Agua and other hidden caves.
→ From Ermita de Santa Ana in Canillas de Albaida take the road into the hills for 3.3km following signs for Área Recreativa.
1 min, 36.8641, -3.9704

MOUNTAIN VILLAGES

16 PUENTE ROMANO, CANILLAS DE ALBAIDA

From this roman bridge over the Río Cajula you can follow the ancient bridleway zigzagging up the green hills and crossing shallow river pools. The Gran Senda de Málaga footpath passes by and links the pretty village to Cómpeta and Frigiliana while smaller footpaths link it to Fábrica de la Luz and great views of the bright white mountain villages.
→ A 7.5km circular path is signed from the end of Calle la Axarquía when it meets Calle

Estación in Canillas de Albaida, you can follow this path 400m down to the bridge.

5 mins, 36.8469, -3.9914 🏕️🚏🚶🔭🌳🚃

17 SENDERO DEL RÍO HIGUERÓN

Hike up the limestone canyon carved by the River Higuerón to find several roaring waterfalls and smooth, rippling stone carved by the abundant water. You'll hike the first part along the dry riverbed, passing caves and views up to pretty Frigiliana, then join the water channel, Acequia de Lízar. After a while you'll reach the cascades but in summer the water levels may be low. You can also hike from Frigiliana to Poza de los Patos using the GR249 Gran Senda de Málaga.

→ The 8km linear route is signed from Calle Boticario off the Plaza de las Tres Culturas in Frigiliana. Walk down to the river and then follow the dry riverbed to the L from here for 8km. It is far, and very wild. It is advisable to download the wikiloc route onto offline Maps.me.

2 hrs, 36.836, -3.8929 🚵🚶🏕️🔲💧

18 PUENTE COLGANTE EL SALTILLO

This 50m suspension bridge, made of wood and steel, is one of the most picturesque spots along the Gran Senda de Málaga footpath. It crosses the Almanchares river and has views out across the Sierras de Tejeda. In summer, flowering oleander covers the riverbanks and the air is heavy with the scent of pine. If hiking from Canillas, carry on along the footpath for another 800m before crossing the bridge to see some waterfalls.

→ Park in Canillas de Aceituno. The 3km footpath is signed from the steps at the end of Calle Convento.

45 mins, 36.8751, -4.06161 🏕️🚶💧

CAVES & SPRINGS

19 NACIMIENTO DEL RÍO CEREZO

A short and scenic walk from Villanueva del Rosario takes you past the hermitage to the spring of the Río Cerezo, rushing with cool water. It is a beautiful place to explore, with hiking routes that lead right up to the via ferratas in the Hondonero mountains and incredible views.

→ From Villanueva del Rosario follow Camino de la Loma for 1km to the Ermita de la Virgen del Rosario. Follow the path from the car park downhill to reach the springs.

20 mins, 36.9855, -4.3553 🚶🎋🏕️🔲💧✝️

20 CUEVA DE LA FÁJARA

A hidden cave by the spring of the River Bermuza. The footpath down the hillside winds

by panoramic views of the Axarquía mountains and through shady woodland with wild herbs. The cave provides a cool spot in summer and if the riverbed is dry, it's great for bouldering.

→ From Canillas de Aceituno take the MA-125 N out of town. At the roundabout take the first exit uphill and continue for 800m until a small layby on R where the cave is signed, park here. Follow the footpath for 800m down to the bottom of the valley, the cave is just before you cross the river.

30 mins, 36.8832, -4.0965 🚵🚶🔲💧▽

LOCAL FEASTS

21 CASA LOLA

An unassuming roadside restaurant opposite the olive oil co-operative in the small village of Mondrón. It is a typical low-key restaurant; the bar staff are friendly and the tapas are generous. Try the *croquetas* or the *puntillitas fritas* (fried baby squid) with a cerveza.

→ Cortijo Las Majadas 2, 29710 Mondrón, 641 935 574

36.9420, -4.2254 🍴💧

22 BODEGÓN DE JUAN MARÍA

A cosy restaurant with excellent malagueño dishes to nourish you after a hike. Try the

chivo lechal malagueño (suckling goat) either roasted in the wood oven or in *ajillo* (garlic). There's nothing better to pair it with than a young red wine from Axarquía.

→ C. Placeta, 6, 29716 Canillas de Aceituno, 952 518 041

36.8724, -4.0820 🍴🚹🚶

23 RESTAURANTE GERARDO

Deep in the sun-drenched olive groves outside Alfarnatejo is this rustic restaurant serving mouth-watering dishes with colourful, local ingredients. A short ramble takes you down to pools in the Río Sabar.

→ Ctra. Riogordo, Km 15,5, 29194 Periana, 630 542 244

36.9498, -4.2531 🈺🍴🚹🛏🏊

24 LA CASONA DE GUARO

A popular bikers' spot in the Axarquía mountains serving hearty food and great migas.

→ MA-156, 1, 29710 Periana, 680 118 615

36.9604, -4.1911 🍴🚹🚶

25 MESÓN LOS OLIVOS

Located on the way into the pretty village of Otívar, this restaurant has mountain views from its terrace. Good for grilled local meats hot off the charcoal.

→ 18699 Otívar, 958 644 588

36.8204, -3.6826 🍴🚹

WILDER CAMPING

26 CAMPO AGAVE

Several safari lodges with incredible views out from the hills to the bright blue sea. You can cook in the open air.

→ Carraspite, 86, 29752 Sayalonga, 656 561 697, Campoagave.es

36.7864, -4.0133 🏕🚻🍴🚹🛖

27 CAMPING CORTIJO SAN MIGUEL

This sustainable campsite is just 300m from the beach at Nerja. Its lack of a bar and pool means it remains a quiet haven. It

sells fresh bread and tropical fruits from the garden.

→ N-340, Km 289, Cortijo San Miguel, 29780, 644 053 891, Campingcortijosanmiguel.com

36.7470, -3.8989 🏕🚻🛖

RURAL HAVENS

28 CORTIJO EL TUNANTE

A beautiful old farmhouse, running off-grid, with olive and almond groves in the Axarquía mountains. Its wide-open vistas across to pretty villages like Ríogordo and Colmenar make it a perfect retreat and good for hiking. A couple of smaller cottages are available too.

→ Partida Rozas Velez, 4, 29718 Riogordo, 711 095 612, Cortijoeltunante.com

36.8969, -4.2437

29 MOLINO JABONERO

Peaceful accommodation in a restored soap mill. Surrounded by olive groves near the Guadalhorce river. Olive-oil tours are available.

→ MA-4100, Km 4, 29313 Villanueva del Trabuco, 652 232 269, Molinojabonero.com

37.0326, -4.2945 🛏🏕🚹🛖🈺

30 LOS OLIVILLOS

Several guestrooms and full board are offered at this rustic mountain retreat and working farm. They also run horse-riding trails into the wilder corners of the Axarquía mountains.

→ Diseminado 476, 29754 Málaga, Los-olivillos.com

36.8336, -3.9386 🈺🏕🐴🏔🛖

19

20

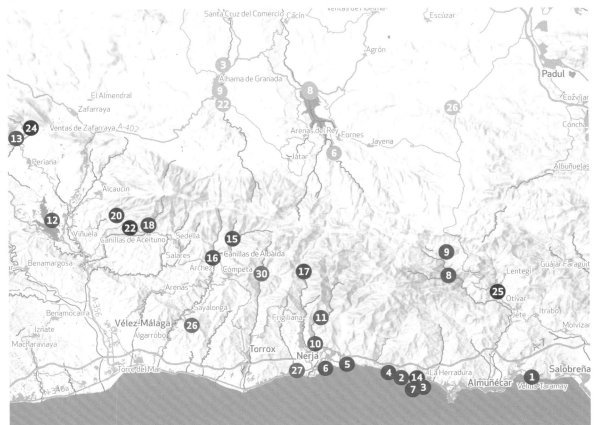

173

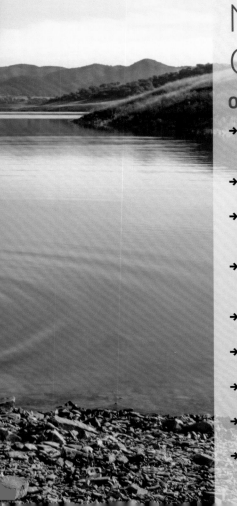

NORTH CÓRDOBA

Our perfect weekend

→ **Wander** through the vibrant streets of Montoro, passing orange trees and flowering balconies to Casa de la Conchas

→ **Hike** up to the sandy-gold castle of Castillo de El Vacar and picnic among its 10th-century ruins

→ **Clamber** into the huge hoop of quartzite rock at Piedra Horadada and look out to the Sierra Morena

→ **Marvel** at hundreds of bright ochre rock paintings by the waterfall at Pinturas Rupestres y Cascada de la Batanera

→ **Dip** into the waters of the Río Guadiato and watch for gleaming blue dragonflies

→ **Feast** on fresh salads and the best Córdobese *flamenquín* at Restaurante El Candil

→ **Retreat** to the most remote of wild havens at the restored 19th-century Hacienda la Colorá

→ **Cross** the old mining tracks at Albergue de Espiel to swim in the deep Puente Nuevo Lake

→ **Stargaze** from the Ermita de la Virgen de las Veredas and wander along the footpaths as wild winds whip the rockroses

The serene landscape of Los Pedroches, north of Córdoba, has been pastoral farmland for centuries. In Arabic the land was called *Fahs al-Ballut*, the 'land of acorns' and cork oaks still provide shelter for grazing animals. The farms beneath Belmez and its rocky castle hide ancient dolmens whose burial stones were raised thousands of years ago by the first farmers to settle here. In the evenings, lanes fill with the clattering and skidding hooves of goats, their coats brown, grey and fawn in the last light.

These hills have seen a lively array of characters and scenes: cave-dwelling hermits, lost caliphal cities, frontline fighting during the civil war and the heart-breaking tale of Marcos Rodríguez Pantoja, a feral shepherd boy raised by wolves. Watch *Entrelobos*, a 2010 film about his early life, to see him in Azuel looking wistfully towards the Sierra de Cardeña y Montoro where he spent 12 years among wolves with no human contact.

Grey watchtowers look down from hills behind Córdoba and once protected the caliphal seat here. Dense woodland also provided refuge for early Christian anchorites and hermits during Islamic rule. They say this hermitic tradition arrived in the 3rd century after the Bishop of Córdoba travelled to Egypt and met with San Antonio Abad and the Desert Fathers. Wander through wildflowers to Torre del Beato, a ruined Islamic tower, later home to a holy hermit.

Ghosts of lost cities fill the valley below. Medina Azahara, the 'Shining City', once stood just west of Córdoba. Built by Caliph Abd al-Rahman III in 929, the city was a dazzling display of 3,400 marble columns and towering minarets. A finely balanced bowl of mercury sat within the palace, and when rocked it would reflect sunlight off golden walls like flashes of lightning. Its opulence was short-lived. Razed to the ground by battling *taifas* in 1010, its stones were quarried during the reign of the Catholic Monarchs. This past, shimmering like a mirage and existing only in stories, is easily conjured by a visit to the Great Mosque in Córdoba, where endless horseshoe arches fade into shadows, or at many enigmatic ruins scattered across Córdoba's wild hills.

Wilder mountain roads connecting forgotten villages and ancient ruins take you back to an Andalucía before new roads cut the land into manageable distances. All but forgotten, these timeless ways wind precariously up to peaks where lakes become distant shining puddles and bumblebees hum across tarmac. You can follow a stage of the GR48 footpath up to Obejo, where low cloud mixes with chimney smoke, or climb to Castillo de Miramontes, where eagles wheel over its decayed towers.

Wander from Cardeña to the abandoned village of Aldea del Cerezo. From here, the Sierra de Cardeña y Montoro runs into the Sierra de Andújar where endangered wolves, Iberian lynx and otters are tentatively returning.

The Alto Guadiato mining villages saw Republican resistance during the civil war. The hideout above Peñarroya-Pueblonuevo was said to connect through old mines to the prison at Hinojosa Del Duque, now a great restaurant; Republican graffiti detailing coded escape plans is hidden under chairs and tables. But it was in Cerro Muriano that Robert Capa and Gerda Taro shot the iconic image 'Falling Soldier' in 1936. Stop at Bar X to see more of Capa's work and feast on local food. Try a *flamenquín*, a typical Córdobese dish of *jamón* serrano rolled with pork loin, breadcrumbs and fried, or *salmorejo*, a chilled soup of tomato and bread.

WILD WATERFALLS

1 PINTURAS RUPESTRES Y CASCADA DE LA BATANERA

Bright ochre paintings of dancing figures from the Bronze Age cover the rocks and caves that lie along the woodland pathways here. Perhaps these ochre paintings were made by the first swimmers here. Below the paths runs the Cereceda river before it tumbles into a waterfall. Follow the footpath along the river to a deep and narrow plunge pool in the gorge. Technically, it is located 4km outside Andalucía, but it's worth it!

→ From Azuel head 13km N on the N-420. Take the R signed 'Pinturas Rupestres' 2km after Fuencaliente and follow the track uphill for 2km to a small parking area by closed gates on the R. Walk down the footpath to reach the river, waterfall and paintings.

10 mins, 38.4343, -4.2885 ⊞🏊🚶⛺🚴♨

2 LOS PILONES

A series of beautiful deep pools and a waterfall by old mill ruins in the Arroyo de Algarrobillo.

→ Access is a little uncertain as it is in farmland. From Villaviciosa de Córdoba follow

Calle Agustín López out of town for 2km. Turn L onto the CO-431a and follow for 1.6km to a track on the L down to the river.

1 hr, 38.0979, -5.0035 ⛺🏊🍴🚶

3 BAÑOS DE POPEA

A tiny waterfall and plunge pool hidden like a jewel in the Sierra Morena. You can also follow the GR48 for 2km from here to find the spring of Río Bejerano or wander on for 500m to the River Guadiato.

→ From Córdoba take the CO-3402 to Santa María de Trassiera. As you come into the town there is a shrine to the virgin (37.9248, -4.8949) near the bus stop (buses run from Córdoba). Park here. The Ruta por Santa María De Trassierra circular trail is signed from here. It is about 2km to Baños de Popea. Continue on the trail for Río Guadiato (see entry) and Venero del Río Bejerano.

30 mins, 37.9381, -4.8955 🏊🍴♨

RIVERS & LAKES

4 RÍO GUADIATO

The River Guadiato widens out and deepens here for a swim. Follow the river upstream for hidden remains of Roman mines. There are many muddy riverbank entrances for a

swim, a few with rope swings, between the gnarly roots.

→ See directions to Baños de Popea and continue for another 500m to the river.

40 mins, 37.9405, -4.8927 ⛺🏊🚴🍴♨

5 EMBALSE DE SIERRA BOYERA

There are a few picnic tables on the shores of this beautiful lake. The entrance to the water is stony but it is a quiet spot for longer swims under views of the Sierra de los Santos.

→ From Peñarroya-Pueblonuevo take the N-432 S for 500m. After crossing the railway take the first L onto the CO-7404 and keep L. At the roundabout take the first exit and then the first R. Keep R at the fork and follow the road straight for 1km through some gates to the water's edge.

1 min, 38.2797, -5.2778

6 EMBALSE DE LAS TEJONERAS

Farmland with grazing sheep and pigs border this lake, which has several private spaces along its banks for a picnic. The lake is a haven for wildlife; keep an eye out for pigs taking a dip along the muddy banks.

→ From Cardeña take the Camino del Aldea de Cerezo. After 3.5km turn L off the dirt track

(at 38.2593, -4.2845). There are some gates but they are usually left unlocked. Park here and walk 1km along the track to the lake.

15 mins, 38.2672, -4.2818 🚶🏕️⛰️

7 PUENTE MOCARRA

The thinnest rib of a Roman bridge, which crosses sparkling pools between river-smoothed rocks, lies along what was once an 800km livestock path linking Soria to Seville. The pastors would use the bread ovens here; you can still see their ruins. There is plenty of shelter for a camp or picnic. Follow the footpath upstream for further pools or deeper swims.

→ A short cycle or good hike from Espiel. Take the smaller bridge, along the CO-4400, over the river from Albergue de Espiel and take the first track on the L, the Camino de los Molinos. Follow for 3.5km to the bridge.

1 hr, 38.1564, -5.0537 🏕️🚶🛖⛰️

8 EMBALSE DE LA ENCANTADA

A large glassy lake with several smooth boulders for drying off in the sun. Located in a residential holiday area with many bars and restaurants, it can get busy in high season.

→ From Córdoba take the C-3408 N into the sierra. After 10km turn R at signs for Urb.

Las Jaras and continue for 4.5km. Turn R and keep following signs for Las Jaras. Park where you can near the lake. There is a good entry point and scrabble down from the road at 37.9680, -4.8401.

10 mins, 37.9674, -4.8405 🚶🅱️

9 EMBALSE DE SAN RAFAEL DE NAVALLANA

Smooth grassy hills run down to this reservoir popular with fishermen. There are many secluded spots with easy entry for a swim and great stargazing on clear nights.

→ From Alcolea take the CO-3103 towards Villafranca de Córdoba. After 4km turn L on to the CH-1 for 5km, cross the bridge over the reservoir and follow tracks on the R to the water.

2 mins, 37.9829, -4.6455 🚶🏕️⛰️

10 EMBALSE DE GUADANUÑO

A large reservoir with grassy banks and a rowdy gaggle of geese – bring bread.

→ From Cerro Muriano take the first L after the military base. After 100m turn R into the parking. A small gate leads to the banks.

1 min, 38.0224, -4.7906 🚶🐕

11 EMBALSE DE LAS BUENAS HIERBAS

A peaceful haven for birdlife and fishermen. Trout bask in its sunny shallows. There is gentle entry to the water and great smooth stones for drying off in the sunshine.

→ From Azuel take the A-3200 towards Conquista for 8km. Turn L at the green gates (38.3646,-4.4061) – remember to close them well as although it is public water it is also private farmland. Follow the track for 100m to the lake and park.

2 mins, 38.3609, -4.4061 🏊🎣🚶

STREAMS & PICNICS

12 LOS VILLARES PARK

Just 8km outside Córdoba are roughly 500 hectares of forest parkland for public use. Streams wind through its rich woodland, where there are picnic tables, BBQs and fountains. In summer there is a simple campsite and a restaurant. See Campinglosvillares.es.

→ From Córdoba take the CO-3408 N for 10km. The parking area is signed 'Los Villares' on your L.

10 mins, 37.9808, -4.8018 🎪

CASTLES & TOWERS

13 CASTILLO DE BELÁLCAZAR

Much of this Gothic castle was destroyed by Napoleon's army but the robust keep of Belálcazar survives. It still dominates the skyline and used to guard the border of Andalucía, where the Sierra Morena falls away into the Extremadura region. During Al-Andalus it was known as 'Gafiq', and the present castle was built in the 15th century. Currently, you can't enter the castle, but it is worth visiting for its beautiful views and intricate carvings.

→ Follow the cobbled street from the town's wash houses, or *lavaderos*, uphill and pass the Albergue Santiago. At the gate there is a small hole in the fence. Follow the stony track up to the castle.

15 mins, 38.5827, -5.1655 🏰📷🏯

14 CASTILLO DE BELMEZ

The ruins of Belmez castle crown a high, streaked limestone outcrop that can be seen from every side of the surrounding flatlands and farmsteads. Once part of the Córdoban line of defence during the Christian conquest, the surviving castle dates from the 15th century and was

uncharacteristically rebuilt by Napoleon's army during its occupation. It barely survived the quarrying which has eroded much of the hillside. A zigzagging path leads up to its beautiful if windy views from the battlements. A heavy iron gate will swing open but watch out for a few sheer drops within the ruins.

→ Park at the end of Calle Castillo in Belmez and walk up a paved path to the castle. Open, not ticketed.
15 mins, 38.2742, -5.2128 🏕️🎒📷

15 TORRE DEL BEATO

Several medieval Islamic watchtowers survive hidden in the undergrowth of the Córdobese hills. This sacred tower, *beato* means blessed, is hidden among herbs and wildflowers and is so named as a holy hermit was said to have lived here. Follow a path to this hideout through holm oak, rockroses and wild thyme.

→ Along the CO-3014 from Córdoba turn R on to a dirt track at 37.9171, -4.8595. Follow for 100m, park and take the path through the bushes on the L.
2 mins, 37.9172, -4.8602 ⛰️✝️📷🚶

16 TORRE DE LAS SIETE ESQUINAS

Part of the same defensive belt as Torre del Beato, this 9th-century Islamic watchtower offers spectacular views across the valley of the Guadalquivir and the ancient routes to Medina Azhara. An enemy would have been seen from miles away. On clear days you can see as far as the snowy Sierra Nevada.

→ From the petrol station at Trassierra take the CO-3314 N. Turn R after 650m and continue to the Mirador de Las Niñas. Park here. Just before the mirador, on the L, is a break in the fence. Follow the footpath downhill through woodland.
10 mins, 37.9074, -4.8546 ⛰️🏕️📷

17 CASTILLO DE EL VACAR

A low, sandy-gold castle crowns the grassy hill outside El Vacar and looks out to the sierra and the reservoir of Puente Nuevo. Built during the reign of the Caliphate of Córdoba, possibly by al-Hakam II in the 10th century or even earlier, it was conquered in the 13th century by Fernando III. Now used as a sheepfold, only four high walls and towers remain. It is an impressive spot for a picnic and the GR48 hiking trail passes by here.

→ From Cerro Muriano take the N-432 N towards Espiel for 14km and take exit 241.

Turn L at signs for El Vacar and cross under the bridge. Follow the road R, parallel with the main road, for 2km to reach a track for the castle. Park where you can and wander up to the ruins.
10 mins, 38.0852, -4.8615 🏕️📷🚶🚴🏕️

HILLTOP HIGHS

18 PEÑÓN DE PEÑARROYA-PUEBLONUEVO

A track winds up through rockroses, wild lavender and olive trees to this limestone crag overlooking the old coal mining town of Peñarroya-Pueblonuevo. Sheltered in the east face of the rock is a cave known as Abrigo de la Virgen with 4,000-year-old cave paintings. They are gated off but the views across to Belmez castle are stunning. The intact machine-gun shelter at the summit beneath the Falange cross is a reminder of its darker, recent past. The land below was the site of a failed Republican offensive in 1939 and a controversial cross still crowns the hill.

→ From Peñarroya-Pueblonuevo follow Calle Almanzor uphill for 1km to its peak, marked by the white cross. For the cave, follow the track down the side of the hill, keeping close to the east face of the rock. After a little way a track on your R (38.3198, -5.2875) leads to the shelter.
40 mins, 38.3196, -5.2880 ✝️📷🚶🏕️

19 CASTILLO DE MIRAMONTES

Surveying the vast rocky belt of the Sierra Morena, Miramontes, or literally 'look at mountains', this ruin was originally a Muslim castle. It later became a stronghold for highwaymen, robbers and later the local lords tasked with their submission. Eventually the Catholic Monarchs razed the rebellious castle to the ground in 1478. What little remains is now lorded over by eagles and vultures. This airy realm feels a world removed from the humdrum of Santa Eufemia below.

→ Take the CO-9027, which runs up the side of Restaurante La Paloma in Santa Eufemia. After 900m turn R and follow the track uphill, park and hike up.
15 mins, 38.6056, -4.9147 🏕️✝️⛰️📺📷

ANCIENT & SACRED

20 DOLMEN DE LA CASA DE DON PEDRO

This colossal passage tomb formed by several huge flint-knapped monoliths is now sheltered by a tin roof. The people who hoisted these stones into place over 4,300 years ago were the first farmers to settle on this land. There are still calves and sheep in the fields so remember to close the gate! The Camino de Santiago passes by.

→ Take the road that runs down the side of the bullring out of Belmez and keep straight on for 2km. The dolmen is signed on the L.
1 min, 38.2492, -5.1994 🏕️🚴✝️🚶

21 DOLMEN DE LA FUENTE DEL CORCHO

Dating from the same time as the Don Pedro dolmen, this long barrow is in a small corral alongside calves and sheep. Open to the sky and with views across to Belmez castle, it lies along the Camino de Santiago.

→ See directions to Dolmen de la Casa de Don Pedro and follow the track for 2km to the dolmen signed at the Godcake, the grassy tuft

in the road, on the R. It is on private land but you can enter. Close the gate for the animals.
5 mins, 38.2295, -5.2019

22 ERMITA DE LA VIRGEN DE LAS CRUCES

Dozens of storks nest in the trees, fences and belltower of Ermita Virgen de las Cruces. There is a small museum here with late Roman, Celtiberian and early Christian findings from the nearby settlement. Opposite is a grassy picnic area with tables and a children's slide. Come on 1 May for the pilgrimage festivities from El Guijo.
→ From the Ayuntamiento in El Guijo follow Calle Virgen de las Cruces north out of town and then turn R onto the CO-7100, follow for 6km until the hermitage. Parking.
1 min, 38.5388, -4.7482

23 PIEDRA HORADADA

This huge, hooped quartzite rock offers a natural seat from which to take in the views of the Sierra Morena around the Guadalmellato river. The rock, stained with malachite and azurite quartz veins, has become emblematic of this town and its copper-mining history. Back uphill towards the town and the Copper Museum, you will pass the ruins of the 19th-century mines.
→ Park by the Centro de la 3 Edad in Cerro Muriano and follow the track through the gates, past the mines and downhill for 300m.
10 mins, 38.0016, -4.7630

HIDDEN CHAPELS

24 LAS ERMITAS DE CÓRDOBA

On the slopes of the Sierra Morena, overlooking the city of Córdoba, sits this prayerful and peaceful hermitage. Founded in the 18th century, it has several monks' cells in gardens filled with cypress trees, memento mori and quotes from Saint John of the Cross. Hermits and monks have lived reclusive lives in these hills since at least the 9th century, seeking refuge under Muslim rule. After a dramatic escape from prison in the 16th century, the poet and mystic Saint John of the Cross was sent by Saint Teresa de Ávila to reform the Andalucían Carmelite order. This hermitage still belongs to the order of the Barefoot Carmelites, reformed by saints Teresa and John, which has roots in the tradition of the Desert Fathers. Donation entry €1.50.
→ From Córdoba take the CO-3405 N into the hills for 10km and turn off at signs for Las Ermitas. Parking.
5 mins, 37.9159, -4.8240

25 ERMITA DE LA VIRGEN DE LAS VEREDAS

A peaceful chapel sanctuary next to the river with grassy banks. The river is covered with white water-crowfoot flowers in spring and rings to a chorus of frogs at night. A footpath runs over the river from the chapel and winds up through rockroses and wild lavender to a cross with views out across the valley. Local legend says a shepherd and his dog discovered a small statue of the Virgin here. Leaving his flock with the dog, he repeatedly ran back to town with the figurine in his satchel, but each time she evaded capture and miraculously reappeared back in the hills with his flock and the dog. Known as the Virgin of the Pathways, she guards those travelling the paths among the wildflowers.
→ From Torrecampo take the CO-7103 N. After 5km turn R at the sign and continue for 3km to the parking.
10 mins, 38.5241, -4.6450

MOUNTAIN TOWNS

26 MONTORO

Rising up above a bend in the Guadalquivir river, Montoro is a beautiful and vibrant town that was under Muslim rule until 1240. Narrow streets and heavy doors hide colourful, flowering patios, dogs watch from balconies and votive candles blink from shrines under the long shadows cast by the sun. Don't miss the Casa de las Conchas: the entire house – stairs, ceiling and flowerpots – is decorated with millions of scallop shells rescued from a truck accident in 1957. It is the painstaking work and legacy of the late owner, Francisco del Río Cuenca. The Archaeology museum, located in the 13th-century church of Santa María de la Mota, is great. The Plaza de España is bordered by the Gothic–Mudéjar parish church and the elaborate facade of the old ducal palace. A couple of bars here offer shade and tapas.
→ Regular buses run from Córdoba to Montoro. There is parking signed off the N-420, along Calle Herrerías, as you arrive from Córdoba.
5 mins, 38.0253, -4.3814

LOST VILLAGES

27 EL TEJAR, AZUEL

Follow a brook into the gardens of José Ruís Cañada on the outskirts of the pretty village of Azuel, with its views of the Sierra de Cardeña y Montoro. Open to the community, the gardens are lovingly tended by Cañada, a local life force and artist. There are lots of nooks and crannies

to explore as well as a grassy outdoor theatre with several kilns set in the earth, like hobbit houses. Keep an eye out for posters in the village as local events are often held here.

➜ Park where the Calle de la Esperanza bends, near the lending library, and follow the footpath behind the sculptures up into the garden.

2 mins, 38.3227, -4.3281 ⊞⏩⊞

28 ALDEA DEL CEREZO

The only way to reach this hamlet, which was abandoned in the 1960s, is along a dusty track from Cardeña. The heavy granite walls of its cottages once offered refuge to local shepherds during the seasonal movement of livestock. Hidden in the Sierra de Cardeña y Montoro Natural Park, it lies at the crossroads of several signed hiking trails. The Sendero Vegueta del Fresno is a great 4.4km walk from the village, following streams and passing through cornicabra olive trees to the Río Yeguas. This wild woodland interspersed with *bolos*, mossy granite boulders, is home to many creatures including lynx, wolf, otter and eagle. Oleander, ash, myrtle and rockroses lead down to the Río Yeguas, which marks the border of the Córdoba and Jaén provinces, the end of the natural park,

and is one of Andalucía's wildest jewels.

➜ From Cardeña take the Camino Aldea del Cerezo for 7km to the village.

1.5 hrs, 38.2557, -4.2526 ⊞⏩⛰⛲

29 CASTILLO DE UBAL, OBEJO

Chimney smoke fills the narrow streets of Obejo, a white-washed village perched on a hill overlooking a sea of olive trees. Hugging the hillside is what remains of the old Islamic castle, its origins obscure; possibly the remoteness appealed to those wishing to hide the spoils of Córdoba's mined mineral wealth. Legend tells of how the church nearby was a permanent hideout for Christians seeking refuge in the last days of the caliphate. The GR48 footpath leads here from Adamuz and passes the Guadalmellato reservoir.

➜ Park at the end of Calle Al-Andalus, at the viewpoint by the church to San Antonio Abad, and walk down the path running alongside to the L, then scramble up the hill to the ruin.

2 mins, 38.1348, -4.8007 ⊞⏸⛲⛲

RUSTIC RESTAURANTS

30 RESTAURANTE BAR X

A welcoming bar and restaurant with guest rooms upstairs, run by Juan José and his family. The food is truly 'soul food', made with the best local produce. The bar itself is rustic and characterful. Juan José has decorated the bedrooms upstairs in the three main themes of the Cerro Muriano: mining, the Camino Santiago and Robert Capa, a photojournalist. It was in Cerro Muriano that Capa, along with his partner Gerda Caro, took the iconic shot 'Falling Soldier' in 1936. The bar lies along the Camino Santiago. Closed Fri.

➔ Calle Carretera, 8, 14029 Cerro Muriano, 957 350 188, Restaurantebarx.es
38.0042, -4.7705

31 RESTAURANTE EL CANDIL

A small, dark bar, relatively unassuming from the outside, hides a sun-filled patio. Here the owner, Paco, grills *carnes de la monte* (fresh local cuts of meat), while further inside is a restaurant with an open fireplace. Try *arroz con javalí* (rice with wild boar), *carnes de la monte* (grilled game) or a lighter option, *sopa de ajo* (garlic soup). Book ahead if you plan to visit at the weekend. Closed Tue.

➔ CO-3402, 18, 14011 Córdoba, 957 730 044
37.9267, -4.8982

32 RESTAURANTE SOL ZAPATILLA

Miguel and María run a foodie's heaven, with views from the balcony over Montoro and the Guadalquivir river. They offer great traditional dishes using local produce, including wild mushrooms and venison, and accompanied by regional wines.

➔ Calle Calvario 2 Montoro, 14600 Montoro, 957 161 279, Restaurantesolzapatilla.com
38.0267, -4.3777

33 MESÓN BRIGADIER EL CONDESITO

A vaulted bar with low ceilings and ancient walls. During the civil war it functioned as a refuge for nuns and afterwards as a prison for Republicans. In the 1960s it existed briefly as a disco and now Quique runs a great restaurant. It was voted Best Local Bar in 2019 and has featured in various Spanish history podcasts. Look out for the floor tiles with Republican graffiti detailing their escape to the Peñarroya caves. The local pork dish, *lechón de los Pedroches*, is excellent. Closed Mon.

➔ Calle Brigadier Romero, 6, 14270 Hinojosa del Duque, 722 502 095
38.5018, -5.1489

34 MESÓN VICTORIA

A small restaurant and bar opposite the parish church offering heaped dishes of fried fish and good local *raciones* for sharing. The *bacalao frito* (fried cod) is great. Closed Tue.

➔ Plaza Iglesia de la Anunciacion, 14240 Belmez, 664 045 124
38.2732, -5.2089

RURAL HAVENS

35 HACIENDA LA COLORÁ

A beautifully remote 19th-century olive-oil estate converted into a guesthouse with generous rooms with high ceilings. Its winding 3km driveway passes through rockroses, wild lavender and endless olive groves before reaching its cobbled courtyard with flowering bougainvillea. As well as a pool, there are pergolas, hammocks and plenty of footpaths down to the Arenoso lake. This is a wild and luxurious haven.

➔ Calle Adamuz, 9, 14600 Montoro, 600 813 031, Facebook.com/Hacienda-La-Color%C3%A1-108300814204810
38.0624, -4.4379

36 CORTIJO DEL ZOCO BAJO

A traditional country house running off solar energy, with a salt-water pool and chickens in the gardens. It is close to many footpaths running into Los Pedroches. Sleeps 18.

➔ Carretera de Pozoblanco Belmez, 14400 Pozoblanco, 630 426 391, Zocobajo.com
38.3665, -4.8667

37 CASA MIRADOR LOS TOMILLOS

The last house in Azuel before the village ends and the sierra begins. The owners, Antonio and Esperanza, are an active part of the native wolf and lynx rewilding projects. Visit the village in early summer for the Noche de San Juan festivities, where the fountains are blessed and filled with flowers.

➔ C. de Bellavista, 24, 14447 Azuel, 637 789 559, Casaruralmiradordelostomillos.com
38.3233, -4.3308

38 POSÁ LA ENCINA

The simple marble steps of this guesthouse lead straight out onto the sun-filled town square. Tables and chairs of three bars spill out onto the cobbles, and the windows of the guesthouse are open to evening birdsong and the bells of the nearby parish church.

→ Plaza de la Independencia, 9, 14445
Cardeña, 652 887 919
38.2706, -4.3236 ⊞¶▮♥⛰

WILDER RETREATS

39 ALBERGUE DE ESPIEL

This converted station house by the overgrown train tracks outside Espiel and next to the Puente Nuevo reservoir is a climber's haven. The line used to serve the once-thriving mining industry but now the limestone rocks of the Sierra de Castillo offer some of the best climbing in Andalucía. This hostel offers bunk beds and dorms, but also a couple of cottages, a treetop adventure park, access to the lake and movie nights at the terrace and pool. There is home-cooked food in the canteen and canoes for hire.

→ Carr. de la Estación, km.3, 14220 Espiel, 957 363 589, Alberg-deespiel.com
38.1767, -5.0467 ⛰🚣▮¶👣⛰♥🌿♿

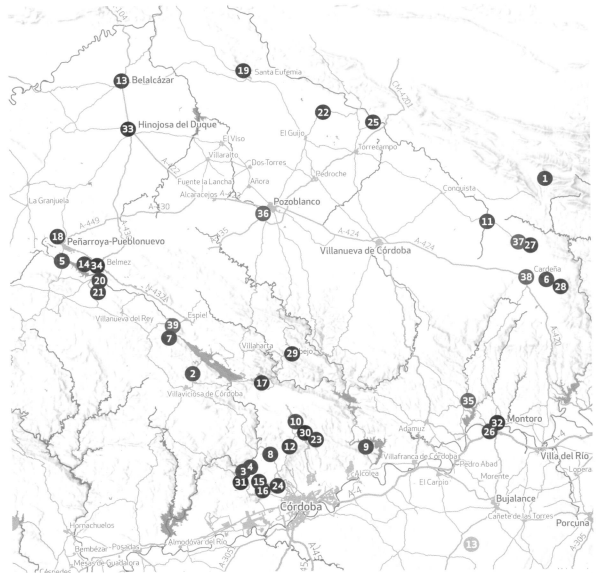

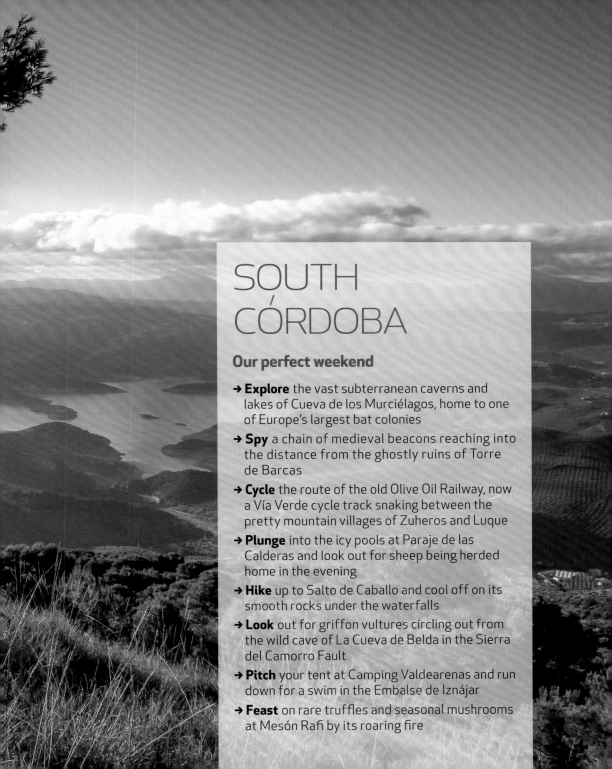

SOUTH CÓRDOBA

Our perfect weekend

→ **Explore** the vast subterranean caverns and lakes of Cueva de los Murciélagos, home to one of Europe's largest bat colonies

→ **Spy** a chain of medieval beacons reaching into the distance from the ghostly ruins of Torre de Barcas

→ **Cycle** the route of the old Olive Oil Railway, now a Vía Verde cycle track snaking between the pretty mountain villages of Zuheros and Luque

→ **Plunge** into the icy pools at Paraje de las Calderas and look out for sheep being herded home in the evening

→ **Hike** up to Salto de Caballo and cool off on its smooth rocks under the waterfalls

→ **Look** out for griffon vultures circling out from the wild cave of La Cueva de Belda in the Sierra del Camorro Fault

→ **Pitch** your tent at Camping Valdearenas and run down for a swim in the Embalse de Iznájar

→ **Feast** on rare truffles and seasonal mushrooms at Mesón Rafi by its roaring fire

The limestone massifs of the Sierras Subbéticas Natural Park lie to the south of the Córdoba province. Over millennia, rivers have eroded this karstic rock to form a landscape riddled with chasms, caves, crags, channels and crevices. Recognised by UNESCO and ZEPA (Zone for the Special Protection of Birds) for its rich history and wildlife, its 32,000 hectares are home to kestrels, eagle owls and peregrine falcons, which nest in the steep ravines, and colonies of griffon vultures, which shelter in the grey- and ochre-streaked cliffs at Las Buitreras. Some of Spain's largest bat colonies live in the shadowy recesses of the caves of Belda and of Murciélago. Pottery, tools and Neanderthal bones were found at Cueva de Belda; it is dizzying to think that these bat colonies saw the arrival of some of the earliest humans to these caves.

Water has played a vital role in forming the Subbéticas. Gigantic folds of an ancient seafloor emerged five millennia ago to form the peaks of Pico la Tiñosa, Peñon del Abuchite and Picacho Virgen de la Sierra, now with its annual pilgrimage. Traces of this Jurassic sea can be seen in hundreds of ammonite fossils, and at Lapiaz de los Lanchares, a bed of oolitic limestone, you can see grains of sand and fossils. With perfect circularity, these peaks once raised by water have been slowly eroded by water to form caves, canyons and sinkholes. Just outside the pretty white village of Zuheros the River Bailón has carved a deep canyon through cliffs. A footpath leads upriver towards La Nava de Cabra, a beautiful karstic depression that leads to the hidden waterfall of Las Chorreras. If you want a longer swim, head south to the glittering, warm waters of Embalse de Iznájar, Andalucía's largest reservoir.

In medieval times the crags of the Sierras Subbéticas provided a natural border between the newly conquered Christian territories and the Nasrid kingdom of Granada. A web of watchtowers, known as *atalayas* or *almenara*, still stands guard over the valleys and ravines, the natural passages through which enemies crept to attack. Looking out on to these hollow ruins in the winter months when low clouds and mists gather in the valleys is particularly evocative, as their history is filled with crackling smoke and hastily lit fires. Rather than providing a line of defence, their purpose was to communicate; fires and billowing smoke would have conveyed the message over the hills faster than any attack. The towers of Barcas, Uclés and Canute are some of the beautiful examples of this heritage and high spots from which to watch the sunset over the olive groves.

More modern lines of connection can be seen in the 19th-century railway once used for transporting olive oil and now converted to a cycle route, La Vía Verde de la Subbética. The cycle path connects the villages of the Subbéticas and was crucial during the Spanish Civil War. It passes through tunnels, picnic parks and ruined bunkers outside Luque, which are eerily quiet at dusk.

Aniseed, marzipan, turron and chocolate are the sweet flavours of the Subbéticas, making it a great Christmas destination. This is especially so in Rute, which hosts the world's largest nativity made entirely from chocolate. It also has the renowned Machaquito distillery, which has been perfuming the streets with its aniseed and cherry drink for over 160 years. After hiking up to the castle at Poblado de Algar, return to Mesón Rafi below to feast on local fare. Some typical dishes of the Subbéticas include *el potaje de habichuelas* (bean stew), *mojete de patatas* (fried potatoes with a delicious garlic and paprika sauce) and *chivo en salsa* (stewed goat).

3

RIVERS & RAVINES

1 PUENTE CALIFAL DE CARCABUEY

This small horseshoe-arched bridge, hidden deep in the olive groves outside Carcabuey, is all that remains of a once busy trading route during the 10th-century Córdoban calipahte. The bridge crosses the Palancar stream to link Cabra, Carcabuey and Priego with Córdoba.

→ The 7km footpath, SL-A 259, passes by on a circular route out from Carcabuey, signed from Calle Arenal.

2 hrs, 37.4608, -4.2702 🌐🚶

2 CASCADAS DE LA NEVERA DE LA TOMASA

Over time the River Genilla has dug a deep ravine through the rock of the Sierra Horconera. It plunges down between abandoned mills and undergrowth. Brambles climb around willow, tamarind and fig trees. In winter the waterfalls course with excess water running off the bordering limestone and it is a popular place for canyoning.

→ Call OcioAventura Cerro Gordo for canyoning, +34 655 614 837, Ocioaventuracerrogordo.com.

15 mins, 37.4419, -4.2378 🏊🚶🏕️📷

3 CAÑÓN DEL RÍO BAILÓN, ZUHEROS

Beyond the Poljé de la Nava de Cabra the Bailón river carves a way through the narrow canyon at this picturesque spot just before Zuheros. Formed over millions of years, the caves and several pools are suitable for short, bracing swims. At this point the river becomes subterranean and there is water only after heavy rain, so it is best to visit in the winter months for a swim. Several walking routes to Las Chorreras and Cueva del Fraile start from here.

→ Parking is available at the small bridge over the Bailón (37.5408, -4.3172) before you enter Zuheros from the direction of Doña Mencía.

15 mins, 37.5396, -4.3168 🚶🏊🚗🥾

2

4 LAS CHORRERAS DEL RÍO BAILÓN

In the middle of the Poljé de la Nava de Cabra, a vast karstic depression, resides this gem of a hidden waterfall. The River Bailón winds through low fields peppered with limestone rocks, known as Lapiaz de los Lanchares, and marshland prone to floods, even sinkholes, to reach this refreshing scene. Hidden by wild olives, a tributary spring falls in thin ribbons over limestone and bright-green moss to fill a tiny pool before joining the river. It's a

4

great picnic stop if doing the 12km hike to Zuheros.

→ The 12km linear Sendero del Río Bailón passes by this waterfall, which is located more or less in the middle of the route. You can either start the walk near the Sanctuario de Nuestra Señora de la Sierra (parking at 37.4836, -4.3756) to walk through the Poljé and marshlands (5km) or start the walk from Zuheros (parking at 37.5407, -4.3173) (see Cañón del Río Bailón entry) to walk through the limestone canyons, following the river (7km). Both are very well signed.
1.5 hrs, 37.5086, -4.352 🔷🧗‍♂️🔦

5 PARAJE DE LAS CALDERAS

South over the Córdoba border with Granada runs the Arroyo de Los Morales, cascading to fill pools along the ancient limestone canyon as far as the village of Algarinejo. Narrow footpaths and wooden bridges follow the river, providing easy access to various spots for a dip. Water energy has been harnessed here since Roman times, but the most lasting change was made during Al-Andalus, with the water channels known locally as 'caces'. In the evening sheep are herded home along the river. Visit on May 15th for la romería de San Isidro, where locals celebrate mass in Algarinejo and follow the river on foot (food, fiesta, flamenco dresses) to reach the source by the 17th-century gardens at Casa Rural El Tajil.

→ The 2km footpath, Ruta de los Molinos y Arroyos, along the river is signed from the church, Iglesia Santa María La Mayor, in Algarinejo, as this is where the pilgrimage on May 15th begins.
30 mins, 37.3362, -4.1617 🔷🔦🧗‍♂️📷

6 SALTO DEL CABALLO

An ancient cattle droveway and Roman way lead up through the gnarled olives of the Caicena valley to a spectacular waterfall rushing over limestone steps to a plunge pool below. This place was considered sacred by the pre-Roman Iberians, and there are several rock-cut tombs at the top of the waterfall.

→ Park at the Museo Histórico-Arqueológico de Almedinilla (itself worth a visit) and follow the footpath signs from Salto del Caballo.
1.2km.
30 mins, 37.4267, -4.0845 🔷🔦🧗‍♂️🚴‍♂️🌿

7 EMBALSE DE IZNÁJAR

A long beach leads gradually down to this glorious freshwater reservoir. At 32km long, it is the largest in Andalucía and the second largest in Spain. Surrounded by low hills and reflecting the sky, the water for all its size is warm, the sun sparkling through gentle ripples. It is a great place for kids, with shallow entry and a small wooden jetty for jumps. You can rent kayaks by the campsite and there are a couple of restaurants nearby.

→ From Iznájar head NE on the A-333, then take the first L signposted 'Escuela de Vela Valdearenas de Iznájar'. Continue for two minutes then turn L at a wooden sign marked 'Playa'. The massive beach is in front of you and to your L is Camping Valdearenas de Iznájar, Campingvaldearenas.es. Kayak rental from Alua.es.
2 mins, 37.2630, -4.3236 🔷🏕️🍴🔷🏖️🛶

8 CUEVA DE LA ENCANTADA

A 40m-deep fissure in the rocks hides Neolithic paintings just down from Plaza de España in Luque. The ochre cave paintings survive at eye level, perfect for kids.

→ Open for small tours on Saturday and Sunday mornings, €1. See Cordoba24.info/luque/html/cueva.html for times or call 957 667 574.
5 mins, 37.5599, -4.2766 🚗🚴‍♂️

11

9 CUEVA DE LOS MURCIÉLAGOS

A vast cave system at the top of the Cañada de Malos Vientos mountain just behind Zuheros. It is dripping with stalactites and stalagmites and has several subterranean lakes. Valued for its beauty and geology, the cave system is home to a stalagmite known as 'the asparagus', which is over 4m high. It is also valued for its archaeology and wildlife: four species of bat shelter here and there are ancient paintings dating from the 6th to 2nd millennium BC. Burial remains show human habitation from around 35,000 years ago.

→ Due to conservation it is necessary to reserve your ticket. Call 957 694 545 or email turismo@zuheros.es, Wed – Sun, 10am – 1.30pm.

3 mins, 37.5421, -4.3040

10 CUEVA DE BELDA

The dark entrance to this 200m-long karstic cavern yawns open at the peak of the Sierra del Camorro Fault. High domes and columns of stalactites lead into darker, humid chambers. At the cave mouth the ochre- and grey-streaked limestone and dolomite cliff drops sharply away. Griffon vultures and peregrine falcons can be seen circling out over the tops of the Aleppo pines below. This massif was formed during the early Jurassic period, about 200 million years ago. The cave today is host to a huge bat colony, which once shared this cave with some of the first humans sheltering here. Bronze Age axes and much older flint tools relating to Neanderthals have been found in the cave. The surrounding hills are host to a network of trails.

→ From Cuevas de San Marcos take the MA-202 towards Embalse de Iznájar. After 300m keep R and follow signs for the Centro de Interpretacion. Park at the centre, follow yellow signed footpath (PR-A 234) on L for 1km to the metal staircase up to the cave.

20 mins, 37.256, -4.4023

11 CUEVA DEL FRAILE

Eagle owls, peregrine falcons and kestrels shelter in the canyon created by the River Bailón just outside Zuheros. There are many caves in the sides of this ravine, but the Cueva del Fraile stands out for the stalagmite at its entrance that resembles, they say, a hooded figure or friar.

→ Starting from Zuheros, this is at about 1.3km following the Sendero del Río Bailón trail signed from the picnic area just before the river as you enter Zuheros from Doña Mencía.

25 mins, 37.5341, -4.3181

8

10

14

12 DOLMEN DE LA DEHESA DE LA LASTRA

A small but well-preserved passage grave made with local limestone and surrounded by epic mountain views of the Subbéticas. Excavations have yielded nothing but a few prehistoric teeth, which might be explained by the presence of a huge colony of griffon vultures just 1km to the west, on the south face of the limestone cliffs of Cerro de Abuchite, Las Buitreras. This dolmen is a great place to watch the birds and can be reached by following the Sendero Las Buitreras, which links Luque with Carcabuey.

→ The footpath Las Buitreras is signed from the town swimming pool at Luque and it is 17km in total. You will reach the dolmen after 9km.

2.5 hrs, 37.5063, -4.2502 🏊🚶♂🦅

CASTLES & WATCHTOWERS

13 TORRE DE ALBOLAFIA

A medieval watchtower, possibly built under Muslim rule, surveys a serene sea of olive groves. Stars of David and crucifixes are graffitied on its masonry, and a couple of owls nest inside the ruins. It's a lovely spot for sunset. Watch out for the opening in the ground to the old cellars.

→ Follow the dirt track from main road for 3km and then park at the crossroads and walk up.

2 mins, 37.8247, -4.426 📷➕🏔

14 TORRE DEL CANUTO

A beautiful, high beacon which would have played a key part in the medieval border struggles. Most likely built under Nasrid rule in the 14th century, it would have had clear views of the road between Iznájar and Priego and been difficult to access on foot. It is a glorious location for sunset, with hazy blue views out to the Iznájar embalse. In spring gorse and wild iris flower on the steep hillside.

→ A 4km footpath, the Sendero Pinar de Rute, is signed from the Area Recreativa Fuente Alta (37.3366, -4.3574). At this picnic park you can see some old Arabic ruins built on the Visigothic remains of old Rute. The footpath winds through the pine woodland and passes a donkey sanctuary.

3.5 hrs, 37.3311, -4.3531 📷➕🚶♂🏞

15 CASTILLO DE CARCABUEY

The ruins of this 13th-century castle crown a rocky outcrop above Carcabuey's white rooftops. Deep in the heart of the Sierra Subbética, this strategically located castle and prominent hill have a history reaching far back to pre-Christian times. The hill has hidden Phoenician funerary urns and Roman tombstones, but most impressive is the Bronze Age long sword now kept in the British Museum. You can look out towards La Tiñosa, the highest peak in the Córdoba province. Visit the second week in September for the procession of the Virgen.

→ A cobbled street called Calle Virgen leads up from the main town square to the hermitage dedicated to the Virgin, who miraculously appeared in the castle walls.

15 mins, 37.4445, -4.2708 ➕⛰🏞

16 CASTILLO DE ALGAR

A footpath leads along olive groves and then through rougher rosemary and rockroses to reach the ruined remains of this 12th-century Nasrid castle. From here there are beautiful views out to the Subbéticas and Sierra de Gallinera with its caves, cliffs and rock shelters. Bronze Age as well as Roman findings here have revealed a long history. The 1.2km SL-A 263 footpath passes by and leads to Algar hamlet below.

→ Park in Poblado de Algar and follow the footpath past Mesón Rafi and up the hill. At

the houses turn L and follow track through olive groves to the castle.

20 mins, 37.4168, -4.3289 🖼🚶⚙📡

17 TORRE DE BARCAS

The remains of a beautiful 14th-century watchtower crown the olive groves north of Priego. Bolstered by heavy masonry, it stands sentinel on what would have been the medieval Christian border with the Nazarí Kingdom of Granada. The River Salado rushes by below, and the small hill commands panoramic views over the green hills and grey watchtowers. Above the entrance sits the Casa de Aguilar crest, a shield, once red and gold, held by a black eagle. A lovely place for sunset.

→ From Luque take the CO-8209 S towards Carcabuey. At the crossroads follow signs for Fuente Alhama and park after 2km at the information board. About 200m up the road there is a dirt track on the R into the olive grove.

5 mins, 37.5011, -4.2008 📡🖼⚙

18 TORRE DE UCLÉS O DE JAUJA

This medieval watchtower is perched on the dramatic limestone ridge surveying what would have been the ancient trade route from Cabra via Carcabuey to Priego. Even today, glimpsed from the road, it is enigmatic. The steep climb is rewarded by beautiful views from the tower surrounded by rockroses and rough herbs.

→ From Priego take the A-339 for 2.5km in the direction of Carcabuey. Turn R at signs for Los Villares. Park after 600m and follow the footpath uphill. At the fork keep right along the tiny track.

20 mins, 37.4382, -4.2409 🖼🚶⚙📡🖼⚙

19 CASTILLO DE ZAMBRA

The thousand-year-old dark ruins of this crumbling castle are visible from miles around. Today an 11th-century keep survives, built towards the end of the Córdoban caliphate, but occupation of this small hill reaches back to the Romans at least. The vanished Roman town of Cisimbrum, once nearby, survives only as a distant echo in the current name, Zambra. Today very little remains but you can crawl into a ruined chamber with great views out to the Subbética mountains.

→ From Lucena, take the A-331 towards Rute and pass through Los Llanos de Don Juan. Turn R for Las Salinas and follow the CP-4 for 700m. Turn L at sign for 'Punto Limpio'. After 1km, park where you can and turn L on to a track. After 90m or so you will reach the

shortest way through the olive groves to the tower. Scramble climb.

10 mins, 37.3907, -4.3944 🖼📧❖❓

20 BÚNKERES DE CERRO DEL ACEITUNILLO

A couple of domed concrete bunkers connected by underground passages and built by Francist troops in the Civil War are hidden in olive groves outside Luque. Now a peaceful spot with sunset views and birdsong, they are a sombre reminder of the Olive Campaign, an offensive led by Queipo de Llano to clear the Republicans from the countryside around Córdoba. The Olive Oil Greenway (Vía Verde cycle route) passes by.

→ From Luque take Calle Pozo Cortes to the N-432. Turn L and after 700m turn R on to the dirt track before Nichol's Hostel and Restaurante. Park where you can and follow the track up and R for 400m. The bunkers are in the olive groves to the R.

5 mins, 37.5744, -4.2567 ❖🖼

FLORA & FAUNA

21 JARDÍN MICOLÓGICO LA TRUFA

A museum and gardens dedicated to the conservation of the fungi of Andalucía.

With over 3,500 types of fungi, the Subbéticas are an incredibly rich mycological site and 'La Trufa' owes its name to the summer truffle, which is found in endemic holm oak woodland. Here you can explore gardens containing wood ear, shaggy ink caps and various boletus, as well as exhibitions recreating the ecosystems of Andalucía.

→ Calle el Batán, 86, 14816 Priego de Córdoba, Córdoba, 671 599 562. Open Tues – Sun, 10am – 2pm.

1 min, 37.4825, -4.2345 ❖🔄

22 CENTRO CICLOTURISTA, VÍA VERDE DEL ACEITE

At this point, the 120km cycle route along the disused Olive Oil Railway passes a picnic park, campervan overnight stop and a great bike rental shop in the foothills of the Subbéticas. There is also a restaurant and children's playpark. The shop sells campervan accessories and local products. Overnight stay with van from €3.

→ Antigua estación FFCC, 14860 Doña Mencía, Córdoba, 691 843 532

1 min, 37.5464, -4.3517 🍴🅿❖🔄

23 IBERFAUNA

Here you can see Iberian wolves, otters, lynx, foxes, roe deer, genets, mouflon, raptors and other species endemic to the Sierras Subbéticas that are threatened with extinction but given a second chance here.

→ Ctra. De la Cueva, km 0.5, 14870 Zuheros, 957 112 487, Iberfauna.es

1 min, 37.5422, -4.3120 🔄💶

RURAL RESTAURANTS

24 RESTAURANTE LOS CABAÑAS

A rustic restaurant in the pretty village of Almedinilla, serving hearty meat dishes and using local produce. Several legs of *jamón* (ham) are usually for sale as well as local oils, honey, olives and cheeses.

→ Ronda de Andalucía, 62 Bajo, 14812 Almedinilla, 957 702 067, Restauranteloscabanas.com

37.4397, -4.0946 ❖🍴❗

25 MESÓN PUERTA DEL CONVENTO

In the beautiful old town of Benamejí this rustic restaurant serves seasonal dishes and hearty *raciones* or sharing plates. Try the *chuletitas de Cordero* or *Chivo a lo Castuera*,

both traditional ways of cooking lamb from the Subbéticas.

→ C. Padre Esteban, 12, 14910 Benamejí, 957 530 864, Mesonpuertadelconvento.com
37.2661, -4.5419 🔲🍴🍷👤

26 BAR CASA ADELINA, CARCABUEY

A friendly bar and restaurant with outside seating on the plaza in Carcabuey. Serves generous classic dishes, *calamares*, *boquerones*, *patatas bravas* and grilled meats at great prices.

→ Plaza de España, 9, 14810 Carcabuey, 600 751 632
37.4437, -4.2733 🔲🍴🍷🚶

27 MESÓN RAFI

A great place to restore your strength after hiking up to Algar castle. Poblado de Algar is a tiny hamlet sheltering in the foothills of the Subbéticas. Visit in winter to try seasonal dishes, such as the *setas*: wild, locally foraged mushrooms with fried potato, egg and jamón. A busy waiter whips around long, noisy tables packed with locals next to the roaring log fire. The *patatas bravas* are also excellent.

→ 14811 Poblado de Algar, 957 553 004
37.4214, -4.3276 🔲🍴🍷🚶

28 ASADOR LA MURALLA, PRIEGO DE CÓRDOBA

With seats spilling out onto the plaza by the 13th-century castle walls at Priego, this a great place to stop for lunch. Specialises in traditional Andalusian cuisine and roasts cooked in its wood oven. Don't miss the chance to visit the parish church next door with the most unexpectedly ornate Baroque chapel.

→ C. Abad Palomino, 16, 14800 Priego de Córdoba, 957 701 856, Asadorlamuralla.com
37.4394, -4.1921 🔲🍴🍷

WILDER CAMPING

29 CAMPING VALDEARENAS

A family-friendly campsite with wooden cabins, a caravan area and a good restaurant. It is right by a beautiful stretch of beach leading to the warm, sparkling waters of the reservoir Izanájar.

→ Playa Valdearenas, 14970 Iznájar, Córdoba, 657 603 704, Campingvaldearenas.es
37.2628, -4.3235 🌿🚣🍷🚻🐟🛶👤

30 CAMPING RAFTING BENAMEJÍ

A great campsite for kids in the hills outside Benamejí. There is a treetop adventure park

with ziplines and rope bridges, a swimming pool and a good restaurant, as well as footpaths down to the River Genil. Several water activities are on offer, including canyoning, rafting, paddle surfing and kayaking. The PRA-160 footpath starts here, passing a ruined medieval castle, ancient watermills and a renaissance bridge. 5km circular.

→ Carretera N-331A, km 495, 14910 Benamejí, 955 110 776, Alua.es
37.2574, -4.5341 🌿🍷🐟🚻🍴🚶🛶👤

WILD RETREATS

31 CASAS RURALES EL CAÑUELO

Five rural houses on the outskirts of the sleepy village of Carcabuey and just downhill from its castle. The bedroom windows open on to astonishing views of the Subbética mountains, and steps lead down into this view with the swimming pool and a garden with roses and lemon trees. A number of footpaths pass through the town leading to Luque, Puente Califal and through the mountains. Sleeps 2–6.

→ Paseo el Cañuelo, 14810 Carcabuey, 687 961 928
37.4434, -4.2689 🛶🚶🛶👤

32 HACIENDA MINERVA

In the heart of the Sierras Subbéticas, with views out to the mountains and the olive groves of Baena, sits this luxurious but wild retreat. The pool uses water from the nearby salt-water spring, and you can enjoy *baños arabes* (thermal baths). The excellent restaurant is in the restored olive oil warehouse at the Minerva watermill and from the terrace you can watch the moon rise over the Tajo de Bailón hills.

→ Carretera Luque-Dª Mencía, Km 9, Vía Verde de la Subbética Km 73,2, 14870 Zuheros, 957 090 951, Haciendaminerva.com
37.5428, -4.3341 🛶🚣🌿🚻🍴🍷🚶👤

33 CASA RURAL EL TAJIL

A cosy and restored rural cottage next to a natural cave and high waterfall that marks the beginning of the footpath Ruta Molinos y Arroyos to Algarinejo, which passes Las Calderas pools. Sleeps 8.

→ Km 36,200, A-4154, 18280 Algarinejo, 610 203 799, Planetrural.com
37.3414, -4.1617 🛶🚣🛶🚶👤

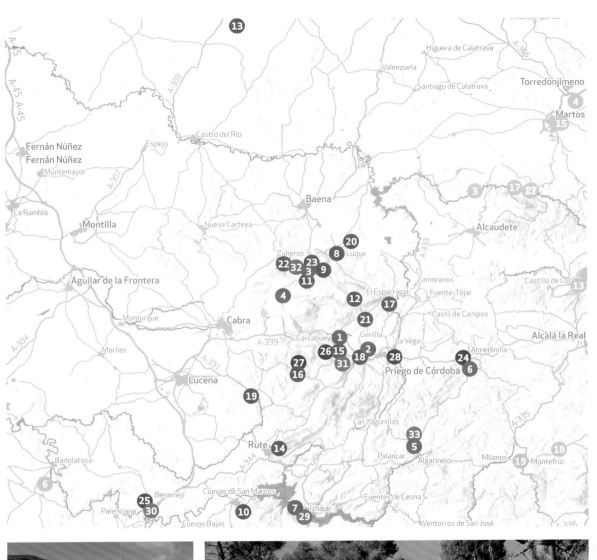

29

30

NORTH JAÉN

Our perfect weekend

→ **Listen** out for the wingbeats of vultures catching thermals as you climb up to the Vacas de Retamoso caves

→ **Enjoy** the peace at the 7th-century chapels carved into sandstone, hidden in olive groves at Valdecanales

→ **Look** down from a neighbouring cliff to the monumental waterfall Cascada la Cimbarra, spraying 20m down rock strata

→ **Picnic** under the shade along the Jándula river and look out for deer drinking from the riverbanks in the dusk

→ **Plunge** into the stone pools at El Piélago beneath the ancient arches of the Via Augusta

→ **Watch** the sun set over the Guadalimar valley from the sacred caves at Cueva de la Lobera

→ **Feast** on freshly grilled meat by the oak barrels and old beams at Restaurante Los Pinos

→ **Follow** the pilgrim way up through pine woodland and rockrose to the Sanctuary of Nuestra Señora de la Cabeza

→ **Bed** down in the cosy wooden cabins in the pine woodland at Paraje San Ginés

A narrow mountain pass that leads from the plains of La Mancha into the north of Jaén has been the scene of some of the most pivotal moments in the twists and turns of Andalucían history. Known as the gateway to Andalucía, the Desfiladero de Despeñaperros gorge is the largest breach for hundreds of miles in the blue backs of the Sierra Morena. Oak trees have taken root in the fissures and clefts of its rock, which have splintered vertically into columns called 'Los Órganos', as they resemble giant pipe organs. For one 19th-century traveller arriving here, his head reeling with tales of wolves and descending bandits, these rocks appeared as "fragments of some ruined castle of the giants".

This once perilous pass, with its sheer drops and hair-pin bends, has seen centuries of footfall. In a deciding battle against Muslim Al-Andalus, conquering Christian armies used the narrow passage's element of surprise to their advantage. They say Napoleon's invading troops halted, stunned by the scene, to salute the view. Overlooking all of this are rock shelters and hollows hiding ochre paintings. At Vacas de Retamoso, now declared a World Heritage Site, you can see some of the earliest cave paintings. Climb up to these caves and the tiny cars gliding along the asphalt river of the A-road far below seem to belong to a different time from that of these hills.

With 60 million olive trees, more than the population of Spain, Jaén is often painted in one brushstroke as a 'sea of olives', but it is much more. As well as being a physical divide between north and south, its high places and craggy peaks, bordering earth and sky, have been sought out as sacred sites for millennia. At Cueva de los Muñecos, a forest path leads down through mastic and kermes oaks, rosemary and rockrose, to a cave where thousands of bronze votive idols once filled its nooks and crannies, hidden for over 3,000 years.

Many modern offerings of flowers, candles and photographs continue to be left by pilgrims at a ruined side chapel at the hilltop sanctuary of the Virgen de la Cabeza. Leafy trees reach through the holes in its vaulted ceiling. Queen of the Sierra Morena, she is regarded as a deity, her *romería* (pilgrimage) being the oldest in Spain. From here you can watch the sun set over the Sierra de Andújar, home to the endangered Iberian lynx, wild boar and deer. Camp out in the sierra below for dark skies and great stargazing. Deer come to drink at the Jándula river in the twilight, and at dawn the trees are alive with forest birds, chaffinches and firecrests.

Follow the GR-48 footpath to reach Baños de la Encina with its mighty 10th-century fortress, Bury Al-Hamma, above a clear blue lake. Playa de Tamujoso is a beautiful place for longer swims and is hidden close to a Bronze Age settlement, Peñalosa, whose slate stone walls crown a grey spur of land above this lake. Fierce warriors would have guarded the land's rich metal resources. A bronze sword, a full arm's length, was unearthed recently. Follow the quiet footpath to Peñalosa and you will cross a Roman road, a real crucible or melting pot of eras.

Throughout all these comings and goings – and older than all the columns and capitals; ancient forts and tombstones; cave paintings and bronze idols – are footprints left in river mud just outside Santisteban some 230 million years old. Calluses, pads and claws of dinosaurs hit the ground in that fleeting moment and left their marks, which you can still find today.

WILDER WATERFALLS

1 CASCADA DE LA CIMBARRA

This monumental waterfall in the River Guarrizas, which charges some 20m down sheer rock strata, comes as a surprise, hidden as it is by the gentle cork and oak woodland. Erosion of the vertical wall of Armorican Quartzite, which was formed 500 million years ago, has revealed fossilised wave ripples, like those on a sandy seabed, and trace fossils from creatures who left their mark on that seabed all that time ago. The pool beneath is wide, deep and green and home to otters and kingfishers. There are many different footpaths you can follow down to the water or up facing cliffs, to marvel from higher rocks. Follow the footpath downstream for further smaller waterfalls. About a kilometre upstream there are some ancient cave paintings called Tabla de Pochico, but access is difficult.

→ From Aldeaquemada, take the J-6110 directly south for 2.5km to the parking. Follow the footpath down to the water.
15 mins, 38.3888, -3.3734 🏊🚶🏔⊞♨🚴

2 MONUMENTO NATURAL EL PIÉLAGO

In winter months the River Guarizzas charges down granite rocks in two fierce white cascades at this spectacular site. The rocks and river are bridged by the arches of a Roman bridge, Puente Romano de Vadollano, which dates back to the 3rd century BC. It fell along with what was the Via Augusta, which made use of ancient paths to connect Cádiz with Rome. Below the remains of an old chocolate factory are deep green pools where the branches of the river meet. Black kites caw overhead.

→ From Linares take the A-312 towards Vilches. After 4.6km turn L at the large junction and continue for 1km. Signed on your R.
1 min, 38.1437, -3.5457 🚴🏊🍴🚻⊞

LAKES & RIVERS

3 DEHESA DE BURGUILLOS

A picnic area in the bucolic fields and meadows around a small artificial lagoon. There are a number of tables and fountains as well as many rounded granite stones known here as *bullos*. Several signed footpaths lead to swims in the Rumblar river about 2.5km away and to trenches from the civil war.

→ From Bailén follow brown signs for Area Recreativa Burguillos for about 6km N, under the A4, to reach the free parking area.
5 mins, 38.1385, -3.8100 🚶🏊🌲

4 PISCINA NATURAL DE MOGÓN

A long, wide pool filled by the Aguascebas river in the small town of Mogón. It doesn't get too deep and the water is usually a clear green. There are a couple of bars nearby and a few grassy areas. Lights come on in the evenings for late swimmers.

→ Cross the bridge into Mogón and the pool is down to your L. Head into the main square and turn L. Continue to small park by river. Park and walk up river.
1 min, 38.0734, -3.0306 🏊🐟🍴

5 EMBALSE DEL ENCINAREJO

Alder, ash and oleander woodland surround this reservoir with several tracks down to the water. Sandy banks make for easy entry and great sunbathing, but the water deepens very quickly. The land here famously holds a wealth of minerals; look out for smoky quartz crystals along the shore.

→ From Área Recreativa del Encinarejo, follow the road along the Jándula river upstream 2.5km to the dam. Continue for 750m and turn

201

R on to dirt track and park. Walk 200m down to water.

2 mins, 38.16891, -3.9899 🏊🚣

6 PLAYA FLUVIAL DEL TAMUJOSO

A slate scurry leads down from pine woodland to this isthmus with easy access into the clear Rumblar reservoir. It is a great spot for stargazing and although the surroundings can seem quite stark, the wooded banks hide secrets. The castle at Baños de la Encina, for example, is one of the best preserved Al-Andalus fortresses, and the Bronze Age village of Peñalosa is nearby.

→ Follow the J-5042 around and under the castle at Baños de la Encina. At the skatepark, before the road does a sharp R, follow signs for 2.3km down to the beach.

1 min, 38.1797, -3.7954 🚣🏕🚶

7 LAGUNA GRANDE

At 25 hectares, this is the largest lagoon in the Jaén province. Built for farmers, it is filled by the River Torres and offers a cool haven for birdlife in the surrounding sea of olive groves. A shaded footpath circles around the lagoon.

→ From Baeza take the road to Puente del Obispo. Here follow brown signs to Laguna

Grande for 3km. In the olive grove, before the entrance to the hotel and museum, take a sharp L and follow to reach the laguna.

1 min, 37.9329, -3.5605 🚣🚶🏕🏊

8 EMBALSE DE GUADALÉN

A good spot under the eucalyptus trees to set up a picnic and swim in the Guadalén. There are views out to Vilches crowning its small hill to the west, and the sunrise over the water from here is spectacular. The place is popular with families and fishermen.

→ From Arquillos, take the A-301 towards Guadalén for 3km and turn R at signs for Vilches. Follow for 2km until the road curves L and here follow a dirt track down to the trees.

2 mins, 38.1628, -3.4728 🚣🏕🎣

9 ÁREA RECREATIVA EL ENCINAREJO

Long grassy banks edge the Jándula river here up to the dam of the Encinarejo reservoir. Follow the river upstream for secluded areas in the deep grass, where there are picnic tables, stone BBQs and easy entry for deep swims and rope swings. Deer live in the cork oak woodland and at twilight come to drink at the water's edge.

→ From Andújar, take the A-6177 N towards the Santuario Virgen de la Cabeza for 23km.

The place is signed after the bridge at about 10km after the visitor centre Viñas de Peñallana. Park where you can and wander upstream for swims.

1 min, 38.1518, -4.0164 🏊🚻🅿️⛺🐕🚣

CASTLES & HILLFORTS

10 FORTÍN DE MIGALDÍAS

The remains of a strongly walled hillfort dating back to the same era as the Bronze Age Peñalosa nearby. They would have communicated by lighting smoking towers all along the banks of the embalse de Rumblar. Patrolled by a few brave and heavily armed warriors, the area was prized for its mineral wealth. There are wonderful views over the Rumblar valley from this elevation, and the enigmatic remains of a paved Roman road lead through the shadowy pine forest back to Baños de la Encina.

→ The fort is signed from Baños de la Encina. Carry on out of town straight past the skate park and follow the footpath for about 1.5km up through woodland to the ruins.

25 mins, 38.1901, -3.7810 🚗🅿️⛰️🚴🚶

11 CASTILLO DE GIRIBAILE

The evocative remains of this 12th-century castle can be seen from all around the Guadalimar river basin. The site of an important Iberian settlement in the 3rd and 4th centuries BC, it controlled the way to the ancient city of Cástulo but was devasted by the Romans. Visigothic settlements were followed by the fortress, which was built during Muslim rule and later handed over to the Christians; this is what remains today. Much of its history remains a mystery as it is pending a full excavation.

→ There is a small museum or Interpretation Centre dedicated to the findings in Vilches. From the Linares-Baeza station, take the J-9007 to Miraelrío and continue, passing the Restaurante Giribaile on your L. Then after 1.4km there is a sign to 'Presa de Giribaile'. Park where you can here. Follow the track uphill; it passes a drinking fountain and some caves. Follow your nose and close gates after you.

1 hr, 38.1223, -3.4834 🏰🏛️🅿️🚶⛰️❓

12 CASTILLO DEL BERREUCO

This ruined castle, surrounded by olive groves, dates from 12th-century Al-Andalus and once stood on the road connecting Jaén with the nearby city of Martos. Although you can't get inside the castle, it is an evocative site with its towers, crenellation and ancient brickwork, lying alongside old farmhouses.

A signed route, la ruta arqueológica de los Torreónes, passes by and is perfect for cycling. It starts on km2.5 of the Vía Verde del Aceite and rejoins at km6, passing important defensive medieval ruins built on Iberian and Roman sites, such as Castillo de la Muña, Berrueco and the Forgotten Tower, to name but a few.

→ From Jaén, head N on the A-311 for 7km. Turn L on to JV-2323 at signs for Garcíez. Pass Garcíez and after 2km at the crossroads, turn R at signs for Castillo Barreuco and continue 7km.

1 min, 37.8653, -3.9387 🏛️🚶🚲

SUNSET HILLTOPS

13 CASTILLO SANTISTEBAN

A grassy, flat-topped hill, about 800m high, rises up above the village of Santisteban, whose white houses huddle below its bulk. It is a beautiful spot to watch the sun set over panoramic views of the valley below. This small plateau was once crowned by an oppidum – or Iberian city – known as Ilurgeia, before the Roman conquest. Now housed in the Museo Arqueológico Nacional, the incredible Perotito treasure was found here: a

silver platter that depicts a human head being devoured by a wolf, surrounded by centaurs and serpents. In the 9th century rebels fighting against Emir Abd-el-Rhaman, the Banu Habil brothers, used the castle as their base. All that remains today is a gentle wind weaving around ruins that date from after the Christian conquest.

→ From Santisteban del Puerto, walk uphill from Calle Murallas for 500m to reach the summit.

5 mins, 38.2488, -3.2100

14 ERMITA SAN GINÉS

Built in 1994, this small mountain chapel is surrounded by wild lavender and rockrose, and its door always stands ajar. The architecture has Arab, Roman and Christian styles, and all pilgrims are welcome. The windows are made from very fine marble, which lights up like skin in the evening sun. Great stargazing spot. The chapel lies along the Sendero del Peregrino footpath, or the Camino Viejo (Old Road), and is a rest stop on the annual pilgrimage to the Santurio Virgen de la Cabeza. The walk is emblematic of the Sierra Morena and can be followed from El Cuadro de la Virgen, Andújar.

→ From Andújar, take the A-6177 into the Sierra. Take the L on to the JV-5011 after the Viñas de Peñallana visitor centre, signed 'Alcaparrosa'. After 8km there are signs up to San Ginés. Alternatively, walk the Old Road from Andújar, following the signed 22km route to reach the sanctuary.

1min-8 hrs, 38.1107, -4.0441

15 CERRO DEL CASTILLO

Holm oaks and pine trees fall away during this gentle walk uphill, leaving rocks, heather and rosemary as you approach the summit. From here you can see out across the entire Despeñaperros park and mountain pass, with Jaén olive groves to the south and Castilla-La Mancha to the north. It is thought there was once an Iberian settlement here which would have controlled the way through the hills. Come in autumn or after the first rains to hear the *berrea* (the bellowing) of the deer in mating season.

→ See directions to Cueva de los Muñecos but follow the right arm of the footpath uphill from Los Órganos.

20 mins, 38.3910, -3.49819

ANCIENT & SACRED

16 CUEVA DE LOS MUÑECOS

Iberian sanctuaries in the centuries leading up to Roman rule were often found at caves,

204 North Jaén

15

sacred forests or by springs. This rock shelter looks out like a stage over its natural amphitheatre of surrounding mountains. Its diagonal shaft slopes back down to shadow under the limestone mass above, a narrow opening, forcing your body to lie and look up at the ancient surface. If you are lucky, you might see a painting of a leaping deer. Over two thousand small, bronze votive dolls were found here, hence its name, and its dark recesses must have held many hundreds of thousands more. A small footpath leads down to the shelter through rockrose, holm oaks, pines, thyme, heather and rosemary. Although it might seem remote, it is located on the east side of the Despeñaperros mountain and has seen much footfall. Over the years people have taken the bronze idols and melted them to make tools or slingshots for distracted sheep, and they barely survived the 20th-century antique dealers. Along with Cueva de la Lobera it demarcated the Iberian territory belonging to Cástulo, now Linares.

→ From Santa Elena take the national road N; it will wind up high into the mountains. After 12km on your L there is a sign for Los Órganos. Park here and take the L arm of the signed walk down through the woodland.

10 mins, 38.3885, -3.4987 🔆🚶‍♂️✝🚴‍♂️❖

17 DINOSAUR FOOTPRINTS IN SANTISTEBAN DEL PUERTO

The footprints in the rock belong to a group of dinosaurs who ran over wet river mud over 230 million years ago. Just outside the ancient town of Santisteban del Puerto the land became a crucible of ancient pathways, but at this spot you can see the imprints left by the pads, calluses and claws of some of the first visitors here. It is not exactly a wild site, and the footprints can only be glimpsed through a window of the old barn, but it is worth a peek if you are passing.

→ From Santisteban del Puerto, take the A-312 towards Navas de San Juan for 1.7km. It is signed on your R.

1 min, 38.2547, -3.2215 🔆🚴‍♂️🏕🏞

18 CUEVA DE LA LOBERA

The caves under a rocky ledge in the fields outside Castellar were an Iberian sanctuary in the 4th century BC. A sacred place, hundreds of small, bronze votive idols about the size of your palm were discovered around these caves. Many of these figures were female with hoods and headdresses, suggesting that the divinity worshipped was female. They contrast with the masculine idols found near Cueva de los Muñecos in

Los Despeñaperros, a site which can be seen on the horizon and which along with these caves marked the edge of Cástulo territory. The furthest shadows of the caves are lit up by the equinox sunsets. A magical place for sunset all year round, the stone turns pink as the sun goes down behind the wide Guadalimar valley. It is a great place to survey the open expanse and is a natural meeting place. Head to the Museo de Arte Ibérico, Castellar, to see the idols.

→ If you head towards Castellar from the E on the A-312, you will pass a large sign for the Cueva. Follow this for a few metres to reach the parking area.

15 mins, 38.2622, -3.1102 🚴‍♂️✝🔆🖼🚶‍♂️❖

19 CUEVA DE LAS VACAS DE RETAMOSO

They say the notorious bandit José María el Tempranillo and his gang took refuge in these caves when he crossed the gateway through the Sierra Morena on his way from Ronda. As he waited to rob the stagecoaches which passed beneath, he probably didn't give much thought to the 3,000-year-old paintings that still stain the stone ochre. The caves look out from the mastic woodland over to the other half of Los Órganos and Cueva de los Muñecos, separated by the river

and motorway running below. Within a few steps the rocks give out to air. Listen for the wing beats of griffon vultures and eagles that circle close by.

➜ From Santa Elena take the N road north for 5.5km. At the roundabout take the 2nd exit and continue for another 2.5km to reach a small parking area just before the tunnel on the L. The walk is signed from here, but after 100m take a sharp R; it is easy to miss. Continue up to a metal gate on R. Close gate behind you. Cave is on L.

20 mins, 38.3922, -3.5071 🚶🏊♿✕†

20 LA ALISEDA PICNIC PARK

Deep in the Despeñaperros woodland lies this picnic area on the banks of the Campana river. Up until the last century the water here was famous for its medicinal properties; numerous springs were said to cure all types of ailments. In the evening the sheep come down through this area and there is wonderful stargazing on dark, clear nights. In the morning the wild olive trees are alive with forest birds, chaffinches and firecrests. The GR 48 passes nearby. Follow the river north for 500m to find a beautiful old ash under the bridge. Footpaths here lead to the Roman

road of El Empedraíllo and to a watermill, Molino del Batán.

➜ From Santa Elena, take the JA-7100 5km W and follow signs to La Aliseda.

2 mins, 38.3308, -3.5760 🚶⊞✕⊡♿

21 CUEVAS DE LITUERGO

They say this series of small caves hollowed into a natural rock shelter in woodland above the Guadalquivir river could be the site of the lost Iberian city of Iliturgi. Destroyed by Scipio Africanus, the ancient city is where Saint Euphrasius preached and was martyred in the 1st century. It would have lain along the road between Cástulo, modern Linares, and Córdoba. In 1945, 183 people were registered as still living in these caves.

➜ From Andújar, take the A4 towards Bailén. Take exit 310, 4th exit at roundabout, and follow for 500m to signs R for Cuevas. Follow dirt track to reach parking. Follow wooden walkway to cave.

1 min, 38.0441, -3.8995 ✕♿

22 YACIMIENTO ARGÁRICO DE PEÑALOSA

On a steep slate spur overlooking the Rumblar reservoir sit the remains of this Bronze Age village. Inhabited from 1850 – 1450 BC, it is formed of tight corridors,

ramps and passages, and cisterns now open to the sky. It is easy to slip on the scurry of slate, but the reinforced wall has preserved the village until now. Like other terraced villages that controlled this river pass, the people at Peñalosa were metalworkers who mined the land for copper. Foundries, moulds and ingots have been found here. The GR-48 passes nearby and makes use of the ancient droving roads and the Via Romana, which meet in this crucible of ancient ways.

➜ There is a beautiful 2.5km walk from Baños de la Encina along the Rumblar riverbank here; it passes a stretch of Roman road. If you are coming from Bailén, it is signed on your L as you pass the entry sign for the village of Baños.

40 mins, 38.1709, -3.7959 ♿⊞🚶✕♿

23 ORATORIO RUPESTRE DE VALDECANALES

A fully developed mystical Christain order reached this area of the Iberian Peninsula in the 4th century. This cenobitic hermitage, or cave monastery, was carved into the soft red rock of the Fuente de la Alcobilla hill, not far from a tributary of the Guadalimar river in the 6th or 7th century. It is hidden by a small terrace among the olive groves, larger uncut rocks and wild figs. The hermitage

lies close to the ancient Camino Real path between Granada and Toledo, so anyone travelling from Granada to the Visigothic capital would have had to pass by. It has a long blind arcade: a series of horseshoe archways superimposed on its wall. It is a beautiful, tranquil place that looks out to the Guadalimar valley.

→ From Arquillos drive south on the A-301 for 18km. Turn R on to JV-6041 at signs for Virgen de Guadalupe and follow for 5.6km. Park where you can. The Oratorio is just visible among the olives. 2 mins, 38.0983, -3.4365 ⚙✝

FEAST AND FIESTA

24 RESTAURANTE LOS PINOS
A popular country restuarant specialising in game. You have been warned, as there are a few antlers and boars' heads on the walls. It can get busy so book ahead.
→ Santuario Virgen de la Cabeza, Km 14, 23740 Andújar, 953 549 093, Lospinos.es. 38.1286, -3.9657 ⊞🍴❗

25 TABERNA MISA DE 12
Surrounded on all sides of the plaza by the Renaissance-style palaces and churches of the old town of Úbeda, this little restaurant appears very humble. But with its tasting menu of Jaén olive oils and a rich array of *tapas* and *raciones* using local ingredients, this award-winning, hidden gem has a lot to offer. Wander down to the nearby chapel of El Salvador afterwards.
→ Pl. Primero de Mayo, 6, 23400 Úbeda, 953 828 197, Misade12.com. 38.0100, -3.3670 ⊞🍴❗

26 BODEGAS CAPELLANÍAS, VINO VITACA
A spectacular winery offering tours and tasting, carrying on the centuries-old tradition which has given the area its name of Viñas de Peñallana.
→ Carr de Alcaparrosa, Km 4,2, 23740 Andújar, 623 002 722, Vinovitaca.com. 38.1037, -4.0086 ⊞❗

27 ROMERÍA DE LA VIRGEN DE LA CABEZA
This hilltop sanctuary with incredible views over the Sierra Morena is the destination of Spain's oldest *romería*: a pilgrimage where the emphasis is tilted more in favour of feasting and dancing than religious solemnity. The walls of its ruined side chapel are encased by an abundance of pilgrim offerings. The legend goes that in the 1st century, Saint Euphrasius brought

with him a portrait of the Madonna painted by Saint Luke. For eight centuries of Muslim rule it was hidden in the most inaccessible mountain, only to be discovered by an arthritic shepherd to the sound of ringing bells. Miraculously cured, he ran back down and spread word. Devotion to the Queen of the Sierra Morena, as she is known, spread wide and the *romería* begins every year in Andújar on the last Sunday of April and finishes here after several nights of parties and sleeping out in the forest.
→ Real Santuario Virgen de la Cabeza, 23748 Andújar. 38.1792, -4.0353 ⊞🏃✝♿

RURAL HIDEAWAYS

28 CORTIJO MONTANO
An elegant, old country house with twelve hectares of gardens and olive groves through which runs the Guadalquivir river. The house sleeps up to twelve and is decorated in keeping with its heritage: dark wood furniture, Andalucían paintings and deep window seats looking out over the fruit trees. There is a pool and it is pet friendly.
→ Camino de Montano, s/n, 23520 Jaén, 685 618 036, Cortijomontano.com. 37.9538, -3.6271 ⊞🍴🚗🏊

29 CASA RURAL LA CARACOLA
Seven simple guestrooms available in an old country house deep in the Viñas de Peñallana area of the Sierra de Andújar. There are many footpaths in the woodland nearby. Pet friendly.
→ La Caracola, Ctra. El Santuario (A-6177), Km 13,800, 23740 Andújar, 953 331 924, Lacaracolahotelrural.com. 38.1256, -3.9533 🍴🚗

30 CASA RURAL LAS CATENAS
A beautiful old house for full rental with nine bedrooms, a swimming pool, barbeques and gardens in the Viñas de Peñallana area of the Sierra de Andújar. Pet friendly.
→ JH-5002, 23748 Andújar, 609 138 918, Lascatenas.com. 38.1317, -3.9676 ⊞🍴🚗🏃

31 CASA RURAL POSÁ LA CESTERÍA
Down the old cobbled street at Baños de la Encina, beneath the protection of its ancient castle, is this rustic retreat, once a busy 16th-century hostel. Rustic and very cosy, with old beams, thick walls and chimneys, there are two bedrooms and the owners offer several artisan workshops.

→ Calle Conquista, 26, 23711 Baños de la Encina, 657 946 010.
38.1700, -3.7746 ⊞ ⏐⏐ ⎰

32 PARAJE SAN GINÉS

Several wooden bungalows with a bar and restaurant under pine trees close to the Santuario Virgen de la Cabeza. Great stargazing and pet friendly.

→ Ctra. de la Cadena, Km 11,5, 23740 Jaén, 657 803 944, Parajesangines.es.
38.1151, -4.0370 ⛺ ⚐ ⏐⏐ ⎰

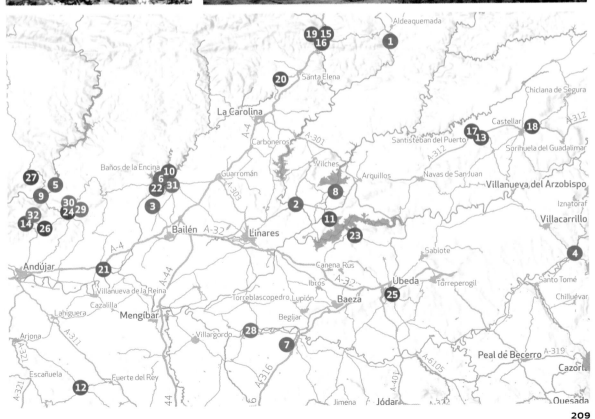

SOUTH JAÉN

Our perfect weekend

→ **Wade** upstream at Los Cañones de Río Frío and discover caves, tunnels and rock pools along its deep gorge

→ **Catch** rainbows in the sun-infused spray of the waterfall at Las Chorreras del Río Vadillo

→ **Cycle** the Vía Verde del Aceite following the old olive-oil railway, crossing tunnels, viaducts and rivers

→ **Duck** under arches of flowering oleander to a hidden picnic spot at Gruta del Río Cuadros

→ **Brave** the clear-as-ice water welling from dark caverns at Nacimiento del Río San Juan

→ **Wake** up to the sound of sheep bells as herds skitter down to drink at the shores of Embalse del Víboras

→ **Trace** the strange Celtic swirls carved into the rock at Cueva del Yedrón deep in Monte la Sierra

→ **Lace** up your boots and hike up to the gnarly, centuries-old gall oak, Quejigo del Carbón, and rest under its extensive shade

→ **Feast** in a subterranean cathedral of a cave system at Restaurante Cuevas de los Majuelos in Pegalajar

Jaén's dusty sea of olive groves rolls on south-east of its city to gentle hills that give way to dramatic limestone crests at Sierra Mágina, and to the dead south dense forest, ravines and lost castles in the Sierra Sur de Jaén. Some of the prettiest and least-visited villages cling to the vast slopes of the Mágina mountains. From Albanchez de Mágina and its medieval castle, you can hike up to the aptly named Miramundos peak. It's a challenging route but worth it for the panoramic vistas of clouds scudding over the landscape below. Numerous *refugios*, or mountain bothies, are hidden along the network of footpaths, perfect for stargazing and waking up to pink dawns. From Pico Mágina, the highest peak of the natural park at 2,165m, you can see the distant Sierra de Cazorla dominating the skies which are home to golden eagles, peregrine falcons and *quebrantahuesos*, or bearded vultures.

Woodland paths lead from these sleepy, ancient villages – Torres, Albanchez de Mágina, Solera and Bélmez de la Moraleda – passing by old stone *chozas* (shepherds huts), *eras* (threshing grounds) and *pozos de nieve* (deep stone wells) used to store and collect ice. Even in midsummer heatwaves, icy waterfalls can be found at Cascada de la Caldera del Tío Lobo and at Gruta del Río Cuadros, where the cascade's billowing freshness emerges from a series of caves beneath a hermitage and old watchtower. These places and villages are notoriously remote, but nearby Bélmez de la Moraleda found fame, and gained a small amount of tourism, from a series of supernatural faces that seeped into the walls of Señora María's house in the early 1970s. They were debunked by *El Mundo* in 2004, but you can still visit a museum to see the strange phenomenon there.

Ruins of 13th-century castles are hidden across the hills here, crumbling grey towers still guarding the valleys at Martos, Mata Bejid and Víboras. Some of the most picturesque castles defended this ancient border of the Kingdom of Granada, loops of lost arches framing sheer drops and dizzying ravines. Castillo de Otíñar lies just south of Jaén, along an epic gorge known as Cañada de las Hazadillas. The Nasrid castle guarded the 'Old Way' connecting Jaén to Granada, and its decimation by Fernando III's army in 1228 was a decisive blow to the Muslim kingdom. You can wander up to Otíñar with its timeless views of the canyon and the hills of Monte la Sierra. Alone among the bricks and ruined masonry, strewn as if the ransacking army has just left, it is easy to feel a sense of vertigo, not just at its airy heights but at the dizzying amount of time that has elapsed and the endurance of these ruins.

The wild hills of Sierra Sur de Jaén clamour and ring with tales of daring exploits and narrow escapes. When Tomás Villén Roldán escaped from the prison in Alcalá la Real in 1940, they say he spent his first night in Cueva del Jabonero, a small karstic cave outside Castillo de Locubín. Roldán, aka 'Cencerro' or 'Cowbell', waged a seven-year guerrilla warfare against Franco across these hills. His tight network of clandestine militia, known as *maquis*, from the Italian for bushes and scrubland, knew the ravines, caves, forests and streams as well as any 19th-century bandolero or medieval light calvary.

A hike through these sierras will reveal much history, lost ruins and ancient caves still used as shady sheep pens during the heat of the day. Break up a hike with a night in a mountain bothy. At Refugio de la Mella you can watch dusk fall over the grey towers of Jaén and its castle. Toast the sunset with a glass of Vino de la Tierra Sierra Sur, regional wines awarded royal warrant in the 16th century, a great pairing with a small tapa of Jaén's famed cornezuelo table olives.

CAVES & CASCADES

1 LOS CAÑONES DE RÍO FRÍO

Follow the river upstream from this bridge to discover several waterfalls and pools along the deep gorge carved by the Río Frío. You'll need to wade, swim and jump at times but the walk also passes through tunnels, caves and the spring of Río Mingo; it's around 2km long.

→ From Jaén, continue S through Puente de la Sierra. Keep R just before the road continues up to Restaurante El Balcón and continue along the road for 500m to the bridge and the beginning of the water route. Parking is very limited.

30 mins, 37.7129, -3.7694 🏊🚶🧍🚴🏃🍴

2 LAS CHORRERAS DEL RÍO VADILLO

A short but beautiful walk through woodland shade along the Río Vadillo. The stream has carved caves, crannies and, at various points, cascades over mossy rocks as well as wooden footbridges and picnic tables. The highlight is a tall, thin waterfall coursing down algae-covered rock making fresh billows and rainbows up close. Medieval fairs are held in the village over August.

→ Parking is available just outside the village near a children's playpark at 37.5859,-3.8060,

and a footpath to Quejigo del Carbón also starts here. Follow the signs for Las Chorreras for 2km along the river and you'll reach the town square with a stone lion fountain.

30 mins, 37.5882, -3.8110 🚴🧍🚶🏃🍴

3 VIADUCTO DE RÍO VÍBORAS

Hidden in the oleanders and beneath a high viaduct lie these shallow cascades leading to small pools in the River Víboras. A little way upstream you will find a much smaller, picturesque medieval stone bridge. The Vía Verde del Aceite passes over the viaduct.

→ From Martos you can take the Vía Verde del Aceite from Area de descanso 'La Tiza'. It is 18km to the viaduct, but take the rocky track downhill just before the viaduct and follow the path L around to the water. For bike rental in Martos, call Viabike.es, 666 451 175.

1 hr, 37.6368, -4.0820 🏊🧍🚴🏃

4 MOLINO DEL CUBO

This once-mighty mill house built by the Order of Calatrava in 1437 is now hidden by olive groves and covered in ivy. In winter the Arroyo del Cubo gushes past and tumbles down through the undergrowth below. You can wander upstream to discover more cascades. The Vía Verde del Aceite passes by.

→ From Torredonjimeno take the Crta de Martos towards the motorway. After 500m on your L the beginning of a 2.5km walk to the Molino is signed. It connects with the Vía Verde del Aceite.

45 mins, 37.7440, -3.9410 🚗🥾⚑🏊🏔

5 CASCADA DE LA CALDERA DEL TÍO LOBO

At the beginning of the Albanchez river lies this cave with a waterfall and several hidden, cool pools inside. It is about a 3km walk along a footpath signed from Albanchez de Mágina. The waterfall rushes down over mossy green rock and is partly obscured by two curtains of limestone eroded over time by the water. The pools are small but the cool air in this haven feels immense after a hot walk.

→ The waterfall is signed from Fuente de los Siete Caños in Albanchez de Mágina. Parking is available here and the 8km circular walk is signed 'Ruta Caldera del Tío Lobo'. It is about 4km to the waterfall.

1 hr, 37.7669, -3.4612 🚗🏊🚶🏃🏔

6 GRUTA DEL RÍO CUADROS

Stone steps lead down from the hermitage to the Virgen del Cuadros and watchtower through fig trees, ivy and oleander to the riverbed. Even in summer there is a little water and within a few steps you can enter an impressive cave with hidden chambers carved by the river and formed from flowstone. At the far end there is a large waterfall and light pouring in. It can get busy on summer weekends but it offers a calm, cool oasis. Follow the river upstream along the footpath for 500m to picnic tables shaded by 8m-high oleander 'vaulting'.

→ From Bedmar y Garcíez take the JV-3222 S for 4km. Follow signs over the bridge to the right-hand side of the river to the parking.

5 mins, 37.7899, -3.4076 🌳⛺🥾🏊✝

MOUNTAIN SPRINGS

7 LA CHARCA DE PEGALAJAR

Since medieval times the town of Pegalajar harvested the water that sprang from the Fuente de la Reja spring; it fed the orchards, olives groves and even the old mills. But in 1988 the aquifer dried up due to overexploitation. A project begun in 2007 has recovered the water source and today tapas bars look out proudly over a large lake which sometimes has boats and is open for swims. On one wall is engraved, "To whom I gave life, I ask not to let me die".

→ Located in the centre of town, you can't miss it. There might not be any water during the summer months.

10 mins, 37.7397, -3.6443

8 NACIMIENTO DEL RÍO SAN JUAN
Cold, clear water surges out of the dark rock to form bright, pebbly pools in the narrow valley just a few kilometres from Castillo de Locubín. People use the stunningly cold water as a spa, ducking in for curative plunges. The picnic area is shady and cool in the narrow valley between La Sierrezuela and La Nava mountains. Holm and kermes oak reach down to the water's edge and there is a small bar and restaurant.

→ From Castillo de Locubín take the A-0650 towards Valdepeñas de Jaén and after 1.5km the turning is signed on the R. Follow signs to the parking.

5 mins, 37.5403, -3.9192

9 NACIMIENTO DEL RÍO ARBUNIEL, CAMBIL
The source of the Arbuniel river is one of the largest and most important springs in the Sierra Mágina. The river wells up from its ground source here and is the pride of the Arbuñelenses, the people from the nearby village to whom the river gives its name.

The water has a salty taste as it gushes up through limestone, marl and Triassic gypsum. Silvery trout glide through its clear turquoise and green depths and crayfish loiter deeper down. You cannot swim here but there are picnic tables in the shade, stone BBQs, a bar and children's play area.

→ From Cambil take the JA-3204 to Arbuniel and follow signs for El Nacimiento. Park where you can near the restaurants and information board.

5 mins, 37.6243, -3.5409

10 ÁREA RECREATIVA FUENMAYOR
A picnic park by one of the many springs in Sierra Mágina. The sweet, searingly cold water gushes out from under stone and cascades into a large pond. While swimming is not permitted, it is a great place to picnic in the shade at one of the old millstone tables, or to rest and refresh under the shade of the oak and walnut trees. In winter months there is water at the Cascada de Zorreón, a short walk uphill with beautiful views of the peaks of Morrón, Aznaitín, Cerro de la Vieja and Cerro Castelar.

→ From Torres follow signs for 6km to reach the parking.

5 mins, 37.7502, -3.5164

LAKES & RIVERS

11 EMBALSE DEL VÍBORAS
Bordered by the hills of the Sierra de la Caracolera, this small but beautiful reservoir lies along the Víboras river. The area is a designated Starlight Reserve owing to a lack of light pollution. The lake is popular with locals for picnics and fishing. In the morning you might be woken by sheep bells.

→ From the plaza at Las Casillas, take the road towards the river and follow signs L towards Mirador Astronómico for about 2km. There are many turnings on your R for easy, sloped access to the water.

5 mins, 37.6382, -4.0039

SUNSET HILLTOPS

12 CUEVA DEL YEDRÓN
Celtic swirls, trislisks, Basque and Sanskrit inscriptions have been carved on to the rock at this tiny mountain shelter deep in Monte la Sierra. At this elevation of 1,150m, the rocks make a great viewing platform of the Sierra Sur de Jaén and the nearby Quiebrajano reservoir.

→ From the hydroelectricity station on the N side of the Embalse del Quiebrajano, head N through the tunnel. There is a fork in the

14

road 500m after the tunnel and a sign for 'Monumento Natural'. Park where you can here and the 4.5km walk to the cave is signed.
1 hr, 37.6499, -3.7514 🛁🏔🚶

13 CUEVA DEL JABONERO
Having escaped the prison in Alcalá la Real, Cencerro spent his first night sheltering in this small karstic cave in Cerro de la Nava. This was the first night of the seven years he spent in the hills waging guerilla warfare against Franco's dictatorship. With views out across Castillo de Locubín and the Valle del Río San Juan, the path passes a ruined hermitage and continues on to a 14th-century watchtower.
➔ From Castillo de Locubín, follow Calle Calvario out of town and straight up the hill. After passing the ruins of the hermitage, now used as a sheepfold, you will come to the cave after 300m.
15 mins, 37.5271, -3.9326 🏔🚶📷✝🎒📷

BORDER CASTLES

14 CASTILLO DE OTÍÑAR
Elegant grey towers and loops of ruined stone arches crown this rocky promontory in the immense canyon of Cañada de las Hazadillas. The path winds by a small gorge where sheep shelter in the Cueva del Toril with its prehistoric concentric carvings. Streaked rock towers overhead, its strata like a collapsed wedding cake. At the peak, are misty blue views and doorways that open out to sheer drops. An almond tree grows from the ruins of a church. Otíñar castle guarded what was known as the 'Old Way', a mountain pass that connected Jaén with the Emirate of Granada. The devastation of Otíñar by Fernando III's army in 1228 paved the way for the siege of Jaén.
➔ Take the road S from Puente de la Sierra for 7.5km. Just before signs for Cañada de las Hazadillas and a graffitied hut on the L, there is a chained-off enclosure to the R where the footpath begins. It is a short but steep climb up to the castle.
30 mins, 37.6714, -3.7472 ✝📷🏔🚶🎒📷

15 CASTILLO DE LA PEÑA DE MARTOS
Many legends are told about this enigmatic 14th-century castle perched on a craggy hill overlooking Martos, and it is easy to see why. This medieval castle was built on the remains of a Nasrid castle, which in turn was built on the remains of an Iberian settlement. It was here that the Carvajal brothers met their gruesome death for allegedly killing Ferdinand IV's knight. An even earlier 12th-century legend tells of how Countess Iréne and her women, dressed in armour, successfully defended the castle from Ibn al-Ahmar, the Emir of Jaén, future founder of the Nasrid dynasty and the first Emir of Granada. The Vía Verde del Aceite cycle route runs nearby.
➔ Follow signs for the castle out of Martos to the parking area before a steep climb.
45 mins, 37.71802, -3.9608 ❓🚶📷❖🎒

16 CASTILLO DE MATA BEJID
A wild walk through ancient olive groves with views of the Cerro de Almaden leads to this ruined castle. Built by Muslims in the 14th century, it was handed over to the Catholic Monarchs after the conquest. Next to the castle is a gigantic stone threshing ground, the best-preserved example in the Sierra Mágina, and a cave known as Cueva del Tocino, or Bacon Cave, owing to the castle's dead pigs being thrown in there.
➔ A 13km walking trail begins at Km13 on the road linking Cambil to the Visitor Centre Mata Bejid. The castle is 2.5km along this path, which continues on to Cascada Zurreón and Área Recreativa Fuenmayor.
40 mins, 37.7053, -3.5107 ❖📷🚶

17 CASTILLO DE LA ENCOMIENDA DE VÍBORAS

The romantic ruins of this 12th-century fortress sit on a small promontory above the olive groves overlooking the Víboras valley and reservoir. Its name might have evolved from the Arabic name, *Bib-Bora*, meaning the Gate of Bora, an ancient turdetano city once located on the hill behind.

➜ From Martos take the A-316 S towards Alcaudete for 10km. Turn L on to the JA-3307 at signs for Las Casillas. After 3.7km turn R at signs for Castillo; it is uneven but tarmacked. After 1km at the bend in the road you can park and walk up through the olive grove to the castle. 10 mins, 37.6418, -4.0257 📷🖼️⊞

18 CASTILLO DE ALBANCHEZ DE MÁGINA

The crenellated battlements of this castle rise up proudly from its rocky hold on the eastern slopes of La Serrezuela in the foothills of the Sierra Mágina. Built in the 14th century, or possibly earlier, it has incredible views out over its village below to the wide valley cradling Úbeda, Baeza and Bedmar; the Sierra de Cazorla can be seen on the horizon.

➜ It is a short but steep stroll up from Calle Rosal where it meets Calle Horno; signed 50m. 5 mins, 37.7903, -3.4679 🖼️⊞📷

19 CASTILLO BÉLMEZ DE LA MORALEDA

With the mountain peaks of the Sierra Mágina rising up from behind, this 13th-century Nasrid castle would have controlled the Jandulilla valley to its south. An old border castle, it suffered numerous sieges and attacks, changing hands many times right up until the Christian conquest in 1492. Many ceramic fragments with a honey-coloured glaze, which can still be seen in the topsoil, date from the Nasrid period. A signed walk to the Cuevas de Baltibañas starts nearby.

➜ From Jódar, head S on the A-401. Turn R just before Km38 and follow the road for 4km, turning R at the junction. Park where you can and the castle can be seen from the olive groves. 5 mins, 37.7496, -3.3837 ⊞📷🚶

ANCIENT & SACRED

20 DOLMEN DE OTÍÑAR

The prehistoric tomb is still covered by earth, its stones set deep underground at the peak of Cerro Veleta and orientated towards the dawn over the epic ravine below. Wander up through scrubland to see the sun set and the moon rise over the

valley carved by the River Quiebrajano. In the gloaming, the stillness of this site has an unearthly quality. Wildlife is the only sound here, the earth disturbed by wild boar and mountain goats.

→ Access is difficult. Take the road S from Puente de la Sierra for 3.5km to the parking on the L for the mirador and the monument to Vitor Carlos III. From this monument the dolmen is located behind the peak of Cerro Veleta. There is no path but the goat tracks in the earth lead close to the dolmen.

30 mins, 37.6907, -3.7664 🐾🏕️🏞️⛰️❓

21 QUEJIGO DEL CARBÓN

This beautiful, gnarly gall oak is somewhere between 500 and 1000 years old, its twisted branches the product of centuries of pruning for charcoal wood. In hills covered with gall and holm oaks, this is one of the largest and it has become emblematic of the sierra and its villages. The oaks look especially striking cloaked in the snow that covers the sierra during winter. It is also known as the Quejigo del Amo in memory of the farmer who was proud to have it on his land. The 11km footpath here from Valdepeñas de Jaén passes spectacular mountain views.

→ See directions for Las Chorreras del Río Vadillo. The 11km route is signed from the parking area.

3 hrs, 37.594, -3.7275 ⛰️🥾👤🏞️

PICNICS & FOOTPATHS

22 ÁREA RECREATIVA LLANO DE SANTA ANA

With views out over Torredelcampo and miles of olive groves as far as the Sierra Morena, the hill of Cerro Miguelico has been occupied since at least the 6th century BC. You can see the remains of a wall of a fortification that once guarded the old road between Martos and Jaén, as well as several rock graves from a Visigothic necropolis, which lie along the side of a grassy spur. There are fountains and picnic tables by the chapel to Santa Ana and a good restaurant. The Vía Verde de Aceite runs nearby, and several hiking routes that lead to the Cueva de Goliat, the Bañizuela forest or the peak of Miguelico are signed from here.

→ From Torredelcampo follow signs uphill for Ermita Santa Ana. The necropolis hill is on your R as you enter before the parking.

1 min, 37.7602, -3.9027 🖼️🚻🚴🥾🚗⛪🅿️

23 CAÑADA DE LAS HAZADILLAS

Under pine tree shade and set deep in the Cañada de las Hazadillas ravine, this grassy picnic area has fountains, streams and BBQs.

It's a perfect woodland hideout. Footpaths lead into the Monte la Sierra.

→ Situated about 20km S of Jaén. From Jaén take the JA-3210 S for 9km. At the roundabout take the first exit for Monte la Sierra and continue for 12km, following signs for Cañada de las Hazadillas to its parking area.

5 mins, 37.6550, -3.7132 ⛰️🥾🚴♻️🅱️🅿️

RUSTIC RESTAURANTS

24 RESTAURANTE LOS CASTILLOS

A great village bar by the old fountain and river serving excellent tapas and *raciones*; try the *croquetas* or *arroz* (rice dishes). It is lively at the weekends and popular with families for Sunday lunch.

→ Calle Huerta de Leonor, 2, 23120 Cambil, 649 144 066

37.6781, -3.5644 📅🍴🍷

25 CAFE BAR MANOLILLO

Situated at the bottom of the coloured steps and in a busy village plaza, the restaurant has views up to the towering mountains by day and lots of kids playing around the tables at night. All the dishes are excellent; they come as heaped plates to share. Try the *albóndigas* (meatballs in sauce).

→ C. Mesones, 17, 23538 Albanchez de Mágina, 695 597 084

37.7916, -3.4674 📅🍴🍷

26 MESÓN ASADOR LA PANDERA

A short stroll from the spring of the Río Frío, this hunters' retreat serves excellent local dishes and wines. There is a shady terrace area and log fires in winter.

→ Cam. de Bellavista, 3, 23160 Los Villares, 953 321 485, Casarurallapandera.es

37.6508, -3.7942 📅🍴🍷

27 BAR MENDOZA

Great food is served in this friendly and lively bar whose tables fill the town square and where kids run about until long into the summer night. All the *raciones* (sharing plates) and dishes are excellent but the *Cachopo*, normally a Madrid speciality, is especially good.

→ Pl. Constitución, 20, 23614 Las Casillas, 953 558 037

37.6391, -4.0017 🍴🍷♻️

28 RESTAURANTE CUEVAS DE LOS MAJUELOS

This restaurant has been running for over 50 years in the spectacular cave system beneath Pegalajar. The underground galleries are lit up

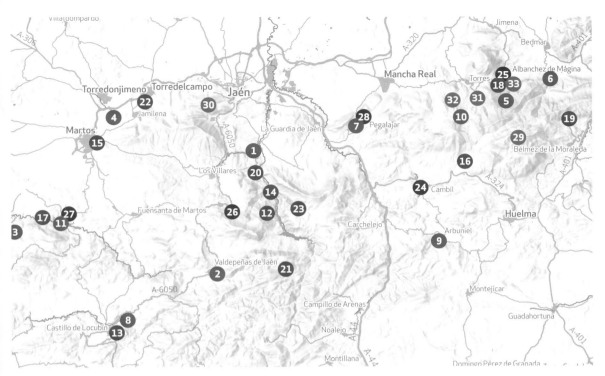

but the natural vault still disappears into the shadows; it's a magical space. Classic dishes and seasonal ingredients are served with flair.

→ Carretera Mancha Real, Km. 0,6, 23110 Pegalajar, 620 286 873, Cuevadelosmajuelos.es
37.7470, -3.6387 🍴🅿️♨️🛏️

BOTHIES & BIVVIES

29 REFUGIO MIRAMUNDOS

This aptly named mountain refuge is located 2,000 metres up the Pico Mágina, from where you can see spectacular views of the Sierra Nevada, la Sierra de Baza and the Parque Natural de las Sierras de Tejeda, Almijara y Alhama. It is a magical spot and the cabin is kept in tip-top condition by the Amigos de Miramundos mountain club. It is a shared, communal space; please be respectful and look after it well.

→ From Huelma take the A-324 towards Cambil for 6km. Turn R on to a dirt track at signs for 'campamento ociomagina' and after about 1km you will see the information board for 'Sendero Pico Mágina'. It is a challenging hike up of about 10km; the refugio is after 8km. The walk-in time is 2.5 hours.
37.7302, -3.4458 ⛺🏕️♿🚶🧗

30 REFUGIO DE LA MELLA

The Cerro de la Mella rises up 1,244m behind Jaén; its long and snaking rocky spine has a dip in the middle called 'la Mella'. Although very basic, this mountain cabin is a magical place to wake up for dawn views over Jaén. The refuge belongs to a family but rather than let it go to ruin, they let people enjoy it, so treat it with care.

→ The cabin is a 4km cycle or hike up the mountain from the Piscina Municipal El Tomillo in Jaén.
37.7583, -3.8253 🚶🏕️🚲🛶

31 ZONA ACAMPADA HONDACABRAS

A grassy area near several signed footpaths to springs. Wild camping is permitted here.

→ From Torres, take the road towards Albanchez de Mágina for 2km and turn R at sign for 'zona acampada'. Parking after 650m.
37.7690, -3.4961 🚶🏕️🅿️

RURAL HAVENS

32 CABAÑAS IMAGINA

A couple of sustainably run cottages with terraces and views over to the Aznaitín massif. Situated close to the pretty mountain village of Torres and numerous springs and streams, they have a swimming pool and pets are welcome.

→ Paraje Nava París, s/n, 23540 Torres, 953 120 328, Casasruralesimagina.com
37.7671, -3.5268 🚶♿🐾

33 CASA LUNARES Y SALINERA

A cosy, family-run guesthouse beneath Albanchez castle on the slopes of the Sierra Mágina, with panoramic views over the village and valley from its terraces. Streets wind down into the lively village tapas bars and plazas, and numerous footpaths lead to caves and waterfalls in the hills. You can book a room or the whole house; pets welcome.

→ Calle Horno, 34, 23538 Albanchez de Mágina, 687 165 648, Casalunaresysalinera.com
37.7910, -3.4676 ♨️🚶🏕️🐾

34 MOLINO DE ABAJO

On the borders of three provinces, Córdoba, Jaén and Granada, this beautiful flour mill situated along the Frailes river has been converted into apartments of varying sizes. It is a short stroll into the tiny village of Ribera Baja.

→ Cjón. del Molino, 7, 23691 Ribera Baja, 625 812 358, Molinodeabajo.es
37.4459, -3.8398 ♿♨️🚶🐾

SIERRAS DE CAZORLA

Our perfect weekend

→ **Listen** out in autumn, after the first rains have fallen, for the *berrea*, the echoing bellows of stags during rutting season

→ **Follow** the old fishermen's way through the caves and hollows carved by the Guadalentín river to green and blue pools

→ **Explore** the rambling battlements, windy views and whispering gallery at the 12th-century Segura castle

→ **Bed** down by a log fire at one of the many mountain bothies along Cazorla's long-distance footpath

→ **Wake** up to a spectacular dawn over the karstic plateau of Campos de Hernán Perea and look out for wild ibex in the early light

→ **Follow** the narrow path down through ash and wild olive to hidden pools at Cascada de la Osera

→ **Leap** from the high boulders at Charco de la Pringue and plunge into crystal-clear water

→ **Sit** still for a moment by the thick, veiny roots of the thousand-year-old yew tree at Valle de los Tejos Milenarios

The Sierras de Cazorla, Segura y Las Villas, in the north-eastern corner of the Jaén province, is the largest protected area in Spain, its 2,000km² encompassing peaks, valleys, rocky gorges and vertical cliffs. Its rich and varied pine forest, interspersed with great, gnarly oaks and thousand-year-old yew trees, is home to mountain goats, deer, wild boar, wolves and Iberian lynx. Countless streams thread through the woodland, while the larger rivers of the Borosa, Segura and the great Guadalquivir spring from the limestone mountains, carving gorges, forming waterfalls and eroding porous stone to create bright-blue plunge pools.

At Río Borosa you can follow a footpath through the river-eaten gorge of Cerrada de Elías to reach the tumbling river at Salto de los Órganos. At Cascada de Linarejos flowstone caves hide behind its plummeting waterfall. At La Toba a travertine stairway leads to a clear spring and cave. And at the birth of the Segura river you can look straight into the earth through hoops of rock behind crystalline, turquoise water.

Its watery nature is reflected in myths and history: fountains spring up at the feet of martyred saints; a great flood in 1694 shattered the church of Santa María in Cazorla, dragging tapestries and sacred ornaments downriver; a Muslim princess forgotten in the damp recesses under Cazorla castle transforms into a scaly, freshwater mermaid known as La Tragantía. Haunting stories are still told in Cazorla and La Iruela about the *buscadores de los muertos*, or 'dead collectors', whose unenviable job was to hunt for casualties in the surrounding sierras. Returning at night they would muffle their hooves against the cobblestone, so as not to disturb superstitious townsfolk and wary dogs.

Threading through all these places is the Bosques del Sur, or GR247, a near 500km-long footpath curling through the park. Sheep droving ways lead through the wild plains of Hernán Perea, passing mountain bothies and timeless castles. It arrives at the ancient villages of Cazorla and La Iruela whose castles are thrust up on rocky slopes, and picturesque white houses cling to the sides of the ravine.

Knotted chains of dried red peppers hang down sun-bleached walls, reminding us that we cannot leave these mountain towns without trying their mouth-watering fare. *Rin-ran* is a delicious dish made with red peppers, cod, potato, eggs and olives. And if you visit during the winter months, a hearty broth made with garlic, peppers, and chorizo, known as *Maimones de Cazorla*, is a great way to warm up. Set up camp in the evening by the calm waters of the Tranco reservoir, its open expanse a perfect place for stargazing and one of several places where wild camping is encouraged in the Sierra.

LAKES & RIVERS

1 EMBALSE DE ANCHURICAS-MILLER

This turquoise reservoir in the Segura river almost seems like a natural lake. It rests between two peaks, Anguijones and Calar de Cobos, with woodland reaching right up to its banks. You can walk here following the signed footpath from La Toba.

➔ Park in La Toba and follow signs from Bar Casa Inocente uphill along the stream. Turn R at the end of the village and follow signs past the Nacimiento de la Toba for another 2km until the dirt tracks begin to head down to the banks of reservoir.

1 hr, 38.1948, -2.5453 🏊🚶🏊

2 EMBALSE DE EL TRANCO DE BEAS

One of Spain's largest reservoirs, the peaceful water reflects the wooded slopes of the Sierras de Cazorla. Before its flooding in 1929 there was a perilous mountain pass known as Tranco de Mojoque. Connecting Segura with Las Villas, it passed along several precipices via precarious bridges over the raging torrent of the Guadalquivir river. It is quite different now, and towards the end of October this is a good place to listen out for the *berrea*, the bellows of the deer in rutting season. Great stargazing; especially dramatic during a full moon, when the whole lake is lit up.

➔ From El Tranco head S on the A-319 for 9km. Park where you can near the white house. Follow the dirt track on L for 700m. Kayaking, rafting, canyoning and more available with El Tranco Centro de Ocio, 34 647 765 420.

5 mins, 38.1220, -2.7933 🏊🚶⛰

3 EMBALSE DE LA BOLERA

Shining brightly under the southern foothills of the Sierras de Cazorla is this clear reservoir, where you can canoe, kayak, fish and swim surrounded by steep wooded slopes. Good for families and kids but it can get busy, so follow the unmarked tracks through woodland for quieter swims. If canyoning floats your boat, then check out nearby Barranco La Bolera. Keep an eye out for peregrine falcons, black kites, golden eagles, Bonelli's eagles and vultures.

➔ From Pozo Alcón drive N for 8.2km on the A-326. After you have crossed the bridge, turn L up the hill where you'll find places to park on the L-hand side of the road. Follow woodland trails down the steep banks of the lake to the water.

2 mins, 37.7629, -2.9014 🏊🍴🏊 B

HIDDEN WATERFALLS

4 CASCADA EL SALTADOR

A hidden paradise deep in the Segura de la Sierra woodland, where a waterfall tumbles over a naturally sculpted fan of flowstone into a green pool. The strange stone has in fact been created by a millennia of mineral deposits, and you can swim underneath this petrified waterfall to a dark mossy cave. Contact Segura Activa for wilder guided routes – 607301716, Seguraactiva.com.

➔ The route here is unsigned. From Siles take the JF-7012 directly S for 10.5km. On your L you will see a green gate. Park here. Follow this track for 1.5km until you reach the stream Andrés. Turn L and follow the stream for 3.5km to reach the waterfall. Access uncertain.

2 hrs, 38.3233, -2.5414 🏊🍴🚶⛰🏊❓

5 CASCADA DE GUAZALAMANCO

A gentle walk leads through ancient Cazorla woodland to this pretty waterfall tumbling over mossy stones.

➔ From Pozo Alcón take the A-326 N. Just before La Bolera reservoir follow signs for 'El Hornico nature classroom' L onto the dirt track and continue for 6km. Park at signs for

the mirador. Follow the footpath to the L for 1.6km to the waterfall.

30 mins, 37.8056, -2.9202 🚶🚗🅱️❓

6 CASCADAS DEL ARROYO DE LINAREJOS

A series of idyllic bathing pools formed by rushing waterfalls under the towering limestone cliffs of Cerrada del Utrero. Griffon vultures soar overhead, and you can clamber up the river or follow the footpath to waterfalls and serene turquoise pools by ancient olive trees. Cascades surge all around and tumble over smooth rocks. Swim under the waterfall to find a cave of crashing water where you can climb up and jump out over the waterfall again. Only attempt to canyon upstream in summer.

→ From Arroyo Frio follow the A-319 S for 2.5km until you cross a little bridge over the Guadalquivir river with an abandoned electricity station on L. Park here and follow the footpath uphill to the waterfalls.

10 mins, 37.9293, -2.9233 🚶🏊🍴🅱️

7 CASCADA DE LA OSERA POOLS

Andalucía's highest waterfall plunges 130m over a steep ravine. Connected to the Aguascebas dam, this fall is now seasonal but beneath are smaller, perennial waterfalls

tumbling into hidden pools. The most beautiful and secret of these pools are canopied over by thick roots and a tangle of branches. The water is searingly cold but clear and worth a plunge.

→ Cross the small bridge over the river beach into Mogón and take first R and follow the small road 3.5km to a bridge. Turn R to cross the river and follow Aguascebas river for a further 5km until road finishes in a parking area. Cross the river on foot and continue uphill on footpath for 300m. You'll pass an entry post into the park and then turn R in a depression into the bush.

10 mins, 38.0510, -2.9600 🏊🍴🏊🏕️

RIVERS & RAVINES

8 CERRADA DEL RÍO GUADALENTÍN

The Guadaletín river carves a deep and dramatic gorge through the Cazorla hills, and this footpath, the fishermen's route, follows a narrow rock ledge a little way above a turquoise river. Wind your way along, stopping to look up at the immense ravine towering above. There are several caves in the river-eaten rock and numerous cascades forming shining blue pools. The mossy, porous rocks where the Arroyo de San Pedro meets the river are perfect for a picnic.

→ See directions to Cascada de Guazalamanco but at the mirador follow the footpath Senda de los Pescadores for 10km along the gorge.

2.5 hrs, 37.8611, -2.8904 🏞️🚶♿🏊🏕️🌄V

9 CHARCO DE LA PRINGUE

A large and clear pebbly pool in a gorge carved by the Guadalquivir river. It is also known as Charco del Aceite as legend tells of a weary traveller whose mule, laden with several urns of expensive olive oil, stumbled and spilt the rich oil into the pool. Today it is sparkling and shallow but deepens at one end for some tall rock jumps. It is popular in summer as there is a bar and lots of picnic tables. Follow the river upstream between boulders for wilder swims.

→ From El Tranco head N on the A-6202 for 5km. Turn sharp L at signs for Charco del Aceite and continue downhill to parking.

1 min, 38.179, -2.8299 🍴🏊🚗🍴

10 RÍO BOROSA POOLS

Here the Borosa river turns a sparkling sapphire blue as it swirls around ancient fossils and tumbles over smooth rocks. Some of the pools reach 5m deep, perfect for somersaults. Follow the footpath upstream for further pools and the beautiful Sendero

de Elías, a wooden walkway through the eroded gorge. It passes cascades and pools to reach the magnificent Salto de los Órganos waterfall and nearby reservoir.

→ From the Torre del Vinagre on the A-319 take the road opposite for 2km to reach the Centro de Visitantes Río Borosa. Park here. The Sendero Río Borosa is signed from here, a linear 9km footpath that takes around 2.5 hrs.

5 mins, 38.0144, -2.8613

11 ARROYO DE LOS MOLINOS

This stream near Hornos is named after the old flour mills which are now hidden in the undergrowth along the narrow pass. It glides a transparent turquoise through the woodland to fill several pools for a short swim or a jump. Follow a footpath along the river to various hidden spots.

→ From Hornos take the A-317 N for 1km. At the first bend in the road there is a mirador. Park here, follow the track downhill keeping R for 1.5km until you reach the stream. Then follow the river upstream to the pools.

1 hr, 38.2177, -2.7002

12 FUENTE DEL RÍO SEGURA

The source of the Segura river is so clear and still that you can look straight down past

the rings of deepening blue into its tunnel underground. Although swimming is forbidden, there is a drinking fountain close by, where the fresh water clouds up your bottle. Up the hill nearby are cave paintings. For guided routes of the sierra contact Segura Activa – 607301716, Seguraactiva.com.

→ From Santiago-Pontones take the JF-7047 S for 4km. Parking after the bend.

1 min, 38.0914, -2.6995

13 CHARCA LAS JUNTAS

The bend of the River Segura offers deeper swims just before the bridge crosses it at Las Juntas. The banks are quite narrow and wooded and steps lead down from the road. The water levels change most evenings, so check for eddies or rapids first and jump out quickly if you see them!

→ From La Toba continue N on the JF-7038 for 17km. Cross the River Segura into Las Juntas, turn sharp R and park. Follow steps down.

1 min, 38.2182, -2.4547

14 PUENTE DE LAS HERRERÍAS

Legend tells how this bridge was built in just one night. In the late 15th century, Queen Isabel La Católica was on a campaign to conquer Baza. She had begun her journey in Quesada but

due to the autumn rains the Guadalquivir had flooded its banks. Her knights built the bridge overnight so she could cross. It still seems to be holding up quite well. The water here runs crystal-clear over shingle, deepening into a narrow limestone pool under the bridge. It lights up beautifully when the sun hits it but remains searingly cold, as it is very close to the source where this great river springs from the bedrock. A couple of footpaths are signed from here and follow the river through woodland.

→ From Arroyo Frio follow the A-319 S towards Cazorla for 6.5km. At the junction take a sharp L and follow for 3.5km. Pass the Chiringuito, cross the bridge and turn R and continue for another 3km to reach parking area after the old bridge.

1 min, 37.9011, -2.9384 🏊⊗↗🏊⊗🌳🏊⛱†

MAGICAL WOODLAND

15 VALLE DE LOS TEJOS MILENARIOS

Thick pine forest cloaks this sheer ravine where several streams, with names like 'cold John' and the 'stream of light', descend from nearby mountains to join the source of Andalucía's most important river, the Guadalquivir. Returning to the roots of this powerful river, you can discover some

equally immense roots, those of a flourishing 2,000-year-old yew tree overlooking the gorge.

→ From Naciamento del Río Guadalquivir follow the road for 1km and park at the signed footpath entrance R (37.8331, -2.9709). Walk along the footpath for 1km.

15 mins, 37.823, -2.9748 🏃🏔🍴

CASTLES & LEGENDS

16 CASTILLO DE BUJARAIZA

The ruins of a 12th-century castle now romantically marooned by the Tranco reservoir. There is a mirador from the road but in summer the edges of the reservoir sometimes silt up, and it is possible to walk to the ruins.

→ Park 100m N of the Parque Cinegético on the A-319 and follow the path down to the L for 300m. Turn L after 100m then turn R and keep the castle in sight.

15 mins, 38.0973, -2.8004 ❓✚

17 CASTILLO DE LA YEDRA

The 14th-century castle at Cazorla houses a great museum. You can see 17th-century tapestries, a beautifully reconstructed 19th-century kitchen, armour and Islamic ceramics discovered under the castle. They say that in the dungeons lurks La Tragantía, a dark

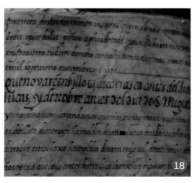

freshwater mermaid who was forgotten hundreds of years ago when her father was killed by Christian knights. If you walk through the tunnel under the castle, you can see signs of her strange transformation.

→ Cam. Ángel, 23470 Cazorla, 953 101 402. 1 min, 37.9075, -3.0015 🚲🐾💶

18 CASTILLO DE SEGURA

A wonderfully complete 12th-century castle with Hammam baths, towers, battlements, a magnificent chapel built by the Order of Santiago and even a whispering gallery. If you're lucky, there might even be some visiting knights of Santiago. For guided tours contact Dani at Segura Activa – 607301716, Seguraactiva.com.

→ Calle Castillo, 23379 Segura de la Sierra. 1 min, 38.2989, -2.6503 🚲🐾✖️💶

WILDERNESS & WOODLAND

19 LOS CAMPOS DE HERNÁN PEREA

The undulating hills of this high plateau are formed of karstic limestone, sinkholes and poljes. This is where the Segura de la Sierra sheds the thick cloak of woodland typical of the Sierras de Cazorla and opens up its bare back to the immense sky. Small rocks cut through the grass like teeth and several *refugios*, mountain

bothies, are scattered across this wilderness for hikers. The best way to see this area is following the GR144 footpath, Ruta de la Transhumancia.

→ The GR144 footpath begins at the Control de Rambla Seca, at 37.9450, -2.7899, and ends after 52km in Beas de Segura. For more information on Segura routes see - Sierradesegura.com/territorio/parque-natural/red-de-senderos/

2 hrs, 37.9995, -2.7463 🏔️🚶🚻

20 ÁREA RECREATIVA GIL COBO

This grassy picnic park, which lies along the Bosques del Sur GR247 footpath, is worth a visit for José's bar alone. It is a haven for hikers wanting to cool aching legs in the small forest pool. There are friendly dogs, cosy chairs and cool beer. Ask about his eagle training and archery bow. If the bar isn't open, knock on the side door.

→ From Embalse de Aguascebas, follow the mountain road north for 8.5km. Signed on L. 1 min, 38.0798, -2.8989 🏊🍴🏔️🚶

HIDDEN CAVES

21 CUEVA DEL AGUA DE TÍSCAR

This spectacular limestone cave has been carved over the centuries by the Tíscar river

25

which plunges through a narrow gorge forming pools below. Huge stalactites count the ages it has taken to create this monumental cavern. Ancient cave paintings are hidden in its darker recesses, and in 1319 the King of Tíscar, Mahomad Abdón, had a vision of the Virgin here, so it is also known as the Gruta de la Virgen. Antonio Machado would later write a few verses on the vision: "And there where nobody goes up, there is a laughing Virgin, with a blue river in her arms...". The GR247 passes by.

→ Head N from the village of Don Pedro and the parking area is signed on the L after 100m. The way is signed and passes down steps and through a 10m tunnel.

15 mins, 37.7686, -3.0235 ⚡B✝

FEASTS AND FESTIVITIES

22 LA ROMERÍA DE LA VIRGEN DE LA CABEZA

A beautiful hermitage devoted to the Virgen de la Cabeza surveys La Iruela from its small hill. Come on the last weekend of April for the festival. Small bars are set up around the hermitage on Saturday night, and pilgrims dance, drink and burn bonfires until the small hours. On Sunday she is processed in all her finery and flowers into Cazorla. The men carry her down but, unusually, the women shoulder her back up to the hermitage.

→ Park in La Iruela and walk up. As it gets busy, take a torch as revellers might drive dangerously.

37.9158, -2.9959 ⚡✝🍴

23 CHIRINGUITO CERRADA DEL UTRERO

A great place to refuel after clambering up and jumping into the Guadalquivir river. There are shady tables and the bar has a panopoly of colourful spirits and hanging dried peppers, garlic and sausages. Try the *carne ciervo* (venison burgers) or the *carne de la montaña*, a hunters' stew to share. Open Thur – Sun.

→ Carretera Nacimiento del Río Guadalquivir, 23479 Vadillo Castril, 617 488 973

37.9236, -2.9288 🍴

24 BAR LOS 11 HERMANOS

A locals' bar with great tapas and a vine-covered terrace facing the River Guadalquivir. A little way downstream by the bridge is a good swim spot too. Inside there is a lot of hunters' memorabilia and wildlife posters.

→ Av del Segura 6, 23478 Coto-Ríos

38.0470, -2.8506 🍴🏠🏊

21

22

25 MESÓN LEANDRO, CAZORLA

A smart restaurant beneath the ruins of Santa María in Cazorla. This is the place to go for local specialities and seasonal dishes with a creative flair. Try the typical Cazorla river trout, pure local olive oils or *rin-ran*, an ancient mountain dish here. The *croquetas de perdiz* (partridge) are heavenly but the restaurant has won awards for its steak cooked on a hot stone. You'll need a siesta afterwards.

→ Calle Hoz, 3, 23470 Cazorla, 953 720 632, Mesonleandro.com
37.9082, -2.9999 🍴🍷

26 MESÓN EL CORTIJO, PONTONES

An excellent bar for tapas, with tables on a little patio outside. The Segura river tumbles past below and old men play dominoes. Try the *ajoatao* as a tapa, a purée of potato, garlic, egg and emulsified extra virgin olive oil.

→ Av. Sierra de Segura, 15, 23291 Pontones, 953 438 3422
38.1189, -2.6718 🍴

27 CASA INOCENTE, TOBA

La Toba is a tiny hamlet of around 40 people but this great restaurant can get very busy with locals and hikers on a Sunday. Sit under the old eaves and feast on local produce with the Segura river gushing past, filling the old village *lavaderos* for clothes washing. Don't miss the chance to see the birth of the crystal-clear river Toba at a tiny cave 250m up the road.

→ Lugar, C. la Toba, 23297 La Toba, 953 433 728, Casainocente.com
38.1827, -2.5604 🍴📶🚲

WILDER CAMPING

28 REFUGIO MAJALSERBAL

Deep in the wilds of the Sierra de las Villas is this refuge for hikers. Well kept with long tables, strong wood, swept stone and deep wide chimneys for hearty suppers. It is spartan but welcoming. There is a fountain outside, a children's slide and simple bunkbeds. Along the GR247

→ Stage 9 of the GR247 begins from here; for more info – Turismoencazorla.com/gr247
38.0716, -2.8966 🏔️📶🚲📶🚶🏔️

29 CAMPING FUENTE DE LA PASCUALA

Old local legends tell of people living in the woodland here, hidden from the world, only emerging for the rare sighting centuries ago. This campsite, with its lamps hidden among the pine trees, seems to keep the spirit of the legend alive. It is a huge space, with a football pitch, hammocks and access to river swims, and many families stay here all summer.

→ Ctra A-319, Km 55, 23478 Coto-Ríos, Jaén, 953 713 028, Campinglapascuala.com
38.0573, -2.8352 🏔️📶🚲📶🚲📶

RUSTIC RETREATS

30 CASA BALBINA

A sleepy cottage with a pool hidden down a lane leading into the village Arroyo Frío. Countless footpaths lead up to wild swims in the Sierra de Cazorla. Sleeps 4, dogs welcome. Various other rural retreats are available at Fuentedelciervo.com.

→ Carretera del Tranco A-319 Km 38.8, 23479 La Iruela, 650 902 232, Casabalbina.com
37.9488, -2.9162 🚲🚶🐾📶🚲

31 CASA RURAL MIRADOR DE LA OSERA

This beautiful, high-ceilinged house with balconies, a pool and a spa has incredible views out over coniferous woodland towards the karst peaks of Navazalto and the Cascada de la Osera. In the evening the sky over the whole park glows pink. Footpaths lead into the hills. Franci has several other houses available too. Ask Domingo for local festivities.

→ 23300 Villacarrillo, 626 496 680, Cazorvillas.com
38.0524, -2.9945 🚶📶🐾🚲📶

32 CALERILLA HOTEL

A beautiful stone and timber hotel with great views out across the Sierras de Cazorla, Segura y las Villas. The restaurant and bar has a terrace where you can enjoy a glass looking out to the sunset over the park. Pets are welcome and there is a pool.

→ Carretera de La Sierra, Km 24,5, 23479 Burunchel, 953 727 326, Calerillahotel.com
37.9504, -2.9458 🍴🍷

33 CORTIJO DE RAMÓN

A rambling 19th-century cortijo beautifully restored by the owners to a peaceful oasis with gardens, a pool and terrace for breakfast in the sunshine. This is a luxurious retreat with polished dark wood and crisp linen. All the details are eco-friendly and a small shop sells local oils, honey, wines and crafts.

→ Ctra. de Beas, Km 23,5, 23293 Cortijos Nuevos, 619 073 925, Cortijoderamon.com
38.2594, -2.7474 🍴🚲

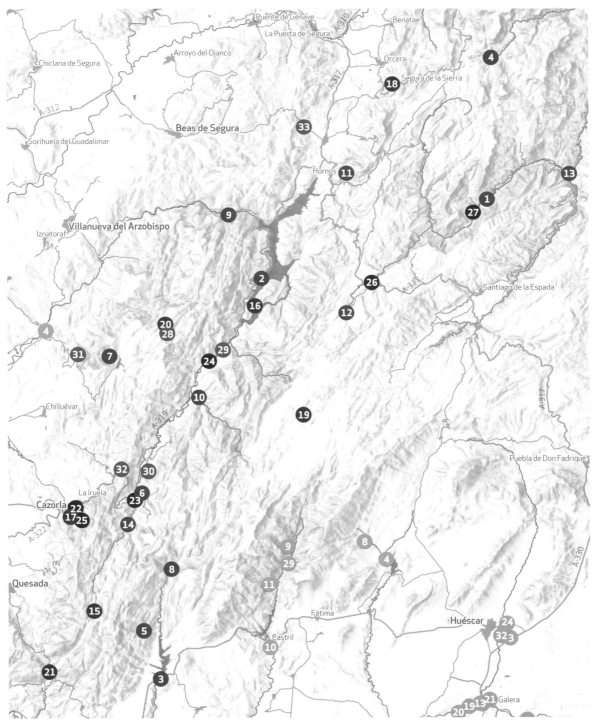

GRANADA

Our perfect weekend

→ **Breathe** in the pure mountain air scented with wild thyme and lavender as you hike up to Cueva del Agua and the peak of Peñón del Asno

→ **Gulp** down cool mouthfuls of the pure mountain water at the springs of Fuente Grande in Alfacar

→ **Soak** in the wild thermal waters at Aguas Termales de Alhama de Granada, curative waters enjoyed as far back as Roman times

→ **Ramble** along the wooden walkway of Ruta del Gollizno, passing cave paintings, gorges and rockpools in the River Velillos

→ **Feast** on local *granadino* mountain dishes, such as *alimoje con bacalao* in Alfacar: cod cooked in a rich pepper and garlic sauce

→ **Look** up to see raptors and perhaps a golden eagle circling above the ancient Nasrid border castle at Moclín

→ **Follow** the eery winding corridors at the Trincheras del Maúllo: windswept civil war trenches with views to the Sierra Nevada

→ **Watch** as the evening sunlight casts long shadows over the *vega* at Beas de Granada

→ **Bunk** down in a cosy cave room at Restaurante El Ventorrillo and follow the footpath down to bracing morning swims

In the centre of the province of Granada, just 20km away from its Alhambra Palace and riddle of ancient Andalusí streets, lies the Sierra de Huétor Natural Park. These mountains are a living museum of the effect of water and time on its porous limestone. Streams and springs run down narrow ravines, seeping into the bowels of the mountains and carving out great echoing caves. Cueva del Agua sheltered some of the first humans in Europe and as you stand close to its ancient stalactites and dark galleries echoing with dripping water, the measure of time here, these first visitors don't feel so very far away.

Later this water resurfaces in the form of springs and thermal waters. One of the most amazing human feats of water engineering dates from the Al-Andalus era, when the hills were used as a summer retreat for the 11th-century Zirid kings of Granada. At Fuente Grande in Alfacar, spring water flows into the Acequia Aynadamar. One of the main arteries of the mountains, it supplies the sparkling drinking fountains at Albaicín in Granada. Numerous springs and footpaths surround the mountain villages of Alfacar, Beas de Granada, Cogollos Vega, Diezma, Huétor Santillán, Nívar and Víznar. Spring water from Alfacar and firewood from its forests have been used for generations to bake its famous bread, pan de Alfacar, scented with wild rosemary and baked in medieval ovens.

But its waters have been muddied by more recent history. The Arabic root of the name Aynadamar means 'eyes welling with tears', possibly a reference to the tiny silver streams of bubbles welling up from the bottom of its pebbly pools. Its melancholic name is apt for a place that saw the death of Federico García Lorca, Spain's national poet, at the hands of Fascists in 1936. The same mountains which attracted the Moorish kings in the 11th century, for their proximity to Granada but also their complicated access, attracted the rebel Fascist troops in the civil war. Remains of their trenches survive across the area, dug at natural viewpoints. At the Trincheras del Maúllo, its overgrown parapets and corridors look out over the Darro valley to the snowy peaks of the Sierra Nevada and appear almost medieval. It is jarring to remember this history is less than 100 years old, buried close to the surface.

The Cerro del Maúllo was the front line between the Republicans and Nationalists for many years. The castle above Moclín defended the ancient border between Nasrid and the medieval Christian kingdoms. From medieval skirmishes to Republicans hiding out in trenches and the last moments of García Lorca, these hills have witnessed some of the most dramatic moments of Andalucían history. Its ravines, caves and streams are home to legends from almost every era. At Baños de Urquízar y Vacamía you can find wild thermal baths built during Nasrid Muslim rule. Legend tells of how they hastily hid a golden cow with diamond eyes at its thundering waterfall. The small cave chapel in Los Tajos de Alhama marks the spot where the Madonna appeared to a knight whose horse had reared up and thrown him down the ravine; hoof marks are still visible on the stone.

"If I die, leave the balcony open…" wrote Lorca in 'Farewell', where he revels in the theatre of life even after death. Wandering along the network of forest footpaths, you will see the forests are filled with wildlife, from its mountain goats on rocky promontories to raptors, including the endangered golden eagle, soaring in the skies. Looking out across these sweeping vistas it's easy to imagine Lorca's balcony, the doors flung open, as you survey the amphitheatre echoing with lives lived out in these mountains.

WILD SPRINGS

1 POZAS DE SANTA FÉ

These wild thermal springs hidden in olive groves have an average temperature of 40°C and views of the snowy peaks of the Sierra Nevada in winter. In the larger dark pool, steam rises around a hub of regular bathers who visit in the early morning. At the other end are waterfalls billowing out their humid heat, splashing the twisted roots of fig trees clinging to the eroded earthy sides.

→ It is on private farmland and access is constantly disputed, so comes and goes. From Santa Fé take the Camino de Ullar out of town for 2.5km. At the junction turn L and continue for 1km to the pools.

1 min, 37.1564, -3.7532 🏠❓🧊

2 FUENTE GRANDE DE ALFACAR

This clear pool in Alfacar is the spring and source of the Aynadamar, which runs along its 11th-century *acequia* (irrigation channel) to the Albaicín corner of Granada. It is a magical site, and they say its Arabic name, meaning 'eyes welling with tears', refers to the silver bubbles rising up from the bottom of the stone pool. It is a bittersweet image and apt, as recent history has cast a shadow over this beautiful spot. If you follow the channel to the nearby village of Víznar, you will pass a monument to the victims of the civil war at Barranco de Víznar, a balcony overlooking a ravine. Federico García Lorca was one of the many victims here who met his death at the hands of Fascists nearby.

→ Fuente Grande is clearly signed and has parking at the end of Av. Alfaguara in Alfacar. The way down to the *acequia* walk starts opposite Restaurante Fuente Grande and you can follow it for 2.5km to Víznar.

1 min, 37.2466, -3.5536 🏠🚲📷

3 AGUAS TERMALES DE ALHAMA DE GRANADA

There are wilder thermal pools in the River Alhama by the gates of the spa hotel. Here you can bathe in the curative waters for free, but it does get busy during the daytime. A beautiful Roman bridge is hidden in the tangle of undergrowth 700m downstream.

→ From Alhama de Granada head N on the A-402. After 500m turn L and follow brown signs for 'balneario'. Park in the hotel car park for a short stay. Cross the bridge and the steps are on the L.

1 min, 37.0190, -3.9833 🏠Ⓑ

4 BAÑOS DE URQUÍZAR Y VACAMÍA

The wild thermal springs in the Lecrín valley have been enjoyed since ancient times. Maidenhair ferns reach down over clear pools, and when the water is still you can see tiny silver bubbles rising up from the bottom. The baths were built during Nasrid rule in the 15th century. Vacamía is the larger bath, also known as Baño Grande, and is filled by a fresh groundwater source. A little further upstream are the Urquízar baths, or Baño Chico (smaller baths), which are filled by a thermal water source of around 24°C. This steep valley would once have been crowned by a medieval castle; little remains now but a ruined watchtower. When it was besieged by Christians, legend tells of how they hid a life-size cow made of gold, with diamond eyes and horns of ivory, in a cave here. It has never been found but you can explore upstream past the springs of Baño Chico and look for a hidden waterfall thundering down from several metres into a plunge pool.

→ At the Ermita de San Blas in Dúrcal, you will see a sign for 'Aguas Medicinales' (Medicinal Waters). Follow the tarmac road, Calle Pensamiento, passing orchards and continuing along the steep hillside, which has incredible views. After 2km you will reach a small parking

area by a wooden signpost for 'Baño Grande and Baño Chico'. Park here and walk to the baths.

15 mins, 36.9738, -3.5825 🏛️🚣🏕️⛰️🚶🏊

RIVERS & WATERFALLS

5 CASCADAS DE PRADO NEGRO

This petrified waterfall can be found in the Prado Negro stream, where the water catapults itself in a 10m drop over long stalactites and moss into a shallow pool. From the footpath, the waterfall is partially obscured by high banks of limestone riddled with caves, so you will need to stop and listen for the sound of rushing water to find the entrance. There are small pools for dips further down.

→ There is an open parking area in a field in the village of Prado Negro. Continue L uphill at the fork and the parking is on your R. Walk downhill, passing Taberna Prado Negro, and continue between the houses on the footpath for 600m. The waterfall is on your R.

15 mins, 37.3175, -3.4557 🚶⛰️📷🚻🚣

6 LA RESINERA

Just south of the Bermejales reservoir lies a quiet stretch of the Río Algar O Cacín. It's a great place for a picnic and for exploring river pools. It is close to Tajos del Río Cacín,

a river gorge where a famous Neolithic vase was discovered, now exhibited in Madrid.

→ From Fornes, head W on Calle Molinos until you reach the GR-3302. Turn L and follow signs for Vivero and La Resinera. The pools are 400m on the L. Park by the side of the road.

10 mins, 36.9418, -3.8618 🚶⛰️📷🚻

LAKES & DOLMENS

7 EMBALSE DE BÉZNAR

A great place for a swim in the calm, deep water of the reservoir. The path leads down from a beach bar and picnic area, popular with family campervans, to a small pebbly shore. For kayak rental call Aventura Alpujarra, 638 597 715.

→ Enter Béznar from Lanjarón on the N-323a and cross the bridge. Continue for 450m, turn sharp L after the bus stop then turn R down a narrow road at a sign for 'Pantano'. Parking is after 700m. Follow the footpath down to the shore behind the picnic area.

1 min, 36.9208, -3.5422 🏕️🚣🏊

8 DÓLMEN Y EMBALSE DE LOS BERMEJALES

In 1958 this ancient passage grave was moved stone by stone to its current location, facing the lakeside, to save it

from flooding. Covered with earth to form a grassy mound, it is a wonderful reconstruction of how a dolmen would have appeared when in use around 3,000 BC. The picnic area here looks out over the lake to the dark blue hills. There are wooden tables, and the lake offers wonderful warm swims with a wooden pontoon popular with kids jumping.

→ From Alhama de Granada take the A-338 into the village of Pantano de los Bermejales. Turn R opposite Restaurante El Cruce and continue for 100m. Turn L, park and walk to the dolmen.

5 mins, 36.9967, -3.8881 🚲🏊🏕🛶🍴

CAVES & CANYONS

9 LOS TAJOS DE ALHAMA

A footpath winds through this dramatic canyon which opens up slowly to stunning views of Alhama de Granada with its white walls and terracotta roofs framed by the yellow stone of the gorge. The riverbanks are wooded with elm, poplars and willow, but there are a few little paths down to frosty swims. Along the path is a 16th-century cave chapel built after a knight's horse reared up and sent the rider over the

ledge. Miraculously he survived and dazed but waking had a vision of the Madonna. The chapel was built to mark the spot. Local guys still ride their horses along the gorge and can point out his 'hoof marks' on the rock.

→ The 2km linear route is called Camino de longeles and starts from the parking zone on Carr. Granada Vieja, Alhama de Granada.

10 mins, 36.9953, -3.9866 🏊🏃🏔🐕✝

10 PUENTE COLGANTE, RUTA DEL GOLLIZNO

This hanging bridge over the Velillos river is hidden deep in the gorge of Tajos de la Hoz and can be found by following the 10km circular footpath, Ruta del Gollizno, which passes rock pools, caves and cave paintings and the great castle at Moclín.

→ The Ruta del Gollizno is signed from the end of Calle Mota in Moclín.

1 hr, 37.3463, -3.7803 🏃🏔🏊🛶🐕

11 HANGING BRIDGES OF LOS CAHORROS DE MONACHIL

Just 2km outside the sleepy village of Monachil lie this dramatic gorge and river walk. Follow ancient *acequias* to waterfalls, plenty of rock pools for

swimming, narrow caves and tunnels and its famous hanging bridges. It can get busy but it is a real Indiana Jones experience for kids. Come in spring to see the apple, cherry and pomegranate blossom, but summer swims are best as the water is searingly cold; it flows from the snowy peaks of the Sierra Nevada.

→ From the centre of Monachil, follow signs to Los Cahorros. The road leads through the historical centre of the village and then upwards into the mountains. After a 2km climb, park near Restaurante El Puntarrón. The walk is signed from here.

1 hr, 37.1303, -3.5326 🚗🏊🏖🍴🔦

12 CUEVA DE LOS MÁRMOLES
A hidden wild cave with stalactites set deep in the Sierra de Huétor.

→ From Huétor Santillán take the A-92 N for 4km. Take exit 259, turn L over the flyover and continue for 400m. Turn R at signs for Sendero del Sereno and continue to the parking. Follow the Sendero del Sereno for 2.5km to the Mirador de los Mármoles. About 500m after this, follow the track to the L to find the cave.

1 hr, 37.2623, -3.5033 🚗🚶🏔🔦

13 CUEVA DEL AGUA
This immense dark cavern, hidden in the limestone hilltops of the Sierra de la Alfaguara, was once inhabited by some of the first humans to cross into Europe. It is a living museum of the effect of water over millennia: stalactites hang from the ceiling and bats shelter in the shadows. It is advised not to enter the cave for conservation reasons, and there is an iron fence at its mouth. However, it is worth visiting for the dramatic rock corridor to the entrance, the woodland hike up and the incredible views from the cave itself.

→ From Granada take the A-92 E towards Guadix. Take exit 253 and follow the A-4002 and then the GR-3101 towards Víznar to the Centro de Visitantes Puerto Lobo. From here follow the track to the Área Recreativa la Alfaguara (37.2599, -3.5299) and its parking. Here the footpath is signed. Follow for 1.3km to the Cueva del Agua.

25 mins, 37.3324, -3.5154 🚗🚴🚲♿🏕🚶🍴🔦♻

BORDER CASTLES

14 CASTILLO DE MOCLÍN
The evocative remains of a medieval Nasrid castle that once stood along the

old border between the kingdoms of Granada and Castile. It suffered heavy damage in the civil war. There are more trenches nearby, but its sandy walls still crown the hill above Moclín and offer beautiful views over terracotta rooftops and Los Agujerones. The Ruta del Gollizno passes by.

→ A short but steep hike up from Moclín, the castle is open only at weekends. See Ayuntamientodemoclin.com for details.
10 mins, 37.3422, -3.7860 🏢🖼️🖵

SUNSET HILLTOPS

15 CONJUNTO ARQUEOLÓGICO DE TÓZAR

In this humble archaeological park just outside the village of Tózar you can see a prehistoric dolmen, a medieval necropolis and a long trench with a machine-gun firing point from the civil war. The dolmen dates from the Chalcolithic era and the medieval rock tombs were used by early Mozarabic Christians. Among the findings, a small oil lamp from the 10th century Caliphate period stands out. It is a haunting place to wander around, especially at dusk.

→ Park along Calle Real de Tózar after the bus stop. A gate near the information panels is usually left open.
5 mins, 37.3678, -3.7754 🐾🏔️🏢

16 TRINCHERAS DEL MAÚLLO

These spiralling trenches were dug by Nationalist troops into the crown of the hill during the civil war. They look out across to the Sierra Nevada, the Darro valley and the old road to Murcia. This important defensive line reached all the way to the Pedroches valley in northern Córdoba. It is a haunting space and one that eerily appears to date back much earlier than the 20th century. Its name comes from the mew of the wild cat, which soldiers imitated at night to indicate their presence. It is a forgotten spot, filled with wind and birdsong.

→ Park at the Centro de Visitantes Puerto Lobo, which has a good museum and hiking information (37.2373, -3.5332), and follow the signed footpath for 1.8km to the hilltop.
30 mins, 37.2375, -3.5190 🏢🖼️🖵◈🚶

17 BUNKER AT ALTO DE VIÑUELAS

This small bunker from the civil war is overgrown and camouflaged behind the long grass of its small hill. It overlooks the *vega* before Beas de Granada and is now, thankfully, a peaceful spot to watch the sunset.

→ From Camping Alto de Viñuelas, walk uphill along the road for 300m. Turn L onto an

unsigned track and continue for 200m until it curves slightly around the hill. Here wade through long grass to the bunker.

15 mins, 37.2251, -3.4921 ▢▢▢

18 DÓLMENES DE MONTEFRÍO

The Peñas de los Gitanos hills, just outside Montefrío, are an archaeological goldmine and hold the footprints of various eclectic civilisations. Apart from its caves, used as a dwelling by the first settlers, it has Iberian–Roman ruins, medieval Visigothic ruins and later Andalusí ruins. Among its five necropolises there are a hundred megalithic burials.

→ From Montefrío take the GR-3410 towards Moclín for 6km to signs on the L for Necrópolis Ibérica. For visitor information, call Laspeñasdelosgitanos.es, 628 305 337.

30 mins, 37.3355, -3.9562 ▢▢▢▢

19 EL PREGONERO

A great stop to refuel, with views of the church and the mountains in Montefrío.

→ Pl. de España, 3, 18270 Montefrío, 958 336 117

37.3209, -4.0108 ▢▢▢

20 KIOSCO LA ALFAGUARA

A popular Sunday lunch spot with a terrace and tables next to a green where kids can play. The typical dish here is *migas*, a delicious recipe of garlic fried bread with pancetta, chorizo and green peppers. The tapas offered with drinks are very generous. Many hiking routes through the Sierra de Huétor meet here.

→ Diseminado Diseminados, 1, 18170, 646 466 365

37.2600, -3.5299 ▢▢▢▢

21 TABERNA PRADO NEGRO

A small dark bar with barrels and seating outside along the footpath to the Prado Negro waterfalls. It offers a huge array of wines and cheeses from all across Andalucía as well as other regions of Spain. Good local dishes for sharing and freshly grilled meats (*a la brasa*).

→ Prado Negro, s/n, 18183 Huétor Santillán

37.3214, -3.4527 ▢▢▢▢▢

22 RESTAURANTE EL VENTORRO

This roadside *venta*, or coach house, opposite the lake in the Alhama river is over 300 years old. It is the place to go for traditional *granadino* recipes accompanied by a wealth of local wines. There are also thermal Arabic baths and lodgings in cave rooms.

→ Carretera de Játar, Km 2, 18120 Alhama de Granada, 958 350 438, Elventorro.net

36.9840, -3.9828 ▢▢▢▢▢

23 RESTAURANTE EL CRUCE

A good local bar to stop for a *cerveza*, served with generous granadina tapas, before a swim in the Bermejales reservoir.

→ Lugar Pantano de los Bermejales, 18129 Arenas del Rey, 958 950 3019

36.9988, -3.8896 ▢▢▢

24 ZONA ACAMPADA LA FLORENCIA

A great place for a picnic or wild camping in a clearing in the Sierra de Huétor. There are tables, stone BBQs, drinking water and a small stream running through the deep grass. The limestone peaks of Altos de Majalijar are just visible above the pine trees.

→ From Granada take the A-92 E towards Almería. After 13km take exit 264 and follow signs for 4km to Las Mimbres. Continue L at Las Mimbres and after 1.8km turn L at signs for Florencia to reach the parking.

37.2943, -3.4752 ▢▢▢▢

25 CAMPING ALTO DE VIÑUELAS

This simple and family-friendly camping ground is surrounded by olive groves and located a short stroll from the sleepy town of Beas de Granada. Occasionally, they hold flamenco nights in the camping restaurant. Dogs are welcome, fresh bread can be ordered for the mornings and there are lovely evening views across the *vega* to the Sierra Nevada.

→ Calle Granada, 17, 18184 Beas de Granada, 958 546 023, Campingaltodevinuelas.com

37.2252, -3.4878 ▢▢▢▢▢

26 NOMADXPERIENCE

Sleep in a tipi, a Mongolian yurt or a gypsy wagon, all with views of the snow-capped Sierra Nevada.

→ Urbanización San Gregorio, C. Olmo, 13, 18640 El Padul, 607 251 946, Nomadx.es

36.9839, -3.7342 ▢▢▢▢▢

RURAL HAVENS

27 CORTIJO BALZAÍN

This rural farmhouse and cottages have won ecological awards and offer a peaceful escape just outside Granada. From the patios and gardens of the old farmhouse there are views to the Vegas de Genil and the iconic Alhambra Palace. The GR7 footpath and horse trails pass by its doors.

➔ Carretera de las Cumbres Verdes, Km 2, 18140 La Zubia, 951 214 858, Balzain.com
37.0994, -3.5631 🏞🚴🏔🧗🐾

28 CASA CUEVA LA ESTRELLA

A beautiful and cosy cave house in Monachil. The kitchen, living room and bedrooms are all hollowed into natural rock, making them naturally insulated in winter and refreshingly cool in summer.

➔ C. Cuevas, 4, 18193 Monachil, 691 412 930
37.1329, -3.5408 🏞🚴🍴💡🐾

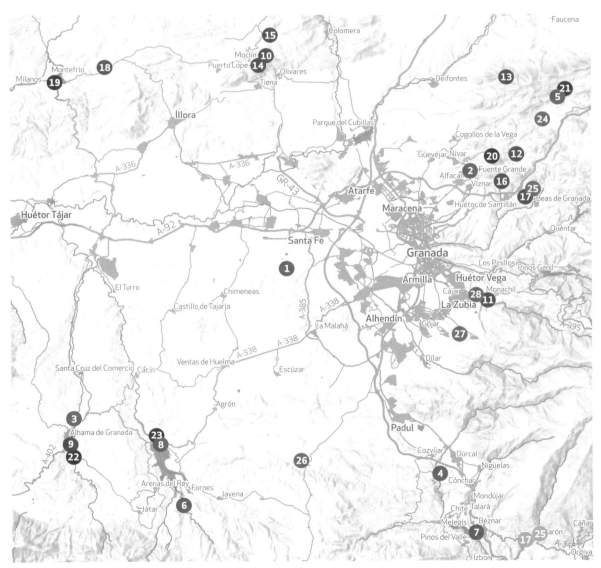

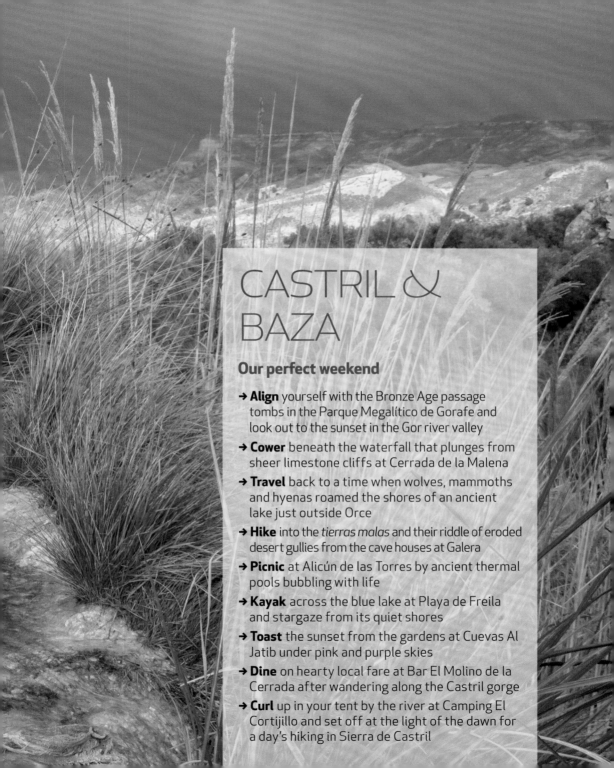

CASTRIL & BAZA

Our perfect weekend

→ **Align** yourself with the Bronze Age passage tombs in the Parque Megalítico de Gorafe and look out to the sunset in the Gor river valley

→ **Cower** beneath the waterfall that plunges from sheer limestone cliffs at Cerrada de la Malena

→ **Travel** back to a time when wolves, mammoths and hyenas roamed the shores of an ancient lake just outside Orce

→ **Hike** into the *tierras malas* and their riddle of eroded desert gullies from the cave houses at Galera

→ **Picnic** at Alicún de las Torres by ancient thermal pools bubbling with life

→ **Kayak** across the blue lake at Playa de Freila and stargaze from its quiet shores

→ **Toast** the sunset from the gardens at Cuevas Al Jatib under pink and purple skies

→ **Dine** on hearty local fare at Bar El Molino de la Cerrada after wandering along the Castril gorge

→ **Curl** up in your tent by the river at Camping El Cortijillo and set off at the light of the dawn for a day's hiking in Sierra de Castril

To the north-east of the Granada province stretches an enigmatic desert landscape of dusty pinks and ochres. Eroded gullies and ravines cover the Guadix-Baza Depression to form a semi-arid desert known as the badlands, or *tierras malas*. Over millennia, rivers have bitten into its terrain forming gaping cavities which still house ancient troglodyte cave dwellings. They say the life of a desert is under its surface, and the Baza mountainsides are dotted with doors and chimneys leading to hidden cave homes, many of which can trace their history back to the kingdom of Al-Andalus over five centuries ago.

On overcast days, when the late afternoon sun pierces heavy clouds, the gullies are thrown into golden relief, conjuring up an atmospheric moment to visit its prehistoric and sacred burial sites. The first people to have dwelt here may have been some of the very first humans from Africa. Findings outside the village of Orce suggest this could have been so. At its small museum you can see sabre-toothed tigers and some of the oldest human fossils in Europe. Much later, these caves saw pre-Roman tribes, *bástulos* or Iberian Celts, whose larger-than-life statue of a regally adorned woman, known as *La Dama de Baza*, now housed in Madrid, was unearthed here.

This parched terrain continues to offer up surprises. Beneath its porous limestone bedrock, a giant aquifer emerges in the form of springs and thermal spas. At Alicún de las Torres, thermal water flows along the top of what appears to be an aqueduct at first glance. Lichen and shaggy moss hang down its sides, disguising the fact that there are no bricks: it is an entirely natural creation built by millennia of mineral deposits; in places it is up to 10m high. Nearby are hundreds of Bronze Age passage graves; it is easy to see why this land was considered sacred.

At Zújar, by the feet of the Jabalcón mountains, thermal baths used since Roman times emerge when the Negratín reservoir levels are low. Meanwhile, locals from Orce and Huéscar cool off in fresh village pools fed by water bubbling up from a ground source and filled with silver shoals of barbel fish.

To the north runs the wilderness of the Sierra de Castril, with waterfalls plunging down precipices, pools as clear as ice and forests filled with wildlife. Look out for mouflon at dusk, when they emerge to pick their way downhill under the cover of twilight to drink at rivers. This beautiful fawn-brown, horned creature is thought to be the ancestor of all breeds of modern sheep. You can follow the coursing River Castril upstream to reach Cerrada de la Malena, a waterfall that plunges over a dramatic escarpment in a remote and unspoilt spot.

After a day hiking in these hills, feast on the locally reared roast lamb at Restaurante El Maño; an area so riddled with caves is going to have at least a few wine cellars, and the red wine from the Galera caves is a perfect match. Soak up the restorative waters in the Hammam baths at Cuevas Al Jatib and bed down deep underground in their luxurious cave houses.

WILD SWIMS

1 PLAYA DE FREILA

A deserted beach by the sparkling blue Negratín reservoir. For kayak or canoe rental, call Manolo at the Nautical Club, 666 086 039. It is a short stroll from Cortijo del Cura restaurant (see entry).

→ From Freila take the GR-8100 N to the main road. Turn L and take the first R. Continue for 3km to reach the beach and parking.

5 mins, 37.5613, -2.9120 🏊🏕️🅿️🍴🛶

2 MANATIAL DE FUENTECALIENTE, ORCE

A small swimming pool fed by the cool River Orce. Children and fishes fill the clear pool which is said to have mineral medicinal properties. As early as the 9th century, Muslim geographers recorded that the farmlands were watered by this abundant spring. The flow rate is 80–170 litres per second.

→ From Orce take the GR-9104 in the direction of Galera. After 1.6km turn R and follow the road 50m to the parking.

1 min, 37.7283, -2.4999 🏊🏙️♿

3 MANATIAL DE FUENCALIENTE, HUÉSCAR

A large natural spring fills this busier pool, which has seating, a restaurant and grassy areas. Barbel fish fill the clean water – fun for kids – and the water can reach around 19°C, thanks to subterranean aquifers. The spring was famous in the 16th century as its large flow, up to 500 litres per second, was used for laundering in the Italian wool industry, which was based here. Special Epiphany swims are held on January 6th. It can get busy but the pool is large.

→ Turn off the A-330 for Huéscar and follow signs for Fuencaliente. Parking.

1 min, 37.8025, -2.5220 🏊🏙️♿🍴🏕️♿

4 EMBALSE DE SAN CLEMENTE

A small pebbly track leads down to the blue reservoir with views out to the ruins of its ancient church.

→ From Huéscar take the A-326 towards Fátima for 16km. Turn R at signs for Coto de Pesca and continue for 5km. Turn L at signs for 'Piscifactoria Las Fuentes' and continue for 1.7km to reach signs on the R for Coto de Pesca. Park here and find your way down to the water. Be sensitive with any people fishing as this is a designated fishing area.

10 mins, 37.8711, -2.6551 🏕️🏊🚣

HEALING WATERS

5 ACEQUIA DE TORIL

This natural water channel, or *acequia*, is formed by the thermal spring water that courses along its top. Over millennia the flowing water has deposited its minerals creating this stunning flowstone phenomenon, which snakes through a desert of scorched ravines. The damp, mossy sides of this natural monument can reach up to 10m in height, and its age is anything between 35,000 and 205,000 years old. There are dolmens and standing stones on either side; could it be these springs were considered a sacred place, hence their designation as a burial site? Approach the area with care and respect.

→ Park opposite the Hotel Balneario in Alicún de las Torres. Walk up the road for 10m and take the footpath to the L at 37.5088, -3.1076. Follow for about 100m until you see the beginning of the wall and follow this.

45 mins, 37.5121, -3.1100 🚶🚴🏃🏊🏔️📷

6 BAÑOS TERMALES DE ZÚJAR

An enormous open reservoir with sparkling blue water surrounded by an almost lunar landscape. The Embalse de Negratín is

245

perfect for stargazing on clear nights or spying out the mysterious caves in the surrounding hills. Just below Restaurante Baños there is access to hot springs when the water levels have dropped. There is also a small swimming pool with thermal waters attached to the restaurant: €2 entry.

→ Park at the Restaurante Los Baños de Zújar and walk down the track curving L to the embalse.

10 mins, 37.5977, -2.8144 🏊🔲✳🏔🏨

7 THERMAL POOL, ALICÚN DE LAS TORRES

Just one of many hot springs in this magic landscape and a tributary of the River Fardes. Under the stone bridge there are a couple of thermal pools with steam rising from the dripping stone.

→ The access is challenging and slippery. Do not jump down the rocks unless you are confident you can get back up. Head S from Alicún de las Torres in the direction of Fonelas. Park on the roadside at the first bridge, about 200m after signs to the 'Piscina', and walk down the track parallel to the road. At the first bend in the path turn L and climb between two large rocks. It's a scrabble down to the pools.

20 mins, 37.5064, -3.1093 📷🚶

GORGES & WATERFALLS

8 SALTO DE AGUA DEL YIYO

Follow the river-eaten passageway of limestone rock upstream, passing little waterfalls and pools in the Río Guardal. It's a very cool swim but in beautifully clear water shaded by woodland, the bends in the river forming private nooks.

→ From Huéscar take the A-326 W in the direction of Fátima. After 16km turn R at signs for 'Coto de Pesca' and 'Embalse de San Clemente'. Continue for 5km, turn L at the fork and continue past the lake on your R for another 5km. Park at the bend in the road where it crosses the Río Guardal. Follow the river upstream.

25 mins, 37.8870, -2.6789 🏊🚶🏕️⛺🍴🚗

9 CERRADA DE LA MALENA

The Arroyo la Malena has a short but dramatic life before reaching the Río Castril. It begins here where the stream has cut a narrow ravine into the Malena escarpment, at the bottom of which is an upwelling of water that fills a clear, icy pool. In rainy months water plunges out of the narrow ravine above to make a waterfall several metres high. Sit still in the evening and

watch for wild rams that come tentatively down the mountainside to drink at the pool.

→ From the gates of Camping de Cortijillo, turn R and carry on up the road. After 800m you will come to some gates and signs for the Sendero de la Magdalena. Follow the track for 1.5km.

40 mins, 37.8825, -2.7631 🏊🚶🏔️🏕️⛺🍴🚗🐾

10 PASARELA DE LA CERRADA DEL RÍO CASTRIL

Follow this 2km circular wooden walkway through the Castril river gorge, where you can run through tunnels, cross hanging bridges and pass numerous waterfalls. It begins and ends in the beautiful mountain village of Castril.

→ There is a parking area along Calle Nueva del Río in Castril and the path is signed from the bridge over the Castril river, a few metres down the road.

10 mins, 37.7946, -2.7816 🏔️🏊🚶

11 SENDERO CERRADA DE LÉZAR

This 2km linear path runs through the Barranco del Buitre gorge. Look up for vultures in the cliffs overhead. The route passes between holm oaks, gorse and cornicabra for a little while until it reaches

16

a wall blocking the canyon. It is a beautiful way to find some river pools. Take care if there have been heavy rains as the currents are strong.

→ From the gates of Camping El Cortijillo turn L and follow the road S for 2.8km. The *sendero* is signed on a path to your R. Follow from here. 40 mins, 37.8480, -2.7837 ⬛🏕🏊👥💬

HILLTOP HIGHS

12 PARQUE DE MERIENDAS EN ALICÚN DE LAS TORRES

A grassy picnic area by the roadside with carved tables, a fountain and views out across the Baza mountains. A via ferrata climbing route begins here and there is a thermal spring as well as a small pond with frogs under the overhanging rock.

→ Park opposite Hotel Reina Isabel and walk 40m downhill to the first curve. The park is to your L.
2 mins, 37.5074, -3.1082 🏞💬

13 LA ERMITA EN EL CERRO DE LA VIRGEN

For 600 years the Muslim population of Galera lived on this fortified hill, now the site of a hermitage overlooking Galera's 'new' village and cave houses. In 1569 it saw bloodshed during the Morisco Rebellion. Moriscos were the Catholic descendants of the Mudéjars Muslims living under the new Christian rule.

→ A great signed history walk, with panels and illustrations (in Spanish and English), starts in Plaza Mayor and winds up to the chapel. Follow signs or download the route from Venagalera.com.
10 mins, 37.7421, -2.5494 🚶🚲🛕🎒💬🏛

14 CASTILLO BENZALEMA

The ruins of this 12th-century castle overlook the Guardal and Castril rivers as they meet the Embalse de Negratín. Following 15th-century skirmishes, it fell to the Christians in 1488. Its legend, if true, goes some way to explaining the ruins. In 1603 a letter in Arabic script was found in a nearby cave house. It read "what great treasure there is in the soil of Benazalema!" The Mayor of Baza took the words literally and ripped up the foundations of the castle, revealing nothing but earth. It turned out that the letter had been written by a Faqih doctor and referred to a nearby spa at Zújar, known to heal skin complaints. The treasure wasn't *hidden* in the earth, it *was* the earth.

17

→ The best place to see this castle is from the tiny hamlet of Las Cucharetas sitting high and haughty on its hill. It is on private farmland and about 3km along the road towards Cuevas del Negro from Baños Termales de Zújar.
30 mins, 37.6006, -2.7872 ☜ ❓

ANCIENT & SACRED

15 DÓLMEN DE ALICÚN DE LAS TORRES 1

This ancient burial chamber drops a few steps underground into a square cavern supported by heavy stone slabs. It looks out over panoramic views of the desert canyons carved by the Gor and Fardes rivers and is now open to the vultures that soar overhead; the only sound is the wind in the long grass. After rain, water pools in the veined rock floor and reflects the sky.
→ Park in the free car park opposite the Hotel Balneario and walk 100m uphill. Turn L up the footpath and continue for another 50m.
10 mins, 37.5102, -3.1082 ❧ ✝ ⛰

16 DÓLMEN DE ALICÚN DE LAS TORRES 2

Lying in a peaceful spot, if a little less dramatic, this passage tomb is wonderfully preserved and surrounded by pine woodland and a shady picnic area.
→ Leaving Alicún de las Torres in the direction of Gorafe, take the first R on to the GR-6101. After 300m park on the L. Walk up the track 30m.
1 min, 37.5065, -3.1072 ❧ ✝

17 PARQUE MEGALÍTICO DE GORAFE

The grassy sides of the Gor river valley fall away to an icy river. The remains of over 200 megalithic funerary stones found in this valley suggest it was once considered a sacred space. At this point many of the stones have been excavated but preserved, still in the form of their dark chambers. Standing at the dolmens signed 'Conquin', you can look straight along the Gor valley to the V-shaped wedge of sunlit badlands beyond. Follow the footpath downhill to reach the River Gor.
→ Park at 37.4485, -3.0210 on the GR-6100 and follow signs along a footpath downhill for the Conquin dolmens and the river or uphill for many other dolmens. Access to the park is free and entrance to the Megalithic Interpretation Centre in Gorafe is €3.
5 mins, 37.4492, -3.0195 ⛰ ✝ ❧ ✛ ✝ ☑

18 DÓLMENES LA MAJADILLA

One of the highest concentrations of dolmens in the Gor river valley, they range in age between the Neolithic and Bronze

Age. They are surrounded by olive groves in a peaceful spot a short, dusty walk from Gorafe. Burial urns, skeletons, flint tools and shells were excavated here. Visit the musuem in Gorafe to see the findings.
→ From the Centro del Interpretaión del Megalitismo in Gorafe follow Calle Granada out of town and straight on to the track to the L, signed 'Grupo Majadillas'.
25 mins, 37.4720, -3.0479 ⛹ ❧ ⛰ ✛

19 CASTELLÓN ALTO

Carved into the soft rock of the hill above the River Galera are the remains of this Bronze Age settlement. One of the most important archaeological sites of the Argar people, it dates from 1900–1600 BC, when Galera was known as Tútugi. Hundreds of graves and two mummified bodies of an adult and child were found in among their houses. The adult mummy had long, dark braided hair. The museum is great and has won awards for conservation. It's a magical place. From Galera, you can walk or cycle to this site just out of town and carry on to the Paleosismitas. The site and museum are open Wed – Sun. For more information see Venagalera.com.

23

24

29

30

30

→ From Plaza Mayor in Galera follow Calle Padre Manjón down the side of the *ayuntamiento* and turn R on to Calle Cervantes. Follow this road for 1.5km to the site signed on the L.

25 mins, 37.7400, -2.5658 🚴🚮💻⊞🎿🚶🏄⛷

ROCKS & TOMBS

20 FORMACIÓN GEOLÓGICA DE PALEOSISMITAS

These wonderfully strange-shaped rocks are the geological result of a prehistoric lake that covered most of the badlands. They sit along a great 12km circular hike, or cycle, from Galera into the gullies and canyons of the wild badlands. For more info see Venagalera.com.

→ See directions to Castellón Alto and carry on for another 1km. After the first bend carry on for 500m, take a sharp L and carry on for another 500m. The rocks are on your R.

40 mins, 37.7344, -2.5732 🚴🎿⛰🚶🏄⛷

21 NECRÓPOLIS DE TÚTUGI, GALERA

This extensive Iberian–Roman necropolis hollowed into the Cerro del Real hill outside Galera was used between the 7th and 5th centuries BC. Many of the chambers and remains were excavated in the 1920s. It was here that the Diosa de Galera was discovered: a small 7th-century BC Phoenician goddess, possibly Astarte, carved in alabaster and flanked by two sphinxes.

→ You can walk from Galera. Take the Camino Puebla over the A-330 and turn a sharp R. Open Wed – Sun. For more information see Venagalera.com.

15 mins, 37.7461, -2.5412 🚴⛲⊞

22 CENTRO DE INTERPRETACIÓN PRIMEROS POBLADORES

Some of the oldest human bones in Europe can be seen in this small museum in Orce. An ancient, vanished lake nearby is the source of its incredible fossils. Rhinos, sabre-toothed tigers, wolves, hyenas, hippos, mammoths and humans came to drink at this lake and ultimately became victims here. The museum houses the fossil remains of this incredible wild biodiversity.

→ Cam. San Simon, 18858 Orce, 958746171, Orce.es

1 min, 37.7242, -2.4758 🚴⛲⊞

WINE & DINE

23 MESÓN ILLUSIÓN

A friendly, traditional restaurant, popular with the locals. Low wooden beams frame a welcoming bar and tables. The tapas, served free along with drinks, are generous and endlessly creative.

→ Calle Manuel García Sánchez, 15, 18890 Gorafe, 676 925 018

37.4799, -3.0431 🍴🍷⊞

24 RESTAURANTE EL MAÑO

Looks deceive at this restaurant on the edge of Huéscar's industrial area, but locals know this is one of the best places for traditional *granadino* fare. Try the *cordero al horno* (slow-roast lamb), which is the house speciality. The *jamón* is cured by the head chef and owner Emilio. A sharing plate of *embotillas* (various cured meats, including the *jamón*) will melt in your mouth, especially the finely sliced *butifarra*, a local style of cured sausage. There is a large cellar of famous Sierra Nevada wines.

→ Polígono Industrial la Encantada, 47, 18830 Huéscar, 647 911 546

37.8136, -2.5224 🍴🍷

25 BAR EL MOLINO DE LA CERRADA

A rustic bar with long wooden tables inside and outside on the banks of the Castril river. They offer hearty fare at the end of the Pasarela del Río Castril footpath. Lodging is available in the historic centre of Castril, a short walk away.

→ C. Villa Baja, s/n, 18816 Castril, 650 356 402, Casarural-laparracastril.es

37.7911, -2.7805 🍴🍷⊞🛏

26 CORTIJO DEL CURA

A good stop for seafood, paella or grilled meats and situated right by the lakeside beach.

→ Cruce Freila, s/n, 18812 Freila, 958 342 358

37.5613, -2.9130 🍴🍷🛏

27 PIZZARÍA LAS 7 FUENTES

Pizzas cooked in wood ovens are on offer here as well as more traditional dishes of *paletilla de cordero al horno* (roast lamb). You can eat outside on the terrace with great views of the Baza hills or inside in the more intimate cave rooms.

→ Paraje 7 Fuentes, s/n, 18800 Baza, 618 266 028

37.4611, -2.7805 🍴🍷

WILDER CAMPING

28 CAMPING LA CABAÑUELA

A cosy campsite on the banks of the Negratín reservoir and just a stroll away from the Playa de Freila beach and the Cortijo del Cura restaurant. A 4km walk south will take you to Freila and its medieval castle.

→ Carril Cortijo del Cura, s/n, 18812 Freila, Granada, 958 063 108

37.5587, -2.9114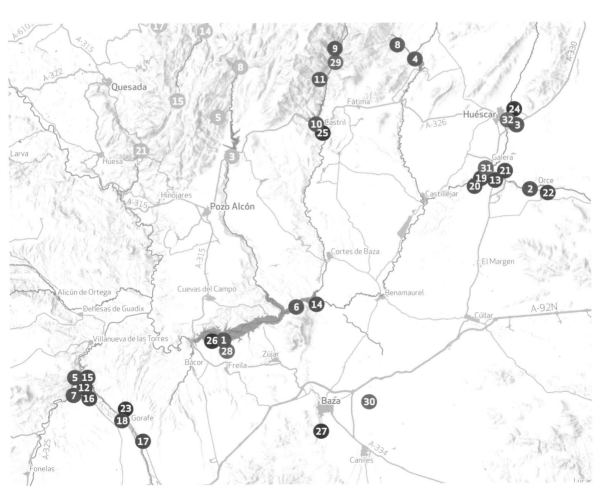

29 CAMPING EL CORTIJILLO

A peaceful campsite, with bungalows and hammocks, on the riverbank in the heart of the Sierra de Castril. Several hiking routes lead from here to some of the wildest places in the mountain range, and the holistic campsite offers a place to disconnect from technology: there is no wifi and they have a very poor phone signal. But they do have a wonderful bar and rustic restaurant next to the river pool. Dogs are welcome.

→ Calle Nacimiento del Río Castril, s/n, 41092 Castril

37.8669, -2.7623

30 CUEVAS AL JATIB

A hamlet of beautiful cave houses each with their own chimney, hearth and kitchen as well as winding passages to cosy bedrooms. Stepladders lead up to ceiling windows where you can pop your head out for dawn views of the Baza hills. The hamlet was abandoned in the 1970s, but the owner, Luc, has carefully restored each dwelling, even adding a rustic restaurant and luxurious Hammam baths in larger caverns. There are several secret passages for adventurous kids, an outdoor pool, gardens and a terrace for the sunset.

→ Arroyo Cúrcal s/n, Camino de Oria, 18800 Baza, 958 342 248, Aljatib.com

37.4942, -2.7162

31 CASAS CUEVAS EL MIRADOR DE GALERA

Surrounded by footpaths and history, these cosy cave houses in Galera have wonderful views and are run by Antonio whose family has lived in the village for several generations.

→ C. Cervantes, 3, 18840 Galera, 639 600 264, Elmiradordegalera.com

37.7427, -2.5514

32 CUEVAS ATALAYA

A rustic complex of beautifully restored cave houses, each one with its own quirks and creative decoration.

→ Cuevas Atalaya, 20, 18830 Huéscar, 615 684 057, Cuevasatalaya.com

37.8029, -2.5288

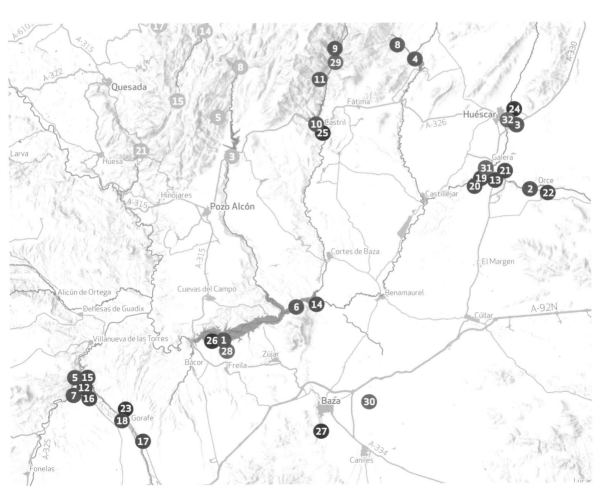

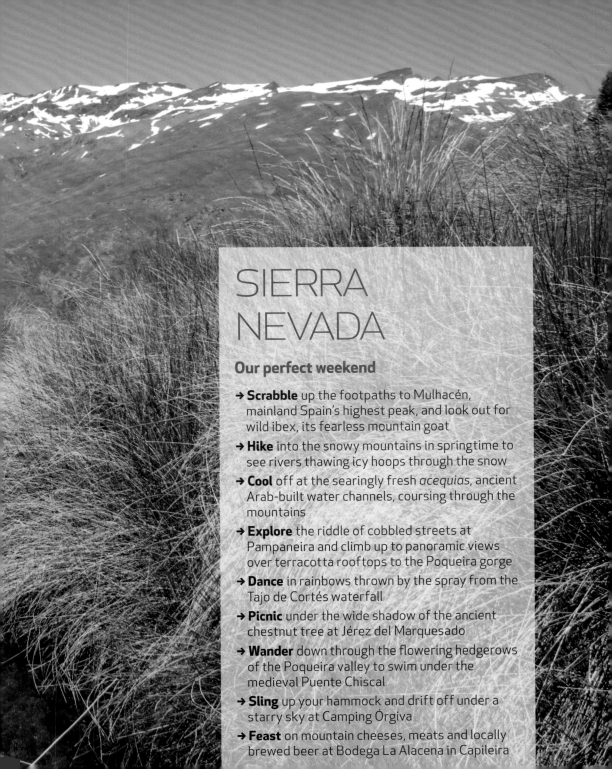

SIERRA NEVADA

Our perfect weekend

→ **Scrabble** up the footpaths to Mulhacén, mainland Spain's highest peak, and look out for wild ibex, its fearless mountain goat

→ **Hike** into the snowy mountains in springtime to see rivers thawing icy hoops through the snow

→ **Cool** off at the searingly fresh *acequias*, ancient Arab-built water channels, coursing through the mountains

→ **Explore** the riddle of cobbled streets at Pampaneira and climb up to panoramic views over terracotta rooftops to the Poqueira gorge

→ **Dance** in rainbows thrown by the spray from the Tajo de Cortés waterfall

→ **Picnic** under the wide shadow of the ancient chestnut tree at Jérez del Marquesado

→ **Wander** down through the flowering hedgerows of the Poqueira valley to swim under the medieval Puente Chiscal

→ **Sling** up your hammock and drift off under a starry sky at Camping Órgiva

→ **Feast** on mountain cheeses, meats and locally brewed beer at Bodega La Alacena in Capileira

The icy peaks of Mulhacén and Veleta crowning the Sierra Nevada are the highest points of mainland Spain. The dazzling heights, glimpsed from dark, narrow streets in Granada, lure with the promise of adventure. If the mountains were an upturned ship, then the area known as Las Alpujarras would run south from the keel. Beautiful mountain villages cling to these green southern slopes. "The place of clear light" the Dalai Lama described it in 1982, and as you wind up mountain roads, these villages appear to be built on clouds rather than rock.

The light of Al-Andalus persisted in the Alpujarras much longer than elsewhere in Andalucía. Pedro Alarcón, a novelist from Granada, described it as a "labyrinth of cliff faces and chasms, in which each rock, each cave, each tree testified" to an episode of its Islamic history. The hills were terraced in the 10th century and an immense network of water channels, known as *acequias*, were built. For a millennium they have fed pastures and supplied the fountains of Granada and countless villages with spring water. Follow these channels of melted snow into the hills and you might spy a monarch butterfly sunning its wings in a mulberry tree, the living legacy of the once booming Andalusí silk trade.

Soon after 1492, when Boabdil surrendered to the Catholic Monarchs, many Muslims were forced to flee. They settled in the remote villages of Pórtugos, Capileira, Atalbéitar and Pampaneira, whose names date from earlier Visigothic times. These ancient villages, with cubic houses, chunky chimneys and roofs serving as neighbours' terraces, resemble Berber villages in North Africa. Narrow passageways are linked by *tinao*, chestnut-beamed tunnels that dip under the houses, connecting a maze of white-washed streets. Peppers and tomatoes dry on clay roofs and at Pampaneira freshwater channels rush through streets.

Almost-forgotten footpaths link these villages. Known as *escarihuelas*, they once acted as medieval trading routes to the coast. You can walk to Atalbéitar from Ferreirola, passing old mills and threshing grounds without touching any tarmac. A beautiful hike follows the Acequía Alta, passing the Poqueira gorge to Mulhacén's steep ascent. These peaks are another vast and icy world where, in springtime, thawing streams carve thick-ribbed ice hoops. Break your journey at the mountain refuge in Poqueira and set off at dawn to hike up Mulhacén; at this hour it will just be you and the ibex, half-seen in the early light.

From Mulhacén the Siete Lagunas glow acid-green below. On the descent you pass the tumbling waterfalls Chorreras Negras and walk through a glacial landscape to reach Trevélez, the highest village in Spain. At Pórtugos, you can slake your thirst at fizzing, ferruginous, mineral-rich springs.

Look out for the Iberian ibex, a sure-footed and not very shy mountain goat. It has a dramatic streak and can be spotted at the crest of almost any challenging-looking outcrop. Visit in spring to see the snowy mountains turn ochre, intense green, russet or purple – there are over 2,000 endemic plant species here. Spy out *violeta de Sierra Nevada* or *estrella de las nieves*, snow stars, whose rosettes of fleshy, white leaves are a symbol of enduring love.

Hearty plates of stews and broths with red peppers, cod, saffron and chickpeas are typical Alpujarran fare, not to mention the *jamón* cured in Trevélez. A drink will typically come served with a good tapa. After a day in the mountains, bed down by the snug hearth at El Gato Negro, a centuries-old house in Capileira, and wake to dawn over the Poqueira valley.

7

STREAMS & PICNICS

1 ÁREA RECREATIVA LA TIZNÁ

A grassy picnic spot where mountain streams join to form the River Alcázar. There are stone picnic tables under the shady trees and several spots for paddling in the stream. Follow the old droving paths along the circular PR-A31 trail from Jérez del Marquesado to reach it. You can follow it on to Balsa de Alcázar, ancient chestnut trees and mountain refuge huts.

→ From Jérez del Marquesado, take the road in the direction of Lanteira. Just before you cross under the aqueduct, 'Sendero 300m' is signed on the R. Follow the walk from here. It's 6km to the Área Recreativa.

1.5 hrs, 37.1391, -3.1856 🎏🏊🛶🏕🏚

2 CASTAÑO CENTENARIO DEL RAMBLON

Autumn is the best time to visit the ancient chestnut groves in the ravines outside Jérez del Marquesado. Watered by the springs and *acequías* rushing down from the Sierra Nevada, this woodland is said to be the home of elves and goblins. This is easy to believe when standing beneath the ancient chestnut tree whose girth suggests it's at least 1,000 years old. Great mushrooming.

→ From Calle Alcázar in Jérez de Marquesado follow footpath signs pointing downhill at 37.1812, -3.1596 with views out to the ancient watchtower. Continue down and cross the river. With the river on your R continue for another 600m to the tree before the bridge over the river.

15 mins, 37.1753, -3.1659 🎏🛶🏊

3 ÁREA RECREATIVA LA ROSANDRÁ

A good place to explore with kids and just 1km from the pretty village of Aldeire in the foothills of the Sierra Nevada. There is a rope bridge, stepping stones, a small cascade in the river, several old chestnut trees and a play park. Plenty of stone picnic tables and BBQs.

→ From Aldeire, follow the road S along the River Benéjar for a few hundred metres to a bridge on the R. Cross the bridge and continue 700m S along the river.

25 mins, 37.1474, -3.0740 🎏🛶🏊

LAKES & RIVERS

4 EMBALSE DE COGOLLOS DE GUADIX

Built in 1978, this reservoir is a recent part of the history of the waterworks around Cogollos de Guadix, which stretches back to at least

Roman times. There is stony but easy access to the reservoir, which is open for bathing and picnics. A few stone BBQs and picnic tables sit under the shade of the pine trees.

→ From the 12th-century Arab cistern (*aljibe*) in the town square of Cogollos de Guadix, head E out of town. At the roundabout, take the first exit onto the GR-5104. After 1.7km turn R and then immediately L onto the dirt track. Follow the track, keeping R, for 1.3km to reach the water. Park where you can on the road.

1 min, 37.2078, -3.1648 🛶🎏

5 BALSA DE ALCÁZAR

A small lake in the ravines outside Jérez del Marquesada surrounded by holm oaks, pine and chestnut groves. Pennyroyal mint grows on its banks.

→ See directions to Castaño Centenario but continue along the path for another 700m.

25 mins, 37.1724, -3.1650 🚶🛶🛶

WILD WATERFALLS

6 CASCADA Y LAGUNA DE LOS LAVADEROS DE LA REINA

The deep winter snowdrifts thaw in late spring here to reveal a black and rocky terrain with rare lichens and algae, rushing

waterfalls and lagoons. These are the headwaters of the Maitena river, an ancient glacier and one of the most spectacular places in the Sierra Nevada. Queen Fabiola of Belgium returned time and again, giving Circo Glaciar de las Covatillas its unofficial name, the queen's bathing spot. Visit in late spring to see thawing snow and ice caves.

➜ The parking for this hike (at 37.1424, -3.3458) is 14km down the tarmac road signed 'Lavaderos de la Reina' in Güéjar Sierra. The 8km route starts at and is signed from the parking. Follow the Acequia Papeles waterway 3km to the peak of Papeles and continue another 5km to the cascada. You will pass the Refugio Piedra Partida should you wish to camp.

2.5 hrs, 37.1284, -3.2718 🏔🚶🏕🏚

7 CHORRERAS NEGRAS

This waterfall tumbles down tiers of black rock and scree from the dazzlingly bright, cold, clear mountain pool of Laguna Hondera. If you're walking the Trevélez–Siete Lagunas path you can wander down the length of its fall, looking out over the Prado Grande meadows.

➜ From Trevélez you can follow the PR-A27 Trevélez–Siete Lagunas footpath to Mulhacén. Please take care in winter as there will be snow,

and crampons and ice axes are required. In summer you will need to carry plenty of water, and as there is very little shade, heatstroke is a danger. The waterfall is 8km along the PR-A27, signed from Calle Horno in Trevélez.

3 hrs, 37.0472, -3.2920 🏔🚶🏕🏚

8 LAGUNA HONDERA, SIETE LAGUNAS

Seen from the summit of Mulhacén, this lake resembles an acid-green inkblot. Descend to its banks and you'll find yourself in a bright-green meadow sprung with lichen. The clear water streams over bright pebbles before cascading down the Chorreras Negras waterfall, which points the way to Trevélez. It is a hidden paradise surrounded by the steep scree of its glacial valley and crowned by the snow-capped peaks above. The water is searingly cold from the melted snow and a couple of springs that fill the pool.

➜ See directions and cautions for Chorreras Negras. Continue uphill for another 500m to the lagoons.

3 hrs, 37.0475, -3.2934 🏕🏔🚶🏕

9 CASCADA DE TAJO CORTÉS

This waterfall plummets into a small pool that can be reached down a few stone steps. Rainbows leap through its spray as it hits

a rock pool large enough for a paddle or a bracing shower in summer. Upstream, and on the other side of the road, are slightly larger pools where the Río Jabalí and Río Chorrera meet to form this waterfall. Follow the Jabalí stream upstream on the right for rockpools.

→ This waterfall is a 3km hike along the circular PR-A29 Sendero Río Bermejo trail, which is signed from the parking on Calle Eras at Pórtugos. It carries on to Capileira and Pitres.

45 mins, 36.9555, -3.3257 🚶🧗🏔⛺

10 SALTO DE PAULA

At this hidden spot the Río Bermejo falls as a fine spray over a limestone ledge into the woodland canopy. In spring it forms a small plunge pool and sometimes in summer the locals from Ferreirola build a dam. Arrive in the summer heat to feel its coolness emanating in waves before you see it. The village footpath passes a couple of drinkable springs: one is sparkling water and the other is very pure, known as Fuente de Paula.

→ From the Fuente Lavadero fountain in Ferreirola walk downhill E, passing the houses, and head out of the village along the footpath for about 1km. You will pass the old threshing floor known as the Era del Trance and there

are splendid views across the hills of Los Picachos. About 300m after the threshing floor take the L fork of the footpath and follow it upstream for about 100m to the waterfall.

30 mins, 36.9313, -3.3068 🚶🧗🏔💧

FOUNTAINS & SPRINGS

11 FUENTE AGRIA AND CHORREÓN DE PÓRTUGOS

The fizzy and ferruginous water at this fountain in Pórtugos make it one of the Alpujarras most famous drinking fountains. The mineral-rich water emerges as a waterfall a few metres downstream, where its iron-rich water has painted the rock a rich rust-red, all the more striking for its mossy green surroundings. It is a spectacular sight even if it is a popular spot and without a place to swim. A tiny market sells handmade leather goods. If you like the taste of the water, fill your bottle at the fountain and it will fizz when snapped open for the rest of the day.

→ Take the road out of Pórtugos in the direction of Trevélez for 400m and park where possible. The fountain is on the L by the chapel and the waterfall is down some stairs on the R.

3 mins, 36.9408, -3.3068 ⛲📖🅱🏞

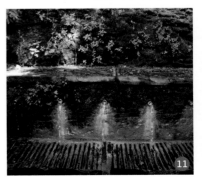

MOUNTAIN SWIMS

12 PUENTE DE ABUCHITE

A thrillingly cold pool in the river Poqueira as it gushes and cascades over rocks at the bottom of its deep gorge. Follow the river 500m downstream to Puente Chiscal with its similar, small sparkling pool. Upstream is the abandoned village of La Cebadilla. The Acequias del Poqueira walk crosses this bridge. It's great for a quick skinny dip as you'll likely have only wild ibex for company.

→ From the car park at the Mirador Sierra Nevada (36.9633, -3.3606) it is an easy 1.5km walk downhill (harder on the way back up!). Follow signs along the footpath for Puente de Abuchite.

45 mins, 36.9721, -3.3627 🚶🏊🔦🍴

13 PUENTE CHISCAL

This low bridge spans the Río Mulhacén where the river swells, pours and eddies over its stones. From the bridge the sheer sides of the gorge look like a drawing from a 19th-century Romantic's tattered sketchbook.

→ Follow the footpath for 1km from Capileira, signed from the bend in Calle Cerecillo.

30 mins, 36.9684, -3.3634 🚻🏊🍴

14 PISCINA NATURAL DE TREVÉLEZ

Located in Trevélez, the highest village in Andalucía, this beautiful, natural pool in the Río Grande is perfect for a dip. Wander up past the curing jamón houses to the higher part of town with its ancient tangle of pretty white streets.

→ Follow the road out of Trevélez towards Restaurante Piedra Ventana, cross the bridge and carry on R down to the water.

10 mins, 37.0004, -3.2624 🏊🍴

WILD RUINS

15 PUENTE ROMANO DE FONDALES

Known as the Roman bridge, this delicate, arched bridge over the River Trevélez probably dates back to the 12th-century Al-Andalus. The remains of a flour mill from the same era can be seen alongside the riverbanks. The GR142 Alpujarra trail passes over the bridge and follows the Camino Real to the distant province of Almería.

→ Park in Fondales and follow the signed GR142 Sendero de la Alpujarra in the direction of Órgiva. You'll pass over the Roman bridge in 500m.

10 mins, 36.9248, -3.3173 ⛰🚶🚻🍴🏊

16 CASTILLO DE ALDEIRE

Crowning a rocky spur on the north face of the Sierra Nevada, this ancient castle has for centuries guarded the natural way from Guadix to the Alpujarras. It is also known as Castillo de la Caba as people say it was at this castle that Florinda, daughter of the Governor of Ceuta, was raped by the last Visigothic king. Legend says that in retaliation her father colluded with Berber Umayyads, easing their entry across the Strait of Gibraltar in 711 and ushering in the Kingdom of Al-Andalus.

→ Access is a little uncertain but from Calle Eras in Aldeira follow signs for Campo de Futbol and on you R look for tracks up the hill.

20 mins, 37.1577, -3.0647 🚻🍴📷

17 CASTILLO DE LANJARÓN

Dating back to the 13th century, possibly the reign of Yusuf I, the remains of this castle crown a dramatic limestone promontory just outside the pretty white village of Lanjarón. Facing south, where the foothills of the Sierra Nevada fall steeply away, it was used to control the trade routes from the sea to the Alpujarras. It fell into decay from 1568 when the last remaining Muslims were forcibly expelled from the Alpujarras. What looks like a scaffold is in fact a metal

framework built to support the ruins and to allow safe entry; it projects the magnitude of the former fortress, while not blocking the incredible view.

→ Entering Lanjarón from Órgiva, turn L after Café Nottingham and continue for 850m to a sign on the L for 'Castillo Arabe'. Follow to reach the parking.
2 mins, 36.9148, -3.4888 ⊞✉️📷

HILLTOP VILLAGES

18 PAMPANEIRA
Find your way up to the top of Pampaneira's riddle of passageways and you'll never find the same way back down. The narrow streets of this pretty white mountain village, known as *tinao*, are as much of a riddle as the snow-fresh streams that course through them. Many of the cobbled streets have a central gutter running with clear, fresh mountain water and there are copious drinking fountains. The springs filling the ancient Arab-built *acequias* of the Alpujarran villages are said to be rich with minerals from the rocks of the Sierra Nevada, which perhaps explains the legend about the fountain next to the parish church:

that drinking from the fountain makes you fall crazily in love.

→ There are several parking areas on the A-4132 just before you get into the village. Regular buses from Granada, as well as many footpaths, connect the Alpujarran villages.
10 mins, 36.9395, -3.3608 ⊞✝️🍴🍷

19 ATALBÉITAR
Atalbéitar, Pórtugos and Ferreirola are some of the most beautiful and less-visited villages in the Alpujarras. Before their modern roads were built, they were connected to the sea via trading routes dating back to at least the 1st or 2nd century AD. You can still walk these footpaths, which follow the ravines and pass the typical drystone *balate* walls that hold up the medieval terraced hills. It is a transportive experience to arrive on foot in Atalbéitar, emerging from woodland into the narrow, white-washed streets, no tarmac or cars in sight. Atalbéitar is a dense knot of *tinao*, ancient passageways built during the Al-Andalus era, which dip to pass under the low chestnut-beamed underbellies of the houses.

→ Regular buses from Granada, as well as many signed footpaths, connect all of the Alpujarran villages.
5 mins, 36.9344, -3.3095 🍴🍷🚶♿⊞🏊⛰

20 CAPILEIRA
The low roofs and chimney pots of Capileira look out to the misty blue Alpujarra mountains and the snowy peaks of the Sierra Nevada. The name Capileira comes from the Latin, *capitellum*, meaning heights, heads or peaks. This is the closest village to the peaks of Mulhacén and Veleta, whose footpaths start from here with incredible views over the Poqueira gorge. Swifts live in the drystone walls and the ancient cottages are built haphazardly on top and alongside one another, stone ceilings serving as terraces for the cottages above. There is a busy artistic community.

→ Regular buses from Granada, as well as many signed footpaths, connect all the Alpujarran villages.
5 mins, 36.9613, -3.3586 🍴🍷♿🚶⊞🚶

21 SOPORTÚJAR
They say witchcraft has been practised for centuries in this tiny Alpujarran village; at least since the expulsion of the Moors from the Alpujarras, when the town was repopulated with people from the north of Spain who brought with them their pagan customs. Fun for kids, the village has cats, cauldrons, serpents emerging from fountains and a life-size Baba Yaga house

on legs. It can get busy. Footpaths lead from here to Órgiva. Visit in the second week of August for its Feria del Embrujo, witchcraft festival, and San Roque festivities.

→ Regular buses from Granada, as well as many signed footpaths, connect all the Alpujarran villages.

5 mins, 36.9284, -4.4061 ⊞⏐🍴⛷️♥🚶🐾🎿

MAGIC MOUNTAINS

22 ACEQUIA ALTA

Icy water from the snowy peaks of Mulhacén fill this ancient waterway coursing along the higher slopes of the Poqueira gorge. Bordered by wildflowers and mulberry trees, home to butterflies, this is the natural heritage of the medieval silk trade from Al-Andalus. Its impressive views look out across a natural amphitheatre, of glacial origin, to the distant peaks of Mulhacén and Veleta. Below, the gentle slopes and grassy ridges, known as Los Corrales de Pitres, are still used for livestock breeding. It's a lovely spot from which to watch flocks of sheep pass below or continue on a longer hike to the Refugio Poqueira. The *acequias* are perfect for refreshment, but watch out for the odd grass snake using them as an Alpujarran highway.

→ The *acequia* lies along the circular Acequias del Poqueira walk, which is signed from Capileira (at 36.9633, -3.3588). It's about 4km from the end of the walk, so you'll want to walk it anti-clockwise if you're not up for the full 19km.

1 hr, 36.9872, -3.3369 ⊞🚶🎿

23 MULHACÉN

At 3,482m, Mulhacén is the highest mountain in mainland Spain and from its windy peak there are dizzying views as the mountain falls away to the glacial lakes below. There is a shrine with prayer flags, flowers, candles and abandoned hiking boots were you can pause and take in the views. The mountain owes its name to the medieval Muslim king, Muley Hacen of the Nasrid dynasty, who is said to be buried here. Look out for ibex, the native mountain goats.

→ See directions and cautions for Chorreras Negras. Take care and be prepared with offline maps, water bottles and suitable weather protection. It is 11km along the signed footpath from Trevélez.

4 hrs, 37.0535, -3.3110 🚶▽⊞🎿⛰️

24 NEVADENSIS

A outdoor adventure company with the best local guides offering ski lessons, trekking

among the peaks or canyoning in some of the wildest places in the Sierra Nevada. Contact them for accommodation during the ski season at the hostel just 3km from the Pradollano ski station.

→ Plaza de la Libertad, 18411 Pampaneira, 958 763 127, Nevadensis.com

1 min, 36.9405, -3.3612 🚶🏔🏊🚴💶

RUSTIC RESTAURANTS

25 BAR LOS FAROLES

A spit and sawdust restaurant located a little walk out of the pretty but touristy centre of Lanjarón. They serve traditional home-cooked dishes at great prices.

→ 18420 Lanjarón

36.9203, -3.4730 🏨📶🍴

26 BODEGA LA ALACENA

This small bar and deli serves plates of local cheeses, cured meats and Alpujarran beer and wines. Cured legs of *jamón*, clay pitchers and drying herbs hang from the old chestnut beams. Thick stone walls and a log fire provide a welcome hearth for autumn hikers, and oak barrels offer a nice spot in the sun for a glass outside.

→ Calle Trocadero, 1, 18413 Capileira

36.9613, -3.3599 🏨📶🍴

27 RESTAURANTE LA FRAGUA

A homely restaurant with rooms available in the pretty white-washed village of Trevélez. There is a nice terrace for a *cerveza* with tapas in the shade at the front or great views of the snow-capped mountains from the restaurant at the back.

→ C. Posadas, 9, 18417 Trevélez, 958 858 573, Hotellafragua.com

37.0025, -3.2660 🏨🚗📶🍴🏊

28 PIANO BAR LA CUEVA DE MORA LUNA

A relaxed, earthy bar just outside Ferreirola, with live music nights and walls covered in signed guitars, artists' photographs and murals. They have a pizza oven and there is a good choice of local tapas and *raciones*.

→ Calle el Rio, 1, 18414 Mecina-Fondales, 958 765 202

36.9293, -3.3211 🏨📶🍴🏊🚶

WINE & DINE

29 RESTAURANTE PLAZA 6

Local Alpujarran products are reinvented and given a new twist under ancient chestnut beams at this restaurant in Bubión. The chef

has worked in Michelin-starred restaurants and the dishes are joyously creative while celebrating the local products.

→ Plaza Pérez Ramón, 6, 18412 Bubión, Granada, 858 990 217

36.9488, -3.3570 🏨📶🍴

30 EL PARAJE DEL CHEF

Lost in the wild hills between the Alpujarra Almeriense and Alpujarra Granadina, a series of hairpin bends lead up to this gastronomic heaven with roaring fires, cosy cabins and footpaths leading into the mountains. Juan Carlos Espejo and his team create a fusion of flavours from seasonal ingredients, fresh from the local markets. Organic wines made by Miguel at the nearby Bodega Fuentezuelas accompany mouthwatering dishes. You'll never want to leave, a hidden treasure.

→ Paraje de las Almagreras, s/n, 18494 Laroles, 629727919, Elparajedelchef.com

37.0090, -3.0264 🏨🚗📶🍴🏔🏊🚴

WILDER CAMPING

31 CAMPING TREVÉLEZ

Surrounded by the snowy peaks of the Sierra Nevada and situated at 1560m, the highest campsite in mainland Spain has some extraordinary stargazing. You can stay in a wooden cabin or camp. A good place from which to hike to Mulhacén or Siete Lagunas.

→ Ctra.Órgiva-Trevélez, Km 32,5, 18417 Trevélez, 958 858 735, Campingtrevelez.com

36.9918, -3.2706 🚗🏊🚶🍴🅿

32 CAMPING ÓRGIVA

A simple and peaceful campsite with grassy areas for tents under ancient olive trees. Wake up to views of the Alpujarras and fall asleep under a starry sky. Bungalows are also available and there is a restaurant at the entrance with great tapas and events.

→ Ctra. A-348, Km 18,900 (Cortijo del Cura, s/n), 18400 Órgiva, 958 784 307

36.8878, -3.4170 🏨🏊📶🍴🅿

MOUNTAIN RETREATS

33 CASA ALOE

An eccentric house in Atalbéitar that has typically grown organically over centuries. Its thick walls, sloping floors and passageways have a labyrinthine feel. The village lanes are car free but you can park a 15-minute walk away. Swimming pool. Sleeps 12.

→ 18414 Atalbéitar, +44 776 765 2903, Albaholidaylets.com

36.9340, -3.3104 🏨🏊🚶

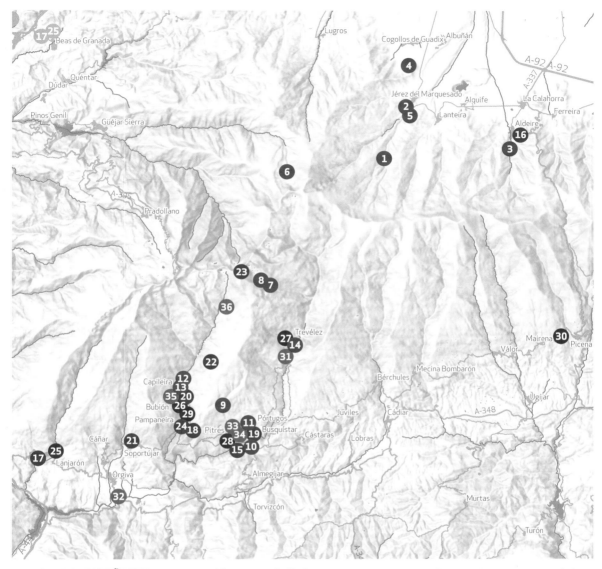

34 CASA RURAL CASTAÑO REAL

A lovely hideaway in Atalbéitar and its tangle of white-washed streets dating back to at least medieval times. The thick walls are made with *tapiar* (a rammed-earth style), providing warmth in winter and coolness in summer.

→ Calle Real, 3, 18414 Atalbéitar, 653 115 519
36.9343, -3.3107 ▢◩◿◿

35 EL GATO NEGRO

A magical mountain retreat with sparrows chattering in the old eaves and an explosion of flowers outside. The house is 350 years old and has traditional low beams and *launa* (river-clay) walls. It's a hikers' haven with a cosy fireplace, and footpaths leading into the Sierra Nevada pass its doorstep. Sleeps 2–3.

→ Calle Cubo, 28, 18413 Capileira,
622045789, El-gato-negro.es
36.9615, -3.3601 ▢◿◿◿◿

36 REFUGIO POQUEIRA

In the foothills of Mulhacén this mountain refuge has incredible views over the Poqueira gorge. Set out in the early morning and it's likely the only other footfall on your path will be some curious ibex. The communal rooms are spartan but clean with bunk beds. A hearty dinner is provided for a little extra as well as a basic breakfast but you need to book in advance. The Sendero Poqueira footpath and Mulahacén hikes lead here.

→ 18413 Capileira, Granada, 958 34 33 49,
Refugiopoqueira.com
37.0275, -3.3237 ◿◿◿◿◿◿◿◿

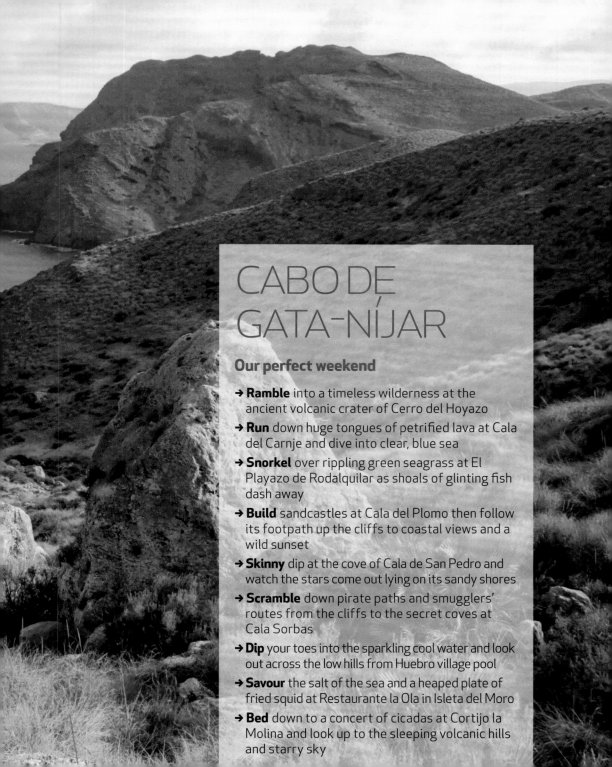

CABO DE GATA-NÍJAR

Our perfect weekend

→ **Ramble** into a timeless wilderness at the ancient volcanic crater of Cerro del Hoyazo

→ **Run** down huge tongues of petrified lava at Cala del Carnje and dive into clear, blue sea

→ **Snorkel** over rippling green seagrass at El Playazo de Rodalquilar as shoals of glinting fish dash away

→ **Build** sandcastles at Cala del Plomo then follow its footpath up the cliffs to coastal views and a wild sunset

→ **Skinny** dip at the cove of Cala de San Pedro and watch the stars come out lying on its sandy shores

→ **Scramble** down pirate paths and smugglers' routes from the cliffs to the secret coves at Cala Sorbas

→ **Dip** your toes into the sparkling cool water and look out across the low hills from Huebro village pool

→ **Savour** the salt of the sea and a heaped plate of fried squid at Restaurante la Ola in Isleta del Moro

→ **Bed** down to a concert of cicadas at Cortijo la Molina and look up to the sleeping volcanic hills and starry sky

The wild and isolated landscape of the Parque Natural de Cabo de Gata-Níjar lies along the most easterly coastline of Andalucía, in the Almería province. Fossil dunes scoop and dip into sapphire waters and eroded teeth of volcanic rock sink into the sea forming rockpools. Twelve thousand hectares of this protected nature reserve lie underwater and are home to one of Europe's best-preserved reef systems. Below the surface are fields of waving seagrass, sponges, and anemones with shimmering fish darting in between.

Dry riverbeds, or *ramblas*, cut down between cliffs to hidden coves; Cala Carbón is a perfect half-moon of a pebbly cove. Pack your snorkel and cycle here from the slightly busier Playa de los Genoveses or Playa de Mónsul. The volcanic rock formations at these beaches were famously the backdrop to scenes in the *Indiana Jones* and *Pirates of the Caribbean* films, while nearby semi-desert hills with prickly pear cactus and sculptural agave, brought over on ships from their native America, were the scene of numerous 'Paella' Westerns. A short walk from these famous beaches leads to the long golden sands of Playa del Barronal, and like many of the hidden coves and beaches here, swimsuits are optional.

This coast has been a wilderness for much of its history. Romans and Phoenicians dropped anchor here and much later the Spanish Armada gathered in the Playa de los Genovese before the Battle of Lepanto. But it was settlers from North Africa in the 8th century who built *norias*, or freshwater wells, making these arid hills habitable. You can follow a footpath along Barranco de la Capitana to a beautifully preserved *noria* under the highest volcanic peak of El Fraile, perfect for stargazing on dark nights.

After the Christian conquest the land became uninhabited again, its people unable to protect themselves from North African pirates. One Tunisian corsair, so fearsome he became known as *Al-Borani*, Turkish for thunderstorm, gave his name to this area of the Mediterranean: the Alboran Sea. You can see the enigmatic ruins of a watchtower built to defend against these pirates at Cala de San Pedro. No roads lead to this hidden cove with its hippy community, dogs, hammocks and freshwater spring; it is accessed only on foot or by sea. Ironically, its watchtower was destroyed in 1743 by an English man-of-war that had given chase to a Spanish pirate ship. After attacking the Spanish ship, the English gratuitously fired on the tower. It remains in a state of disrepair and a small pirate flag now cheekily flies from its top.

Parallels with the Wild West continue at the abandoned gold mines at Rodalquilar, briefly mined for gold and iron ore during the 19th century. Wander along a footpath, passing tunnels and the old mining houses of San Diego, to reach the dusty crossroads at Cortijo del Fraile. This evocative, decayed farmhouse, built by Dominican friars, was the setting for numerous Westerns starring Clint Eastwood and Lee Van Cleef. But it witnessed a real-life crime and tragic shooting during the elopement of Francisca Cañada in the early 1900s, immortalised in Federico García Lorca's famous drama, *Blood Wedding*.

Run back down these hills in the evening to Rodalquilar, where you can feast on heaped plates of fried fish at Lola's lively bar, Restaurante El Cinto. Or come in from the beaches to Asador La Chumbera and watch sunset while dining on grilled mussels and red prawn *croquetas*. Rest at nearby Cortijo La Joya de Cabo de Gata, with its secret gardens, natural pool and silky daybeds looking out to the Wild West hills.

VOLCANIC BEACHES

1 PLAYA DE LA FABRIQUILLA

At this long stretch of quiet sandy beach gentle waves roll in and the volcanic hills of Cabo de Gata rise up behind. Located just south of the desolate-looking Iglesia de la Almadraba, a picturesque church tower, and before the dramatic hills and near the ancient traps of the tuna migrations, it is a perfect place to watch the sunset. There is often a small collection of campervans on the corner where the coastal road diverges.

➜ From San Miguel de Cabo de Gata, head S on the coastal road for 5km. There is parking by the campervans in the fork of the road.

1 min, 36.7384, -2.2084 🏖️🌊📷

2 EL PLAYAZO DE RODALQUILAR

Wonderful snorkelling can be had at this sandy beach, where the water remains shallow over a reef rich with sea life. The fossilised sand dunes to the north form smooth yellow shelving that turns golden in the evening light. Wander past the 18th-century fortress of San Ramón, now a private home, to where these rocks really stack up some height. Here there are cliff jumps of up to 15m, usually frequented by kids gathering courage, and scooped seats for beautiful views along the coastline.

➜ From Rodalquilar take the AL-4200 towards Las Negras. After 1km turn R at a brown sign for 'El Playazo' and follow the road for 1.5km. Parking at the beach.

2 mins, 36.8628, -2.0051 🐚🚫🍴🚗🏖️

3 CALA DEL PLOMO

The fossil dunes and hills protecting this beach are straight out of a Spaghetti Western. A pitted, dusty 7km track leads down past ruins of old *cortijos* to the sandy cove. A 4km footpath to Cala de San Pedro begins here and loops over the cliffs. Hike up a little way to see great views of the Mesa Roldán mountain.

➜ From Agua Amarga take the AL-5106 for 5km towards Fernán Pérez. Turn L at the junction (36.9532, -1.9798), and after 200m take the second L and continue along the dirt track for 7km to parking.

2 mins, 36.9232, -1.9549 🚫🚶🏖️🚗

4 PLAYA DE LOS GENOVESES

This beach takes its name from a Genovese fleet of 200 ships that was anchored in the bay for two months in 1147 while waiting to attack an Andalusí settlement in Almería. In 1567 the Spanish Armarda gathered here in the bay before the Battle of Lepanto, which brought to an end the Ottoman control of the Mediterranean. A more popular spot now, it is beautiful off-season. Continue along the coastal path for other quieter coves near Cala Carbón. A 1km footpath leads to this beach, starting at the end of Calle la Morra in San José; it hugs the coastline and passes civil war bunkers.

➜ From San José regular buses travel 5km S along the coastal road, passing the paths that lead to the beaches of Genoveses, Mónsul, Barronal and Cala Carbón. Car access is limited and restricted to certain hours. It is best to either take the bus from San José or cycle or walk. From the bus stop a signed path leads down to the beach.

20 mins, 36.7486, -2.1198 🅱️🏖️🚫🚗

5 PLAYA DEL BARRONAL

This sandy beach is hugged by basaltic rocks that have been weathered over millennia into marvellously strange shapes. The water is crystal clear, with hundreds of shimmering fishes and

a gently sloping shore. As with many quieter beaches in the area, nudism is the norm. Follow a path to the left (facing the sea) or clamber, dip and swim around the shore to discover further coves and sea caves hidden under the towering black basaltic columns.

➜ See directions to Playa de los Genoveses. If taking the bus from San José, continue for 2km to the bus stop and a signed dirt track down to the beach on the L.

15 mins, 36.7296, -2.1396 🪧🏞️🏊🏕️⛰️

6 PLAYA DE MÓNSUL

This most iconic beach of Cabo de Gata was made famous by Sean Connery's seagulls-crashing-a-plane scene in *Indiana Jones and the Last Crusade*. Its marooned volcanic rock formation resembles a sea monster heaving itself out to sea. Swim out in the warm, shallow water for views of the Spaghetti Western backdrop.

➜ See directions to Playa de los Genoveses and continue along the coastal road for another 2.5km to a signed path on the L. It is advisable to either cycle, hike or take the bus from San José as car access is restricted.

15 mins, 36.7310, -2.1459 🏊🏖️🅱️

COVES & ROCKPOOLS

7 CALA CARBÓN

A perfect half-moon of a pebbly cove filled with clear, calm water. A long, winding track descends through tumbleweed and Sergio-Leone-style hills; the cove is usually deserted. The seagrass underwater is almost neon green and so alive you realise it can remain 'untrodden' like grass or fresh snow.

➜ See directions to Playa de los Genoveses and continue along the coastal road for 3.5km to a signed dirt track on the L. It is advisable to either cycle, hike or take the bus from San José as car access is restricted. You can also access it from parking near Torre de la Vela Blanca, from the other direction, and cycle downhill from there.

40 mins, 36.7299, -2.1566 🏞️🏊🐚⛰️

8 ARRECIFE DE LAS SIRENAS

Beautiful black volcanic rocks jut out of the crystalline water here. Dive under with a snorkel to discover a seabed teeming with life and colour: a busy mosaic of shells, colourful seaweed and shoals of fish. The reef owes its name to the sirens, or mermaids, fishermen saw here, which were

probably monk seals that once lived near this reef.

→ From San Miguel de Cabo de Gata take the coastal road S for 8km. Park outside the lighthouse and walk down beside the information bureau, following the old rusty rail tracks into the water.

5 mins, 36.7216, -2.1905 ⬛B⬛⬛⬛⬛

9 CALA HIGUERA

Seen from the small cliff above, the water of this tiny cove with its pebbly shore is a piercing blue. There are clambering rocks for perching, jumping or letting the waves wash over you. A 6km coastal footpath starts from here, at the Hotel Los Escullos, and passes many secret coves en route to Higuera before looping inland around the Los Frailes volcanic massif.

→ Entering San José off the AL-3108, take the third exit at the roundabout and turn L on to the Calle Cala Higuera and follow signs. It becomes a dirt track. Parking.

2 mins, 36.7651, -2.0939 ⬛⬛⬛⬛⬛⬛⬛⬛⬛

10 CALA DEL CARNAJE

This is a beautiful and quiet pebbly beach. Huge tongues of ancient lava scoop down to the right as you approach and make

fantastic jumping rocks into the deep, blue sea. Colourful seaweed, shoals of fish and shimmering stones make it worthwhile bringing your snorkel and flippers.

→ From Rodalquilar take the AL-4200 towards Las Negras. After 200m turn R at a brown sign for Cala de Carnaje and continue 1km along the road to the parking (36.8449, -2.0196). This is also an easy walk or cycle. Follow the pitted track 1km down to the beach.

15 mins, 36.8353, -2.0132 ⬛⬛⬛⬛⬛

11 CALA DE SAN PEDRO

A beautiful, hidden cove with the ruins of a 16th-century pirate watchtower, hippy shacks and a small community who live here. In summer months, there'll be a sprinkling of tents in the woodland for folk staying a month or so. There is a freshwater spring and a small bar with hammocks and heaps of books near the ruins of an old fortress built to defend against Berber pirates. The beach itself is sandy, dog-friendly and swimsuits are optional.

→ From Las Negras follow Calle Bahía de las Negras and turn R on to the track at 36.8859, -2.0060. Follow for 2km to the parking lot. Walk 1km along the narrow cliff path to reach San Pedro. You can also kayak

here; see Buceolasnegras.com for details and kayak hire.

20 mins, 36.9035, -1.9790 ⬡🏊⛰🏖🏄🚗🐟✳

12 CALA HERNÁNDEZ

This hidden cove is just before Cala de San Pedro (see entry) if you are walking from the parking area to the south. It is best to kayak; Buceolasnegras.com for details and kayak hire.

➜ See directions to Cala de San Pedro. The track begins 150m after the parking area on the R. Follow the track for 1km to the cove.

20 mins, 36.8919, -1.99438 🐚🏊🏖⬡🏄🐟

13 CALA SORBAS

This small, secret pebble beach is filled with brilliant-blue water and accessed via a narrow rocky path winding down the high cliffs. You can also follow the path as it forks right to reach Cala Arenas, which is a slightly larger sandy beach, also quiet.

➜ From the parking for Arrecife de las Sirenas follow the ALP-822 towards San José for only another 500m, turn R and park or follow the dirt track as it curves L for another 200m. From the end of the track there is a small goat path down to the cove.

15 mins, 36.7210, -2.1834 🏖🐚🏊🏖⬡

14 CALA DE LOS TOROS

A beautiful hidden cove with great snorkelling. To its west side are the black, basaltic columns at the cliffs of Barranco del Negro. The 7km Sendero Requena, which leaves from the car park, is a beautiful way to see the stunning volcanic geology.

➜ From Rodalquilar take the AL-4200 towards San José for 2.5km. After the *mirador* there is a small parking area signed for the beach. Follow the track down along the dry *rambla* to the cove.

20 mins, 36.8226, -2.0432 🏖⛰🚶🐟⬡⬡

WILD SWIMS

15 HUEBRO VILLAGE POOL

Huebro is a beautiful *pueblo blanco* high in the hills with the wild Sierra Alhamilla rising up behind. On hot days the locals here bathe in the *alberca*, a large water tank filled by mountain springs from above. If you ask permission, they are usually happy to let you enjoy a dip.

➜ Park outside Huebro and walk in. The roads are very narrow. From the square outside the church follow the road running downhill for 20m. Turn L and the pool is on your R.

20 mins, 36.9866, -2.2227 🏊🏖

CRATERS & LAGOONS

16 CALDERA VOLCÁNICA MAJADA REDONDA

A 3km footpath leads inland from the sleepy village of Presillas Bajas along the pebbly *ramblas* to this vast crater. You'll pass giant agave and prickly pear cacti; it's easy to see why this immense landscape has been used for filming so many Westerns. From the centre of this striking crater you can see the terraced sides, still being farmed less than a century ago as the high walls would channel the occasional rains down to the fields.

→ From El Pozo de los Frailes take the AL-3108 then the AL-4200 towards Rodalquilar. Just after the Km3 post, turn L following a sign to Caldera de Majada Redonda. At Presillas Bajas turn L at the recycle bins and park near the old threshing ground. Follow Calle Perdigal out of the village. The way is signed for 3km along the *rambla* to the crater.

45 mins, 36.8250, -2.0897 🏕🚶🎦

17 CERRO DEL HOYAZO

The proximity of this six-million-year-old volcanic crater with the nearby autovía and 'Cuidad del Motor' in Campohermoso is oddly surreal. But it feels amazing to plunge into this other wild world. Turn off onto the dusty track and you can hike up the gorge into the crater. Within seconds you are lost in the timeless wilderness of the Sierra Alhamilla. The volcano is also known as La Granatilla, a corruption of *granate* or garnet, due to the small precious crystals found in the earth. Do marvel at them but please don't take them!

→ From Campohermoso take the A-7 with Ciudad del Motor on your L and then immediately take exit 481 towards Níjar. After 300m turn R onto a dirt track and layby at 36.9513, -2.1877, next to signs for 'Níjar 2', and continue for 2km or, depending on how uneven the track looks, park here. After 2km there is an information board and the footpath turns L into a gorge. From here it is 1km into the crater.

45 mins, 36.9595, -2.1706 🏕🚶🎦

18 LAS SALINAS DE CABO DE GATA

This salt water lagoon is an important sanctuary for breeding and wintering birds. Separated from the coast by a long sandbar, it is home to hundreds of flamingos. The beautiful volcanic skyline stetches out behind this roadside bird hide.

→ From Cabo de Gata head E on the AL-3115 for 500m. It is signed on the R.

10 mins, 36.779, -2.2330 🐦🚗

21

WILD WEST RUINS

19 NORIA DE SANGRE

One of the best-preserved *norias de sangre*, literally 'blood-powered water wheels', so named because beasts of burden – donkeys, mules and sometimes oxen – were used to turn the wheels that brought the water to the surface. Early medieval Arabs were the first to tap into the region's aquifers, and hundreds of these *norias*, once the most important water sources, remain in the natural park. This is a peaceful place in the evening, great for watching the moon rise over El Fraile. A dry riverbed leads to the hamlet with sculptural agave. Great stargazing.

→ From the parking in front of Hotel Los Escullos, with your back to the hotel, head inland on a wide dirt track directly opposite. After 1.5km you'll pass Camping Los Escullos on your R. Keep on the foopath, following the dry riverbed, Barranco de la Capitana, for 1.8km until you reach the tiny hamlet of Los Cortijos Grandes. The *noria* is 40m off the footpath to the R.

45 mins, 36.7984, -2.0963 🏕🚶🎦🔆🚗

20

20 MINAS DE RODALQUILAR

The dusty road linking the disused gold mines at Rodalquilar with those at nearby San Diego takes in a hauntingly beautiful stretch of the

18

stark hillsides above the abandoned mines. Gold was first discovered in the lead smeltings at Rodalquilar at the end of the 19th century. The metal was eventually refined using the cyanidation method, and the mines were nationalised after the civil war, eventually closing in 1966. Climb higher up the road, following the Sendero Requena for another 2km, to reach a small tunnel through the hillside leading to the abandoned miners' houses of San Diego. This same path continues for another 3km to Cortijo del Fraile.

→ From Rodalquilar follow Calle Bocamina to the Ecomuseo La Casa de los Volcanes (great geology museum). Park here. Mines are behind the museum and the road leads to further abandoned ruins.

5 mins, 36.8532, -2.0466 🏞️🚶🅿️

21 CORTIJO DEL FRAILE

The stately ruins of this rambling farmhouse, built by 18th-century Dominican friars, emerge from open desert at a crossways. Its decayed courtyard and chapel were used as the location for hideouts and shootings in classic 1960s Westerns: *The Good, the Bad and the Ugly*, *A Bullet for the General* and *For a Few Dollars More*. But in the early 1900s it was the scene of a tragic and very real crime immortalised in Federico García Lorca's most famous work, *Blood Wedding*. On the eve of her wedding to a man she didn't love, Francisca Cañada Morales escaped from this house with her cousin, whom she had loved her whole life, only to be betrayed by the brother of her groom. As they fled on horseback, her cousin was shot. She was badly beaten, left for dead, but survived and lived out the rest of her life nearby, never speaking to the press.

→ See walking directions to Minas de Rodalquilar and continue following the Sendero Requena up the hill for another 3km to the crossroads and this striking farmhouse.

1.5 hrs, 36.8657, -2.0750 🏞️🚉🧭🚶

FRESH FISH

22 RESTAURANTE LA OLA

A great place to sit outside and look out to sea with a heaped plate of fried squid, whitebait or *adobo* (sherry-marinated dogfish). This sleepy Cabo de Gata fishing village is a quieter alternative to the buzz of San José.

→ Calle Rinconcillo, 04118 La Isleta del Moro, 950 389 758, Laolarestaurante.es

36.8142, -2.0511 🍴🍷🅿️🐚

23 RESTAURANTE EL CINTO, RODALQUILAR

This bar and restaurant, the lively social hub of Rodalquilar, offers fantastic plates of fried fish and endless tapas with cool beers. Sit at tables in the street by the chalked-up specials. Even if it's extra busy, they'll try to find a chair for you. Lola, the owner, is loud, fun and you can't leave without trying her homemade *tarta de queso* (cheesecake).

→ Calle Sta. Bárbara, 13, 04115 Rodalquilar, 687 507 154

36.8467, -2.0403 🍴🍷🏞️🚶

24 RESTAURANTE LA HOYA

Even during a power cut this busy bar offered cold beer and grilled fish with heaps of fresh prawns. There are no sea views but it is off the tourist trail and has a simple terrace on the street. Great food at a good price and reassuringly busy on a Sunday.

→ Ctra. Carboneras, 7-9, 04149 Agua Amarga, 648 261 942

36.9410, -1.9352 🍴🍷

25 ASADOR LA CHUMBERA

Surrounded by the rolling hills, this restaurant offers dining under olive trees and stars. Traditional Almeriense food is given a twist with the chef's creative flair. Try the *carpaccio de pez lecha* (a finely sliced Mediterranean amberjack). The grilled mussels with alioli and the *croquetas de gambas roja* (red prawn croquettes) are divine.

→ 04149 Agua Amarga, 634 676 298, Asadorlachumbera.es

36.9453, -1.9263 💶🏞️🚶🍴🍷

26 RESTAURANTE EL FARO

A great stop for paella or squid-ink rice, with sea views from the terrace. It is an easy walk to beaches, the Cabo de Gata lighthouse on its rocky promontory and Arrecife de las Sirenas.

→ Carretera del Faro de Cabo de Gata, s/n, 04150 Almería, 950 160 054

36.7246, -2.1929 🚶🍴🍷

RURAL HAVENS

27 CASA RURAL CAMPO FELIZ

A beautiful guesthouse with thick stone walls and chimneys, hammocks under its shady terraces and colourful Moroccan pottery and glass. A peaceful and sustainably run haven.

→ Carretera AL-3108, 04117 Boca de los Frailes, 635 797 432, Casaruralcampofeliz.es

36.8090, -2.1345 🏞️🚶🅿️🚲

28 EL JARDÍN DE LOS SUEÑOS

A restored farmhouse next to Rodalquilar. An exotic garden and hidden pool make it feel far more remote. Several walking paths run close

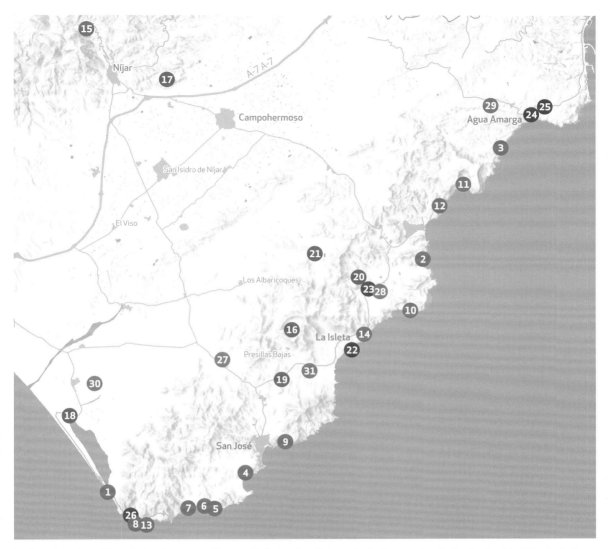

by, through the desert hills to the beaches. Eckhard, the owner, ensures this is more of a place for quiet couples than wild children.

→ 04115 Níjar, Almería, Eljardindelossuenos.es
36.8463, -2.0354 👣🏄

29 CORTIJO LA JOYA DE CABO DE GATA
Several elegant bohemian houses with terraces opening to views of the Spaghetti Western hills. Rambling gardens hide daybeds, tropical fruit trees, a collection of sculptures and secret shrines before opening out to a long pool with a fountain and a jacuzzi. Weekly dinners are hosted for guests and dogs are welcome. Run by

Charo and Tania, her niece, their passion for the place shines through in all the details.

→ Paraje La Joya, 04149 Agua Amarga, Almería,
619 159 587, Lajoyadecabodegata.es
36.9459, -1.9614 🏔🏄⚗🧺👣🏄

30 CORTIJO LA MOLINA
Lovingly restored farmhouses, close to the sea and surrounded by olive groves, look out to the volcanic Cabo de Gata hills. There is a real sense of peace here, cultivated by its connection with the rhythms of nature. A fountain runs from the old Arab-style mill into a large *alberca*, which makes a generous swimming pool. This pool

waters the farmland and at night reflects the stars above. Bed down to the concert of cicadas.

→ Calle San Miguel, 04151 Pujaire, 670 809
545, Cortijolamolina.es
36.7962, -2.2170 🏔🏄⚗🧺👣🏄🏕

31 CAMPING LOS ESCULLOS
A simple, pet-friendly campsite next to several footpaths and close to beaches.

→ Paraje Los Escullos, s/n, 04118, 950 389
811, Losesculloscabodegata.com
36.8031, -2.0784 👣B🏄🐚🏕

ALMERÍA & TABERNAS

Our perfect weekend

→ **Cycle** through the arid, semi-desert ravines of a Spaghetti Western following the Via Verde de Lucainena de las Torres

→ **Watch** desert tumbleweed roll through the scorched Desierto de Tabernas

→ **Slide** through the wild cave systems at Cuevas de Sorbas, where unexplored caverns will leave you spellbound

→ **Picnic** by alder roots reaching into the clearwater springs at the Nacimiento del Río Andarax

→ **Climb** up to the ghostly ruins of the Islamic citadel of Alcazaba de Senés in the Sierra de los Filabres

→ **Travel** back to Roman times at the aqueducts of Carcáuz hidden deep in the Sierra de Gádor

→ **Celebrate** the feast day of San Roque at Sorbas, where his garlanded statue is paraded

→ **Taste** the Alpujarra de Almería in a glass at the organic vineyards of Cortijo El Cura Eco-Bodega

→ **Wake** up to a frosty, clear dawn at the mountain bothy of Refugio de la Polarda in the foothills of the Sierra Nevada

Just 20km inland from the coastal city of Almería the eroded gullies and sun-scorched earth of the Tabernas desert begin. Its dusty canyons, cacti, and *ramblas*, or dry riverbeds, have been the backdrop to numerous Spaghetti Westerns, most famously Sergio Leone's *Once Upon A Time in the West* and *A Fistful of Dollars*. But you will also find snow-capped mountains in the Alpujarra Almeriense, with mountain bothies for stargazing, or ancient cave paintings at Cueva de los Letreros. The magical *indalo* figure, painted at these caves, is the official symbol or talisman of the province and looks out to an endless sea of desert gullies.

Eight million years ago the Tabernas desert was covered by a real sea which left behind sand, loam, limestone, and gypsum. Over the millennia it eroded to desert but at Sorbas, rainwater has eaten further into the *yesos*, or gypsum, carving a secret underground world with over a thousand interconnected cavities: a spectacular and diverse universe of stalactites, stalagmites, crystalline columns and corals. Its most famous cave is Cueva del Agua, the largest gypsum cave in Spain, with siphons and galleries running for 8km, yet much more waits to be explored. It extends under the hillside village of Marchalico Viñicas, abandoned in 1969 due to lack of water. Shafts of sunlight pour through collapsed ceilings, and wild goats pick their way through smoky crystal shards of gypsum.

After the river's subterranean passage, it emerges at the Nacimiento del Río Aguas, smelling slightly of crypts and cellars, where it fills deep plunge pools formed in karstic stone. In 1986 a small community investigating renewable energy took up residence in the ruined mills downstream, filling the riverbanks with treehouses and colourful gardens. Oleanders, reeds, and white poplars also grow along the river and native turtles can be spotted here.

Hot thermal springs emerge south of Tabernas, in a sleepy hamlet near Pechina on the slopes of Sierra de Alhamilla. The source itself still runs at 58°C into a tiny fountain by its plaza. In the 9th century, Pechina became a Maritime Republic under the Córdoban caliphate and flourished with its silk trade and wealth gained from the plundering corsairs. One corsair, and it is unlikely she ever had a Pechina licence, was Malika Fadel ben Salvador, whose fearless marauding across the Alboran Sea would significantly delay the Christian conquest of Almería.

The *taifa*, or Islamic principality, of Almería was one of the most powerful in the kingdom of Al-Andalus, its green-and-white striped flag the forebear of the official Andalucían flag today. Head north of Tabernas to the foothills of Sierra de los Filabres, where the lost ruins of a medieval Islamic citadel, surrounded by ancient almond trees, overlooks Senés. Or follow the footpath at Urrácal winding through its towering gorge and medieval *acequias*. These ruins bear witness to the aftermath of the Rebellion of the Alpujarras, where Morisco communities were forced to flee their villages, castles and livelihoods in these hills.

Head to the eastern slopes of the Sierra Nevada to explore the Alpujarra of Almería – Padules, Almócita, Beires – with their excellent vineyards and clearwater springs at Laujar de Anadarax. From Padules follow a leafy track down to the marlstone gorge of Las Canales, with sparkling pools in the Andarax river and its rustic bar, El Molinillo de la Abuela. In springtime, these hills are white with almond blossom. On summer evenings wend your way to the ancient settlement at Los Millares and watch as the last rays throw the dusty pink gullies into golden relief.

RIVERS & GORGES

1 LAS CANALES DE PADULES

A series of idyllic hidden pools and cascades following the smooth rock chasm scoured over millennia by the River Andarax. Cheerful, rustic Molinillo de la Abuela (see entry) down in the gorge is open in summer months.

→ From the *ayuntamiento* in Padules follow the road downhill, keeping R, out of town for 2.5km. It will take you right down to the beautiful gorge.

40 mins, 36.9871, -2.7742 🏊🚶🏞️🏠

2 SUNSEED COMMUNITY AND RÍO AGUAS

After tumbling through the immense network of Sorbas' caves and siphons, the Río Aguas emerges at its spring to flow into several deep, dark plunge pools with high karstic sides. A small community called Sunseed took up residence in the abandoned village downstream in 1986 with the purpose of investigating green energy and permaculture. They are off-grid and use the river water and solar power to generate energy. The gardens of the old mill houses are now reanimated with colourful plants and pets while kids run about in the veg gardens. Ask for permission and you can wander down through these gardens and treehouses to the River Aguas. The swims are very cool, with a slight smell of old crypts and cellars, the water having just emerged from its subterranean passage. The circular 9km PR-A97 footpath leads into the karstic landscape.

→ From Sorbas take the main road past the cemetery and turn off on to the A-1102 at signs for Cuevas de Sorbas. After 5.5km park in the layby by the recycle bins to the R, cross the road and walk down into the community. Follow signs to 'río' and ask for permission to swim in the river.

10 mins, 37.0884, -2.0723 🏊🚶🏕️✨

HILLTOPS & STARGAZING

3 LOS CAÑOS DE SERÓN

The ruins of this abandoned hamlet, once used as storehouses for charcoal burners, cling to the steep hillside deep in the Sierra de los Filabres. Its terraced slopes have been called the Machu Picchu of Almería. It was finally abandoned in the late 1960s, once the mines at Las Menas were closed.

→ From Serón take the A-1178 S for 7km. Turn R on to the track for the Cementerio de La Loma and continue 6km to the cemetery.

Park here and continue to the hermitage. From there take the R track and continue for 5km. Download offline maps to see the route before you go.

1 hr, 37.2872, -2.5723 🏞️🏔️🏕️🚶

4 CASTILLO DE TABERNAS

The ruins of the castle where the Catholic Monarchs Ferdinand and Isabella stayed during the siege of Almería rise up on a dusty, barren hill above the town, once a strategic position along ancient lines of communication. An almost endless eroded wilderness falls away below. Legend tells of secret passages between the castle and the town below. It is a beautiful spot to watch the sunset.

→ Entry to the castle is free. If you park at the Tabernas Sports Stadium (37.0532, -2.3924), you can follow a footpath up to the castle.

10 mins, 37.0521, -2.3948 📷🏔️📸

5 TABERNAS

These empty semi-desert plains, far from the lights of any village, are perfect for stargazing. There are beautiful sunsets over the Sierra de Alhamilla hills and Tabernas castle is lit up at night, sometimes with fireworks displays during summer festivities.

7 YACIMIENTO ARQUEOLÓGICO FUENTE ÁLAMO

This early Bronze Age hillfort in the foothills of Sierra de Almagro was abandoned in 2,000 BC. Built by the Argaric people who lived here, it would have controlled mountain access along the Almanzora valley. It is a magical place with incredible views across the low hills.

→ For more information and to see the artefacts visit the Museo Arqeológico in Cuevas de Almanzora. The walk to the archaeological site is 6km and starts on a dirt track opposite the roundabout entry into La Portilla on the A-332 at 37.2904, -1.8634. Park here and walk 5km until the track ends. The way to the site is signed with white guiding poles.

1.5 hrs, 37.3294, -1.8581 ✝♿▨▦

8 CUEVA DE AMBROSIO

This wild cave near the Sierra de María-Los Vélez houses Palaeolithic paintings that are around 17,000 to 22,000 years old. Painted in red ochre, the clearest image is of a horse created with bold strokes. They are well protected behind a fence, as they should be, but it is a beautiful site none the less.

→ From the Centro de Visitantes Almacén del Trigo in Vélez-Blanco, follow the road out of town and take the R fork signed to Cuevo Ambrosio. Follow the road parallel to the main road, following signs for Cuevo Ambrosio, for about 30km. The track is in poor condition in places and you may need to walk. It is advisable to download an offline track map.

15 mins, 37.8319, -2.0955 ▨▨◫▨▦♿?

→ From Tabernas, take the N-340a towards Sorbas for 4km. Pass Restaurante Route 66 on the L and after about 300m there is a dirt track on the L. Park here and walk into the open valley for about 1km.

15 mins, 37.0856, -2.3499 ▨▲▨

6 YACIMIENTO ARQUEOLÓGICO DE LOS MILLARES

The mysterious itinerant Beaker people left their mark at this Copper Age (pre-Bronze Age) hilltop settlement. Dating from 3200 to 2200 BC, the ruins of 13 hillforts crown the hills which flank the Rambla de Huéchar and the River Andarax. The full moon rises above these forts which guarded entry to several megalithic passage tombs in the plateau below. Its wild and primal landscape throws you back in time, but it is just a short walk from the road and can be visited from Wed – Sun, 10am – 2pm. Free entry.

→ From Alhama de Almería take the A-348 towards Almería for 4km. Take the A-1075 at the junction and then turn R on to the AL-3411 for the Yacimiento Arqueológico and parking.

15 mins, 36.9660, -2.5191 ♿▦✝▨

9 LA CUEVA DE LOS LETREROS

This wild rock shelter, with prehistoric ochre paintings dating from around 5,000 BC, is located high up on in the limestone massif of El Maimon. It shelters the original painting of the 'indalo': a figure with outstretched arms holding a rainbow above its head, along with other horned creatures and figures. The indalo has become emblematic of Almería, a magical symbol representing the province, but it only carries luck if the charm is presented as a gift. The cave lies behind gates, for conservation, but you can phone ahead for a tour – call 694 467 136.

→ The meeting point for these tours is at the main entrance of Camping Pinar del Rey, 5km N of Vélez-Rubio on the A-317.

10 mins, 37.6808, -2.0951 ♿▦🚶▨

10 CUEVAS DE SORBAS

This cave system in the karstic rock under Sorbas hides over a thousand cavities carved by underground rivers. A number of caving routes are on offer here with accredited local guides. See Cuevasdesorbas.com.

→ From Sorbas take the main road past the cemetery and turn off on to the A-1102 at signs for Cuevas de Sorbas. The parking area is signed in 300m on the R.

5 mins, 37.1024, -2.0714 🚷🧗‍♂️♿🏕🍴

LOST RUINS

11 MARCHALICO VIÑICAS

Abandoned due to a lack of water in 1969, this ruined village is frequented by goats that pick their way past the fireplaces and dressers of these deserted houses. It clings to the eastern end of the Tabernas desert hills, with views to the Sierra de Cabrera. The smoky crystal shards beneath your feet are gypsum, as these hills form part of the karstic system around Sorbas, eaten away into sinkholes and chasms below. Carob and almond trees grown by the farming community now run wild across the remains of the two neighbourhoods. The children here would have gone to school at

La Herreria, the hamlet directly opposite on the facing hill, whose drinking fountain still flows. Watch out for one particularly territorial white goat.

→ Take exit 510 off the E-15 coming from Venta del Pobre. Cross under the flyover and take the second exit at the roundabout uphill. Follow for 1km and park where you can. The village access road is chained off but you can follow the track to the ruins on foot.

10 mins, 37.1056, -2.0430 🏔✛♿🚻🖼

12 ERMITA DE LOS DESAMPARADOS

This wild hilltop chapel, surrounded by olive and almond trees, is a jewel in the Alpujarra de Almería. It is known as the hermitage of the three villages and from its grassy knoll you can see the white houses of Padules, the Mudejar church at Almócita and the rambling streets of Beires. In September it is the site of a pilgrimage in which newborns are blessed, floral offerings are laid and bonfires are burnt into the night. A 13km circular footpath, the PR-A 360, passes by linking Almócita with Padules, Beires and the Las Canales gorge.

→ Park at Bar El Rincón de Almócita, just as you enter the village from the A-348, and follow a small track uphill for 500m.

10 mins, 37.0074, -2.7917 ✛🔔🏕🖼❓

13 ACUEDUCTOS DE CARCÁUZ

Three wild and overgrown Roman aqueducts in the dry riverbed of Rambla de Carcáuz, the most beautiful of which is known as the Acueducto de los Viente Ojos, 'of the twenty eyes'. Nearby, there is a via ferrata climbing route up to the Peñón de Bernal, a limestone peak where they filmed a sequence for *Conan the Barbarian*.

→ From the A-7, in the direction of Almería, take exit 420. At the roundabout take the first exit and head through the industrial area for about 2km. At the end there is a road that runs along up into the hills; follow this for another 1km until the tarmac runs out. Park where you can. The first of the aqueducts is 1km ahead to the R.

25 mins, 36.8265, -2.7033 🖼🚶🏔❓

14 PARAJE NATURAL LA CERRÁ DE TÍJOLA

You can follow a dramatic ravine carved by the Río Bacarés to reach several wild caves and the ruins of a medieval Islamic castle and town, Tíjola la Vieja. The castle was located just outside Tíjola, guarding this ravine, but it suffered a heavy attack when the town joined the Morisco Rebellion of the Alpujarras in the late 16th century. Follow the *acequia*, or water channel, south for

500m and a path leads up to the caves; the largest of which is called Cueva de la Paloma de Bacarés. You'll pass the ruins of the old castle too and the Vía Verde del Valle del Almanzora passes nearby.

→ From Ermita del Salvador in Tíjola, follow the narrow footpath for 1km down the hill to the ravine. Turn L towards the bottom and continue following the water channel. After about 500m there are footpaths up on the left-hand side of the gorge to caves and the castle. Take care as there are small drops into brambles.

30 mins, 37.3360, -2.4463 🔲🚶🏕️⛰️🔲💧

15 RUINAS DE LA ALCAZABA DE SENÉS

The vestiges of this medieval citadel of Senés, or Hisn Xenex, lie in the southern foothills of the Sierra de Los Filabres and just north of the pretty village of Senés. Built in the 12th century by Abú Isaac Ibrahim Albolafiq under the rule of the Almohads, this powerful base was constructed from the naturally occurring slate stone which shimmers underfoot in the sun, the same stone used in the village below. Evocative ruins, some with carvings in Arabic, look out towards the Valle del Andarax. The GR-244 long-

distance trail passes by, linking the Sierra de Los Filabres with Sierra Alhamilla. Café Bar El Mirador does great tapas post-hike in town.

→ Follow the blue graffiti of a fortress image, it marks the Sendero Hisn Xenex footpath which leads up to the ruins and is signed from the *ayuntamiento* in Senés. First, follow Calle la Fuente but don't head down to the fountain, take the R fork, and it is about a 2km walk slightly uphill.

45 mins, 37.2071, -2.3517 🚶🏕️⛰️🔲💧

16 TORRE DE ALACÍN O DE MONTALVICHE

A ruined 15th-century watchtower surrounded by wildflowers looks out to the rocky outcrop La Muela and Murcia. When Murcia fell to Christians in 1244, Vélez-Blanco became the last, north-eastern defence for the Kingdom of Granada. Fire and smoke signals would have shot back messages along a chain of watchtowers. Ancient woodsmoke now only a distant memory, it is a beautiful spot for picnics and stargazing.

→ From Vélez-Blanco take Calle Desengaño out of town. At the T junction with the cemetery turn R and continue straight on along this track for 2km until the asphalt runs

out. Continue straight on for another 1km, then turn L and follow for 1km until a sign on L with a red triangle, the track leads up to the tower.
1 hr, 37.7078, -2.0662 🎪🖼️🖼️🏔️⊞

HIKING & BIKING

17 VIA VERDE DE LUCAINENA DE LAS TORRES

This 15km cycle trail links the beautiful village of Lucainena de las Torres to Venta del Pobre. It follows an old railway through ravines and *ramblas*, passing old mines, watermills and farmhouses, with views of the Sierra de Alhamilla.

→ Entering Lucainena from the N, or A-340a, the cycle route is signed off Calle Bilbao and the school or old station house. Parking is before, signed to the R.
5 mins, 37.0434, -2.2020 🚴⊞🚶

18 VÍAS VERDES VALLE DEL ALMANZORA

This 98km cycle trail follows old iron mining railways along the Almanzora river valley and links El Baúl in Granada province to Arboleas in Almería. Just north of Serón it passes thermal springs called El Aljibe de Serón.

→ The cycle way is well signed from the Serón Planetarium which lies along the AL-6404 from Serón in the dirrection of El Hijate.
1 day, 37.3599, -2.5668 🚴⊞🏊🚴

19 EL NACIMIENTO DEL RÍO ANDARAX

A beautiful picnic area under dense alder woodland with tables and paths down to the spring of the River Andarax. The Sendero de Monterrey, PR-A 35, starts here and leads through pine woodland and almond trees, through gorges and tunnels to incredible views of the Alpujarra de Almería. You can return along the Sendero de la Hidroeléctrica, PR-A 36; it is 8km in total. Restaurante El Nacimiento is a great stop here, with a log fire.

→ Follow Carretera Nacimiento out of Laujar de Andarax for 1km.
15 mins, 37.0063, -2.8892 🚶🏔️🎪🍴

20 EL ESTRECHO DE URRÁCAL

Urrácal is a pretty mountain village often overlooked in the Almanzora valley and foothills of the Sierra de las Estancias. A couple of beautiful footpaths, signed from the *ayuntamiento*, follow its *acequias*, or farming water channels, up through its hills. You can also walk through a narrow gorge,

eroded by water and wind, whose great weathered walls hide ancient fossils and tower overhead.

→ The path down to the gorge starts just before you cross the bridge, heading in the direction of Somontín.

10 mins, 37.3924, -2.3647 🚶🏻‍♂️🎒⊞

21 DESIERTO DE TABERNAS

This 9km, circular walk, the Sendero del Desierto, passes through the gullies of the Tabernas desert following its *ramblas* to abandoned cave houses and tunnels carved into soft rock gorges. The gentle walk begins at the Oasys Mini Hollywood film set, and now theme park, but the real Wild West scenery is out here. These canyons were the backdrop to *For a Few Dollars More, Indiana Jones, Lawrence of Arabia* and *The Thief of Baghdad*, among many others. Best walked in springtime before the heavy summer heat.

→ Park opposite the Oasys Mini Hollywood. The footpath begins here and leads down in the direction of the dry river. It is signed but in summer it is best to download the route on offline maps.

1 hr, 37.0307, -2.4453 🏔️🚶

WINE & DINE

22 BODEGA BAREA GRANADOS

A family-run bodega with vineyards along the Andarax river and in the heart of the Alpujarra Almeriense. They also run a lively restaurant with garden tables, which is only open weekends.

→ Calle Hernan Cortes, 11, 04458 Padules, 950 510 356

37.0002, -2.7772 🍴⊞

23 CORTIJO EL CURA ECO-BODEGA

The Cortijo El Cura winery was founded in 1998 with the aim of making the first organic wines in the province of Almería – or at least the first organic wines for a few centuries. The vineyards are a beautiful way to see the Alpujarra de Almería mountains and several tastings and tours are available. A welcoming place.

→ Paraje de Ojancos, 04470 Laujar de Andarax, 620 785 618, Cortijoelcura.com

36.9746, -2.9274 🍴⊞

FEAST & FIESTA

24 FIESTA DE SAN ROQUE, SORBAS

The rambling streets and pretty squares of Sorbas come alive on August 16th for the feast day of San Roque. His garlanded image

is paraded through the town under a rain of blessed *roscos*, or doughnuts, and water thrown from balconies. The doughnuts not trampled into the cobbles are shared and eaten. Every bar hosts its own little party, spilling out onto the streets where a musical band, or *la charanga*, weaves in and out of the tables.

→ The main events happen around Plaza de la Constitución but you'll find festivity everywhere.

37.0982, -2.1238 🍴🎒⊞📍⊞

25 BAR SIERRA ALHAMILLA

Not much happens in this sleepy hamlet up in the sierra; however, right next to the ancient medicinal fountain and spa are a couple of bars that have become a bit of a foodie pilgrim site. This restaurant does the best tapas and you should try the *migas* (breadcrumbs with garlic, wine and pork), *conejo con ajo* (rabbit with garlic) or the *papas a lo pobre*, the best potatoes you'll ever try.

→ Plaza Doctor Campello, 2, 04259 Pechina, 950 160 275

36.9607, -2.3964 ⊞🍴📍

26 EL MOLINILLO DE LA ABUELA

You can spend the whole day in the River Andarax as the girls at this hidden leafy bar, under the oak beams of the old mill, serve some of the best tapas and coldest beer around. Open in the summer months only.

→ 04458 Padules, 610 302 915

36.9870, -2.7738 ⊞🍴🏔️🚶

RURAL HAVENS

27 LA POSADA DEL CANDIL

Several beautiful rural houses, all sustainably run using bioclimatic architecture and natural materials, with gardens and footpaths into the Sierra de los Filabres.

→ Paraje El Angulo, s/n, 04890 Serón, 675 987 242, Laposadadelcandil.com

37.3271, -2.5016 🏔️🚶⊞🔆

28 CASA DE LA ENCINA Y EL ENEBRO DEL CERCADO

A couple of beautiful family houses sleeping 6-8 in the valley just outside Vélez-Blanco. Flowering gardens surround a swimming pool with views out to the mountains La Muela and Maimon. Each house has cheerful, elegant rooms, old beams, window seats and terraces.

→ El Cercado de Alcocer, 27, 04830 Almería, 973640571, Luderna.com

37.6893, -2.0471 🚶⊞⊞🔆

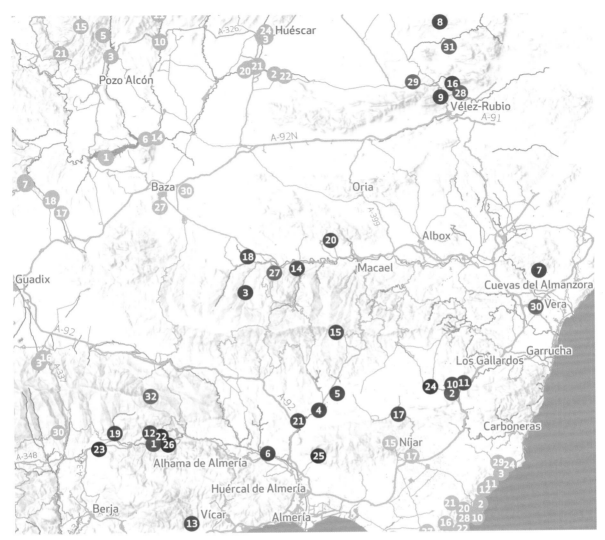

29 CORTIJO VENTORILLO

From their beautiful cortijo in the Sierra María Natural Park, Manel and his wife Rosa run six day courses in ceramics and 3D printing along with massage therapies and yoga. No experience of printing, ceramics or yoga is necessary. Bed and breakfast or full-board options available.

→ Contact potterholyanda@gmail.com. 37.7114, -2.1626 🖼️🍴📍⊞👤➕

WILDER CAMPING

30 CAMPING VERDEVERAS

A friendly eco-camping site running off solar and wind power, with bell tents, hammocks, caravans and van spaces available. They run several volunteer programmes too.

→ Pago San Anton, 6, 04620, 634 317 910, Verdeveras.es

37.2551, -1.8663 🖼️➕📍

31 ZONA ACAMPADA LAS ALMOHALLAS

A beautiful woodland hideout where camping is permitted in the Parque Natural Sierra María-Los Vélez. Oak and pine trees provide shade, and footpaths lead from here towards Cueva de Ambrosio. Perfect for stargazing and there are fountains, BBQs and toilets.

→ See directions to Cueva de Ambrosio. Area is signed Zona Acampada Libre from Vélez-Blanco.

37.7815, -2.0737 🔺➕📍🏕️

32 REFUGIO DE LA POLARDA

This mountain bothy sits at 2,199m on the peak of Polarda in the Alpujarra Almeriense. Several hiking trails pass by through the foothills of the Sierra Nevada. It is often under snow in winter and there are a couple of other bothies close by.

→ It lies along stage 12 of the 300km GR240 long-distance hiking route of the Sierra Nevada. The Pista da Floresta leads 10km up here from Ohanes.

37.0805, -2.8023 🔺➕📍👤

Wild Guide Andalucia
Hidden Places, Great Adventures and the Good Life

Words:
Edwina Pitcher

Photos:
Edwina Pitcher & those credited

Editing:
Victoria O'Dowd

Layout & Proofreading:
Rae Malenoir
Daniel Start
Tania Pascoe

Distribution:
Central Books Ltd
50, Freshwater Road
Dagenham, RM8 1RX
020 8525 8800
orders@centralbooks.com

Published by:
Wild Things Publishing Ltd.
Freshford, Bath, BA2 7WG

Contact:
hello@
wildthingspublishing.com

Author acknowledgements:
I would like to thank Julio Baños Barrera, who appears with Roller throughout this book, for his love, spirit of adventure, and ability to produce a cold beer in any terrain. To Leti and Sara and all my *gaditana* family for their love, expert Andalucían knowledge and making Cádiz home. To Betty Röther for her friendship, getting us to the peak of Mulhacén and the hours shared in Seville library. To Niki and Simon for their friendship and showing me a wilder, feathered, side to Andalucía. To César Cuadros and Alejandro Rosado Alcarria for their knowledge of the sierras. And to my mother for sharing desert roads and quarantine with me in Almería.

Thank you to Dan and Tania at Wild Things for believing in this book from the start and for your tireless hard-work and encouragement in making it a reality. Thanks also to Rae and Victoria for their attention to detail in design and editing.

Thanks to the Diputación de Jaén, Seville, Málaga and Granada for their support and wonderful guides. Thank you to all my hosts across Andalucía for your generosity. And lastly for their wild spirit, love and support Antonio Suarez, Michael and Soledad, Duncan and Verity, and of course, my Dad, brothers, and cousins.

Health, Safety and Responsibility:
The activities in this book have risks and can be dangerous. The locations may be on private land and permission may need to be sought. While the authors and publishers have gone to great lengths to ensure the accuracy of the information herein they will not be held legally or financially responsible for any accident, injury, loss or inconvenience sustained as a result of the information or advice

WILD guide
the award-winning, best-selling adventure travel series, also available as iPhone and Android apps.